Contextual Media

Technical Communication, Multimedia, and Information Systems
Edward Barrett, editor

Contextual Media

Multimedia and Interpretation

edited by Edward Barrett and Marie Redmond

The MIT Press
Cambridge, Massachusetts
London, England

First MIT Press paperback edition, 1997

This book was set in Sabon by Publication Services, Inc., and was printed and bound in the United States of America.

Library of Congress Cataloging-in-Publication Data

Contextual media : multimedia and interpretation / edited by Edward
Barrett and Marie Redmond.
    p.   cm.
    Includes bibliographical references and index.
    ISBN 0-262-02383-0 (HB), 0-262-52239-X(PB)
    1. Multimedia systems—Social aspects.   I. Barrett, Edward.
II. Redmond, Marie.
QA76.575.C67   1995
303.48'33—dc20   94-23791
                                                CIP

Contents

Series Foreword

Technical Communication is one of the most rapidly expanding fields of study in the United States, Europe, and the Pacific Rim, as witnessed by the growth of professional societies and degree-granting programs in colleges and universities as well as the evolving status of documentation specialists in industry. The writer, and writing, are no longer mere servants of science and engineering but rather partners in the complex matrix of forces that go into the construction of knowledge and information. And the audience is not a passive but an active player in this transaction. Furthermore, computational science has delivered a powerful tool for the creation, presentation, exchange, and annotation of text—so powerful that we speak not in terms of a text but rather of a hypertext, of seamless information environments that integrate a variety of media.

The MIT Press Series in Technical Communication, Multimedia, and Information Systems will present advanced research in all aspects of this rapidly expanding field, including hypertext and hypermedia systems, on-line documentation, information architecture, interface design, graphics, collaborative writing in distributed networks, the role of the writer in industry, scientific and engineering writing, training and education in technical writing. Only in addressing such a wide range of topics do we begin to understand the complexity and power of this field of expertise.

Edward Barrett

Acknowledgments

Many of the chapters in this volume were presented as papers at the conference on "Culture, Technology, Interpretation: The Challenge of Multimedia," held at Trinity College, Dublin in 1993. This conference was jointly sponsored by the Department of Computer Science at Trinity College and the Program in Writing and Humanistic Studies at MIT. We would like to thank Professor John G. Byrne, Chair of the Department of Computer Science at Trinity College, for his generous support, which made this conference possible. To the staff of the Multimedia Centre at Trinity College—Rachael Corcoran, Fergus Creagh, Tom Hopkins, Eoin Keith, Dermot Rogers, Blaise Smith, Niall Sweeney, and Neil Williams—we would like to express our admiration and sincere thanks for their professionalism and generosity of spirit. We are also grateful to Professor Alan Lightman, Head of the Program in Writing and Humanistic Studies (WHS) at MIT, Rebecaa Chamberlain (administrative office of WHS at that time), and Cindy Haverstock and Nick Altenbernd of WHS, for their support. As always, we are grateful to Teresa Ehling and staff of the MIT Press for their friendly and invaluable guidance in bringing this volume to print.

For his gentle yet unwavering support, which made it possible to convene an international conference devoted to humanistic issues in computer science, we dedicate this volume to John G. Byrne, Chair of the Department of Computer Science at Trinity College.

Hiding the Head of Medusa: Objects and Desire in a Virtual Environment

1

The computer textualizes everything. The phrase "information superhighway" tricks us into believing that it's all about delivery and movement, about access and possession, about abundance and automatic knowledge. There is an enforced passivity as we watch cable and communications companies tangle for control of a metaphor. As if environment did not precede it, as if place, this time, this view, this thought, my words, our world, language did not precede it.

The computer textualizes everything: it is our writing of the world as we know it, a map of illiteracy. It must always contain a blank space, a margin in which to write "Yes" or "No," or "Today, a crowd, fierce as angels. . . ."

The computer is an angel of history.

2

What is the space we devote attention to? Really, the question is, I have thoughts I want to give shape to, embody, adore, situate, leave behind, and revisit. This one makes me happy, this one makes me cry, this one is more powerful than a Roman breastplate or the cheekpiece of a horse. Where is the museum of my thought, where is the wall I can write on?

We are angels of history. We walk, invisible, through galleries of mute paintings. We read words in silence. We sit in the dark watching films. We read each others' minds on the Underground or the Dublin DART or the T. We wait to speak.

In Dunquin, on the west coast of Ireland, the government built a museum to the men and women who used to live on the Blasket Islands, which lie a few miles offshore. The islanders wrote an alternative history to the twentieth century. The museum is called an Interpretive Centre. You can stand inside it and look at the walls, the texts, the photographs; hear music and voices. At the far end you can stand near a big window and look out at the islands. The Interpretive Centre is either an interface for what lies outside of it, or a shield barring you from a world you will never really know. The body of Tomás Ó Crohan, one of the most famous Blasket Island authors, lies in an untended grave in the churchyard not far from the Interpretive Centre. The local schoolmaster teaches only in Irish, or more correctly, a dialect of Irish, which can differ from county to county, profuse yet dying, the only real connection to the world of the islanders. The local pub used to have carpets on the walls to hide the water stains, the wet world seeping in from the islands offshore.

3

On Tuesday, September 8, 1992, four months after the riots in Los Angeles following the verdict in the Rodney King case, the *New York Times* published a story about a mural some local teenagers had painted on the walls of a building in the Dorchester section of Boston. The mural depicted the chief events surrounding the case: "a man driving a car, a video camera, four white police officers clubbing the black motorist, a courthouse and jury, a tipped scale of justice, a city burning in bright orange flames." In a photograph of the mural, you can see one of the panels. Surrounding this particular panel are various icons, depicted in a style reminiscent of ancient Egyptian hiero-glyphics: an eye, an ear, a hand-held video camera, a head. The reporter writes: "In the background bordering the final panel, in huge white letters, is the word, 'History.' " The mural symbolized the conflict of interpretations surrounding the videotape that had come to dominate, night after night, the national imagery of the U.S. The content of the videotape of the beating of Rodney King (and later, the videotape of the beating of Reginald Denny) seemed absolutely clear. Yet the trials that followed these beatings offered interpretations for what our eyes had seemed to reveal unambiguously. The trials suggested that the videotape could not be understood so easily, that direct sensory input could not be relied upon out of context, that experience required extensive mediation to be forced to deliver up its meaning. And each side provided a context for the images on the tape—the body of evidence—a context for meaning, a different version of the truth.

For many Americans the trials were a lesson in textualization and annotation. We had been through this before in the Anita Hill–Clarence Thomas hearings on the confirmation of Judge Clarence Thomas to the United States Supreme Court. We made decisions about who was telling the truth and who was lying. We listened to evidence, we scrutinized images of faces, trying to read into those images a character. We felt one had to be right, one wrong. We believed in, and more importantly, we were being asked to decide in favor of, absolute categories of truth and falsehood.

As the *New York Times* was publishing its story about the mural in Boston, I received a telephone call from a former MIT colleague, Marie Redmond, who now lived and worked in Dublin, the city of her birth. She had given up her teaching duties at MIT, as well as her senior position in management at Digital Equipment Corporation, in order to return home to pursue an advanced degree at Trinity College, Dublin. In addition to her academic course work, she also headed a new Multimedia Centre at Trinity. Ireland, as well as the rest of Europe, was engaged in debate over the signing of the Maastricht Treaty, a document which laid the foundation for a new European community, a powerful political and economic confederation which could transform intra-European politics and the role of Europe in international affairs.

Marie asked if I wanted to co-direct my next conference on computational technology and the social construction of knowledge at Trinity. Frankly, at the time I felt I had covered this topic in a series of MIT-sponsored conferences resulting in a trilogy of volumes devoted to a new paradigm for viewing computer development (Barrett, 1992, 1989, 1988). The flavor of the month in industry was now "multimedia" (outstripping hypertext and hypermedia). "Multimedia," as a term, I felt, was a retrenchment. Hypermedia could be discussed with reference to a rich tradition of textual criticism (Delaney and Landow, 1990). Multimedia, as a term, implied nothing more than a collage of media types—it seemed useful mainly for product development.

However, Marie and I felt that discussions of multimedia needed to be expanded. We wanted to know, for example, how artists and humanists could use this technology. We wanted to know how multimedia technology might be used to place the conflicts of our respective cultures in some sort of meaningful context for analysis and understanding. We wanted to know how this delivery mechanism was itself transformed in the mix of media: transformed into an extension of ourselves in the human enterprise of interpreting and constructing "reality," "truth," "knowledge"—the enterprise of constructing ourselves in our world, a two-way street of human-computer interaction, each affecting the other.

I thought about the court testimony in the King case. Frame-by-frame interpretations were applied to the tape of the beating. The trial was a series of annotations as delicate, as contrived, as intricate as the illustrations in a medieval text of the Gospels. The trial was an illuminated text. Flesh (image) was made word (annotation) in a kind of reverse incarnation. Winners and losers became secondary. We had entered into a world of continual interpretation and annotation.

One body politic was tearing itself apart. Another was debating how to assemble itself anew.

We called our conference "Culture, Technology, Interpretation: The Challenge of Multimedia." The challenge was our human need to make sense out of the welter of experience, whether in riot or in treaty. What tools could the computer give us to analyze this process of sense-making, to add voices to it, to create new contexts for understanding a specific action, or image, or object—to archive voices, images, thoughts that could be lost, marginalized, defeated, or could assume the status of a core? How could we modify those tools to suit our human needs?

4

It is not so easy moving discussions of computers away from a technological base because that base is continually budding anew. Technology is always more accessible than trying to imagine how this technology might actually be used. How do you contextualize cyberspace? For cyberspace is a realm of desire, disembodied, an Ovidian theater of love and metamorphosis that entails nothing. It is where Medusa, the objectifier, the body, is slain. Yet all programming points to "objects" in some fashion. Direction is remarkably linear in cyberspace, it's just that you have more arrows of direction in your quiver. If you surf the Internet, interfaces are muddy, clunky; syntax sophomoric. Contexts presented online are often too limited for what we really want: an environment that delivers objects of desire—to know more, see more, learn more, express more. We fear being caught in Medusa's gaze, of being transfixed before the end is reached; yet we want the head of Medusa safely on our shield to freeze the bitstream, the fleeting imagery, the unstoppable textualizations. We want, not the dead object, but the living body in its connections to its world, connections that sustain it, give it meaning.

Between sessions at the main conference hall at Trinity College, we'd duck out to the Long Room of the Old Library where the *Book of Kells* is on display. You'd stand in line waiting to view one page, a book in a glass case, with a guard standing nearby. The book of course was no longer a book but a sacred object. It was unreadable, or more correctly, no longer meant to be read, and existed only as a presence to symbolize cultural heritage. Possession of it implied coherence and continuance in one's self. A fixed image to latch on to. An object. A body. It was a statement of what its absence would mean to a particular culture, and its location therefore conferred power. It could not be transferred or duplicated. Copies were meant for others who did not know how to use it.

One evening, as the conference sessions for that day were concluding, a group of Dublin women held a rally at Trinity to protest a bombing in Northern Ireland earlier that week in which an innocent child had been killed. I tried to imagine how this demonstration could be interpreted by various individuals within and outside the Republic of Ireland. What did it mean to have a pacifist rally in the south? What did it mean that it was a rally by women? How did this demonstration fit within the context of what we now know were a series of secret talks going on then between the British Government and Sinn Fein? There was the object, the body. What annotations or treaties could anneal its wounds? Here, too, was one page of a book opened before me, a text dense with imagery and illumination and darkness. Its meaning a question of context.

5

The computer is an angel of history. It textualizes everything, reducing multimedia to unimedia (Hawley), a bitstream collapse of space and time. The computer sorts and categorizes and duplicates and transmits this dimensionless text; it shapes and filters and contextualizes whatever can be recorded and reflected. Each contextualization implies a narrative, a story, an interpretation. The computer is language: it embodies and inflects thought; through it we talk to ourselves or to others.

The virtual environment is a place of longing. Cyberspace is an odyssey without telos, and therefore without meaning. The head of Medusa is hidden there, as if cybernauts feared the embodied, the instantiations of desire in an object. Yet cyberspace is also the theater of operations for the reconstruction of the lost body of knowledge, or, perhaps more correctly, not the reconstruction, but the always primary construction of a body of knowing. Thought and language in a virtual environment seek a higher synthesis, a re-imagining of an idea in the context of its truth.

References

Barrett, Edward. 1992. "Sociomedia: An Introduction," in E. Barrett, ed., *Sociomedia: Multimedia, Hypermedia, and the Social Construction of Knowledge.* Cambridge, MA: MIT Press.

Barrett, Edward. 1989. "Thought and Language in a Virtual Environment," in E. Barrett, ed., *The Society of Text: Hypertext, Hypermedia, and the Social Construction of Information.* Cambridge, MA: MIT Press.

Barrett, Edward. 1988. "A New Paradigm for Writing with and for the Computer," in E. Barrett, ed., *Text, ConText, and HyperText: Writing with and for the Computer.* Cambridge, MA: MIT Press.

Delaney, Paul, and George P. Landow, eds. 1990. *Hypermedia and Literary Studies.* Cambridge, MA: MIT Press.

Hawley, Michael (MIT Media Lab and Laboratory for Computer Science). April, 1994. Address to the MIT Computers and Humanities Group. MIT, Cambridge, MA.

The New York Times. "Teen-Agers' Mural of Beating Angers Boston Police." September 8, 1992.

1

Interactive Transformational Environments: Wheel of Life

Glorianna Davenport and Larry Friedlander

Introduction

Collaboration often calls on circumstance. In the summer of 1992 Friedlander came to MIT as a Visiting Professor of Literature and Media Arts. Both he and Davenport had long been fascinated by the literary and artistic possibilities of interactive technology, and both were intrigued by the idea of creating an *Interactive Transformational Environment*. They agreed to design and build such an installation in the Villers Experimental Media Theater at the Media Lab in MIT as a project for Davenport's upcoming *Workshop in Elastic Movie Time*.

The collaboration began with a series of questions concerning the future of interactive technologies and interactive environments. As technology becomes more "intelligent" and more precisely responsive to a user's wishes and actions, its functions can increasingly be distributed throughout the everyday environment. Eventually, might not the computer itself dissolve into the very fabric of our environment? Could we not imagine a world thoroughly permeated with hidden functionalities invisibly available to us? What would it be like to be in a world that "knew" we were there, and that was totally responsive to our every move; a world that literally transformed itself as we traversed it? What kind of rules might pertain in a landscape dominated by change and by transformation?

These ambitious musings helped us formulate some initial goals for our project: first, we would create an interactive world situated in a real space outside of the computer box, a kind of museum installation *cum* theater-set. This space, however, would retain many of the functionalities of the computing

Figure 1.1
Behind the scenes of the Wheel of Life.

environment. Visitors would immerse themselves in this world with their whole body, mind, and feelings. We hoped that it would feel as though they were walking through a computer monitor into a magic landscape.

Second, we decided the space should contain or embody a narrative, and that the narrative should be actualized by the transformative actions of the visitor moving through it. After much discussion, we settled on an overarching theme: *the wheel of life, the cycles of change and continuity that whirl us along in the journeys of our lives.* The space would be broken down into four subspaces, each containing a distinct story but each connected to the space as whole. Each subspace would take as a starting point for its design one of the traditional elements—earth air, water and fire—and each element would be associated with a set of attributes—emotional, historical, technical.[1]

Finally, we wanted to explore the connection between this new kind of place and traditional computing environments. What if we had two kinds of participants: explorers, who would in fact enter and explore the space, and guides, who would sit at a workstation outside of the space and, using the computer, help the explorers navigate through the different areas? And what if, to make matters more interesting (and frustrating!), these two would have to communicate not through words but through the matter and media of the world itself, its colors, sounds, images? Perhaps these constraints would force the participants to find new methods of expression and communication and would encourage us, as designers, to push at the limits of interface and spatial design.

By stipulating a human guide, we also wanted to reexamine the way expert "presences" have been used in the multimedia interface.[2] Could we establish a collaborative, democratic partnership between the makers and users of this world by having guides who did not stand above and aloof from the experience but were as involved and as vulnerable as those they guided? Human guides would provide a model of how guides might learn as they went along.

Organizing the Project

The *Workshop in Elastic Movie Time,* which Davenport has taught since 1984,[3] offers a perfect venue for this kind of collaborative project as it had always centered around the collective design of an interactive media experience. In it, students jointly explore the interrelationship of content, form, audience participation, technology and tools, as they create a multimedia system. This is a demanding and rigorous class, for the collaborative process requires significant commitments of time and patience, as well as a willingness to work in a group. Students are carefully screened before being accepted, to insure that the final group will be highly motivated and will represent a broad spectrum of fields such as computing, film-making, and design.

Typically the group begins by defining the aim and methodology of the project and then divides itself into parallel groups centered around specific aspects of the project. Early exercises build student confidence and understanding of the complexity of the design task, and a significant portion of class time is devoted to student presentations and discussion. An important goal of this style of teaching is to hone student understanding of a fabricated world, and to build communication skills which are necessary for collaboration. This process keeps ideas fluid and ensures that all subprojects will eventually merge into a single expression.

In the current workshop, students were divided into three teams;[4] each team formed subgroups to work on expressive design and on technical

Figure 1.2
The guide helps the explorer navigate through the spaces.

design. The expressive task was to "develop a model of the experience for one of the elements—water, earth, air—including the feel of the terrain, imagery, sound, objects, riddles and other aspects relevant to the journey of the explorer and the experience of the guide." In parallel, the technical tasks involved designing and eventually constructing the physical world, creating an electronic network and connections between the inner space and guide station, and developing the software to control the image-projection and sound systems.

Class sessions alternated between presentations by experts on issues such as lighting, construction materials, sensor devices, filming methods etc.; reports by the students of their progress; and exercises designed to provide insight into conceptual issues.[5] The class also studied the techniques used by some modern artists, particularly the Surrealists, to create starling and unexpected visual experiences: for example, the juxtaposition of dissimilar objects; the deconstruction or reconstruction of such objects; the alteration of viewers' perspectives; and creation of totally imaginary worlds.

Process and Challenges

The challenges facing each group were enormous: the students, who had strong technical backgrounds, had to turn themselves into set designers, sculptors, story-tellers, and theater people. They had to both develop a workable conceptual scheme and build a large-scale installation, all in a short space of time. Basically students were working in the dark; plans might look good on paper, but until we opened the installation we would not know if visitors would be able to read and interact with our designs. In fact, it took many weeks to evolve and iterate the various narrative concepts.

The first job was to create the conceptual framework for the piece and to develop detailed plans for its implementation. The initial challenge was to envision a space that was also a story, an embodied narrative world with self-defined rules and procedures that expressed the symbolic content of the area—water, earth, air. Moreover, while the space would seem open for free exploration, it would in fact have to lure the visitors through it in a fixed sequence of interactions, or else the transformations could not take place. Here, the role of the guide was paramount.

But, first the groups had to define the specific relationship between explorer and guide. The guide, seated at a workstation outside of the space, was to direct and intervene in the explorer's progress. Given the complexity of the final spaces, it was technically difficult to give the guide a precise sense of the explorer's movements (except by using a camera); creatively, it was challenging to search out new and surprising ways for the guide to "talk" to the explorer. And, to be fair to the visitor who became a guide, we had to find really interesting things for her or him to do, tasks as complex and as engaging as wandering through the actual installation.

The second challenge was the actual construction of the installation. The Villers Experimental Theater is a big, boxlike space—50 × 50 × 60 feet—located at the center of the Wiesner building. The space was a tabula rasa—vast, empty, and symmetrical—that demanded large but simplified and dramatic shapes to energize it. Our students were mainly programmers and filmmakers who had almost no experience building large-scale walk-through installations. The time available for the building such ambitious structures was very brief—a matter of a few weeks, during which the same students also had to create a multifaceted network that linked all the areas to our computer, lighting, and computing systems.

As it turned out, each group developed its ideas and constructed its area in decidedly different ways: some areas were strong on spatial effects and atmosphere, others on story, others on technical wizardry. Some groups had ingeniously difficult puzzles for the guide to solve, others concentrated more on allowing the guide to participate in the explorer's experiences.

The Areas

The Water Group

The water group began its design process with a strong sense of the feel of its world: dark, prenatal, engulfing. To create the impression of an abrupt descent into a watery world, the group decided that as the explorers entered into a totally dark space they would suddenly be confronted with a huge video image, projected on the opposing wall, of a hand that seemed to reach down, pick them up, and throw them into the watery deep.[6] The visitor, surrounded by images (projected on the walls) of people and other marine beings staring inward, would feel trapped in a watery enclosure. The space itself developed as a kind of giant fishbowl made of scrim that twisted upwards until it almost disappeared out of sight in the reaches of the ceiling. (When this environment was actually built the fishbowl shape rose forty feet in the air!)

To devise a suitably aqueous atmosphere, the group played with methods of creating shifting reflections. After rejecting as impractical the idea of covering the space with water itself, the group designed a hoop covered with mylar, a semireflecting material, which was set at the top of the fishbowl form; a small fan was then used to vibrate the surface, thus creating watery-like reflections on the walls and floors below. This, together with some ingenious lighting and a floor littered with "drowned" objects made for quite a powerful and eerie feel of underwater space. A seventeen-foot whale (created out of rebar, mesh wire, and painted muslin) with a shocking-pink fluorescent mouth dominated the area; by entering the mouth, the visitor activated a radar system that made the whale talk and sing.

Finally, Ariel's song from *The Tempest* suggested a narrative.[7] The whale sang these lines[8] but the song remained indecipherable until the explorer

World: rippling light, mysterious images peeping through the scrim, half-buried objects, haunting underwater sounds.

Action: plunging down to the bottom of the sea; escaping from the depths.

Interactions: deciphering the whale's song; exploring the inside of the whale's head; encountering the animal guides.

The Guide: choosing and choreographing the images and the animals.

Figure 1.3
The Water Guide Interface and Explorer's Environment.

learned to communicate with the whale and sing back to it. By accomplishing a set of tasks in a prescribed order, the explorer freed herself or himself from the watery world.

The guide's part in all this was to direct the explorer towards each area where a task had to be accomplished. The guide's computer was linked to a camera that showed the movements of the explorer. In order to direct the explorer through the space, the guide could place image-messages on specific television monitors which surrounded the water environment; these images were inserted interactively into the regular image stream for that monitor. Initially the group hoped to use gestures from habitants of the aquarium—a penguin waving its flippers to the left, for example; however, for readability, the group finally settled on a combination of a child's hand gesturing with a whisper "come here" or "go left." If the explorer did not succeed within a certain amount of time, the air reserve would run out, and she or he would be figuratively expelled from the space.

The Earth Group

In contrast to the vertical water piece, the earth space was a long, slightly curving rectangle of scrim and wood, designed to suggest an infinitely long featureless landscape. The group's vision was of a world of objects buried in sand, of ruins under a hot sun, of the remnants of technology littering a wasteland. In keeping with this area's theme of growth, decay, and renewal, however, new life would eventually spring from these ruins. The explorer and guide had to collaborate to effect this renewal.

The first plan went like this: each abandoned object would contain a hidden camera that, when set off by the guide, would capture different elements of the explorer's body. These images would then be sent to the guide station where they would be rearranged into a whole image of the explorer. This image in turn would trigger changes in the environment, restoring the wasteland to its former fruitful state, and the explorer would be freed.

While this design had appealing aspects, particularly the idea of capturing and redisplaying the explorer's image, the narrative was weak and it was unclear how the explorer could be made to move from one object to another in a predetermined order.

However, the idea of a ruin did suggest Shelley's poem *Ozymandias,*[9] which in turn suggested a different scenario: the task of the explorer would

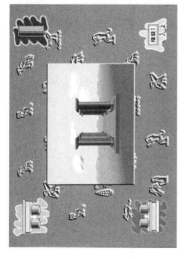

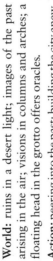

World: ruins in a desert light; images of the past arising in the air; visions in columns and arches; a floating head in the grotto offers oracles.

Action: peering into the past; building the city anew.

Interaction: making the column talk; dancing on the stones; heeding the oracle.

The Guide: teaching the right sequence; speaking the oracle's voice.

Figure 1.4
The Earth Guide Interface and Explorer's Environment.

be to reconstruct this lost kingdom. Instead of capturing and assembling the body of the explorer, the explorer would summon up and connect pieces of the past into a final image of its full splendors.

Here is how it worked: the explorer, by entering the space, triggers a sensor. A voice—seemingly coming from the ruins of the world—recounts the history of the lost kingdom and asks the explorer's help in restoring the palace. At first, all the explorer can see is a broken column, dimly outlined in dawn light. Drawn to the column, the explorer has to discover how to make a film, hidden within it, play. Once that is accomplished, the lighting brightens and the space widens out as if under a noon sky, revealing a stone archway with a sundial. There another task awaits. Once completed, the lighting changes again, and the explorer spies the last object, a ruined wall and window, silhouetted under the twilight sky.

Each time the explorer successfully executes a task, a part of a large-scale computer image appears in the sky. Piece by piece the ruined palace seems to be rebuilt: first the floor, then the walls, then the roof. The moment all the pieces come together, the entire space transforms into a springlike garden, filled with sounds and light.

The guide actively leads the explorer by choosing different films to play in the arches and stones. One set of films shows the past of the world, the other describes its downfall. As the explorer learns how to evoke the films, the circle is complete and the area metamorphosed.

It was particularly difficult, in this section, to design interactions that the explorer could easily decipher. For example, we placed four light sensing diodes (later replaced by buttons) and a video monitor on top of the broken column. Our idea was that the explorer had to discover and unlock the secret of the column by moving his or her hand around the edge of the column in a specific direction; as the hand blocked the light from each diode, the explorer was rewarded with a short film element. What we wanted was a smooth unfolding; however, constraints of the technology required that rather than mapping a smooth unrolling of the film with the sweep of the explorer's hand, we had to break the film into granular elements and offer the reward for each individual interaction. This fragmentation, made the task more difficult for the visitors.

The second interaction was more complex than the first because the guide was engaged to send messages to the explorer. The interaction required visitors to stand on different parts of a floor compass[10] in a predetermined order (north, south, east, west) and in response to audio clues, bits of poetry that contained the names of the directions as in "I am as constant as the northern star" or "It is the east, and Juliet is the sun."[11] Almost all visitors, including children, found this interaction difficult, in part we believe because of the slow system response time. The difference between adults and children seemed to be that children would play for longer without giving up.

The Air Group

In response to the themes suggested by our schematic chart—human intelligence, technology, and risk-taking—the air group envisioned a complex puzzle-filled environment—a bar in an airship, a bridge over misty fog, and a cylindrical space in which one would seem to rise up into sky. This space proved unworkable: it was at once too literal and too cluttered, and the scenario provided no clear tasks for the explorer. After a few sessions the group decided to concentrate on creating the airship itself, with a bridge that would lead to the fire space, envisioned as a video wall in which fire images rose to the stars.[12] Once the group as a whole focused on the airship, the vision evolved at a steady rate. The ship itself was created by using an electric fan to keep a mylar balloon inflated. The interior that resulted was magically shimmering and translucent, and the colored videos glowed in the air.

The group developed the most intricate scenario of all the spaces. This was the story: the airship was caught in a red nebula; the captain and four crew members were in shock or trance, the "red" state. In order to save the ship and the crew, the explorer had to bring all members of the crew into the "blue" or active state at the same time. The crew members would be visible in videos placed along the sides of the cabin; each crew member would show up on a different monitor. The explorer could change the state of a specific crew member by stepping on a sensor which would be placed in front of the monitor. The trick was that the segment length of blue state varied in length for each character, and therefore their sensors had to be triggered in a specific sequence in order for all the crew members to be simultaneously in the blue state which, in turn, would release the captives. In order to help, the guide needed to solve a puzzle that paralleled this idea of duration on the computer; the guide could then signal to the explorer by turning lights on in front of each monitor in the correct order.

World: a silvered capsule; images trapped in light; speed and motion.

Action: saving the ship; freeing the crew.

Interaction: triggering the character's change of state; keeping the images running.

The Guide: solving the monkey puzzle; lighting the way for the explorer.

Figure 1.5
The Air Guide Interface and Explorer's Environment.

As in the other spaces, significant frustration and confusion was introduced by the delay between stepping on the hidden sensor and playing the required video clip. Visitors had difficulty connecting their action with the change in the state of the crew member. This seemed to be aggravated by the fact that visitors were overwhelmed when they were introduced to the narrative before they were able to explore the space. Concurrently we optimized the network, and adjusted the digital audio track which situated the narrative so that it played out in two sections; the second section explained to participants that in order to save the ship all of the characters had to be in the blue state at the same time.

The Visitor's Experience

The Wheel of Life was open in January 1993 for 10 consecutive days from 12 noon to 6 p.m. Sign up sheets were placed on the door of the Villers Theater so people could come in and book a reservation; people could also call in. Because this installation was open for such a short time and because the IAP[13] period at MIT increases general campus circulation, we were saturated with visitors. In the early stages we estimated we could take about 12 people an hour. That number waxed and waned in accordance with how the technology fared on any given day. In general, visitors were fascinated by the experience and worked to solve each puzzle with determination. This often took longer than we initially anticipated.

In the beginning, each group entered a small waiting space in which a rotating mandala animation[14] spun round high on a scrim. In this anteroom, one of the students greeted the visitors and introduced the concept of the transformational environments, encouraging the explorer to seek out and solve some puzzles, and encouraging the guide to help by sending messages or solving their own puzzle. These introductory comments proved essential in situating the visitors for the experience which followed.

On average groups of six people entered the space at a time—three explorers and three guides. This group size had strengths and weaknesses. Social interaction tended to strengthen resolve. For instance we frequently observed that participants would hesitate before entering the whale's mouth; however, once one member of the group entered and triggered the light which made the pink throat fluoresce, every one else in the group would

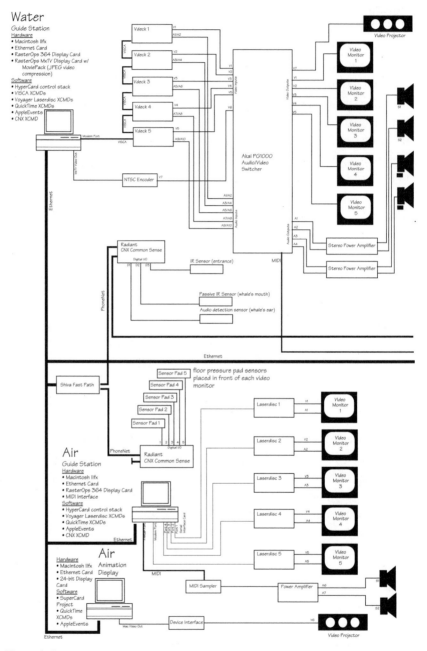

Figure 1.6a
Block Diagram.

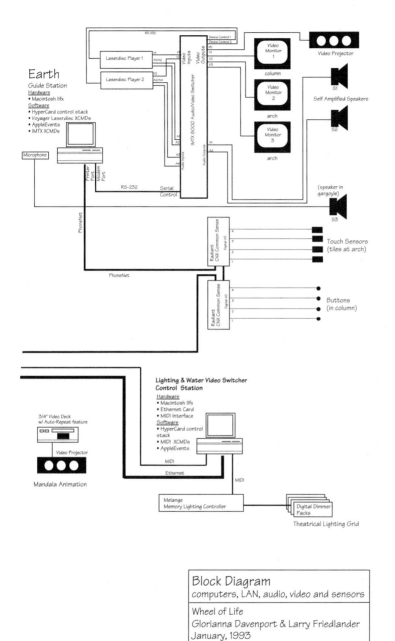

Block Diagram
computers, LAN, audio, video and sensors

Wheel of Life
Glorianna Davenport & Larry Friedlander
January, 1993

Figure 1.6b
Block Diagram

enter. In Earth, we found that participants talked through the interaction at both the broken column and at the compass; this shared approach to problem solving helped them understand the nature of the transformation. However, having more than one explorer in the space at the same time also created inconsistencies in the narrative which for the most part had been designed for one person. For instance, when the guide sent a message "Go left" into the water space, the multiple explorers were unsure who the messages was meant for. In air, sometimes participants rushed to stand in front of different monitors which made it more difficult to decipher the relationship between the length of the video pieces. At other times the participants moved as a group which tended to be slow and unwieldy.

Some explanation was offered at each guide station although some guide groups immediately understood the Earth interaction. Air offered the most obscure mapping between explorer and guide. The paradigm of a board game, while it provided a real puzzle, was startling in the context. In addition, this interface was clearly designed for a single user. A short piece of audio which the guide listened to on headphones explained the narrative—all the logs needed to be launched in the river in order to provide a bridge which the monkey could use to cross to the other side. Because only one person could hear the instructions and because the game moved quickly, the two other partners in the guide group had difficulty participating.

Our achievement and lack thereof can be evaluated in light of visitor feedback. For the visitor, the experience was one of learning and understanding—learning the rules of the experience first, and then perhaps contemplating why the experience mattered. The simpler the introduction of the activity and clearer the direction through the space, the more quickly visitors grasped what to do. Children in particular truly enjoyed the magical way in which each of the spaces talked to them. While most adults grasped the activities at the guide stations fairly quickly, the experience of being an explorer tended to cause anxiety.

From a research standpoint, the fact that visitors insisted on playing both roles—explorer and guide—allowed the visitors to reflect deeply on their experience. Over and over, we discovered that visitors gained situated knowledge which included the schema of each space when they took on their first role of either explorer or guide; this knowledge made them more relaxed when they participated in the second role. The explorer role in general was more baffling to those participants who had not first served as guides. One participant who started as an guide stated "You don't know how interactive you have to be. You think you have a mission." When participants who started as explorers with a mission could not discover how to control the environment, they often became completely baffled and virtually gave up until some outside observer offered a whispered hint. In some cases these reactions occurred in relation to a specific interaction and the visitor was able to work through to a new level of understanding. For instance, one visitor described feeling a little silly walking into the mouth of the whale, but then reflected that "it is only when you understand the whale as a character, that you understand that the whale is talking to you and think about how to talk back."[15]

Evaluation

At the outset we sensed that we were on the brink of a long and fascinating journey but we found we had underestimated the complexity of our task: as we refined and reiterated our conceptual design we were forced to continually adjust our software designs and modes of construction. When we opened the installation it became clear that we needed another substantial period of refinement before the installation would be truly hospitable for visitors. Some of the problems were technical, for we had little or no chance to test and correct the installation. We also realized that as our designs grew increasingly complex, we lacked strong graphical scripting tools which would enable us to pre visualize the impact of a new idea on the complex environment.

Other problems arose from the visitor's reactions to an unfamiliar experience. With so many different kinds of people moving through the space, we discovered a whole range of problems in providing a unified way of orienting them to the experience and teaching them how to participate.

Several limitations were clear: we had relied heavily on puzzle-solving as a way to engage the visitors and have them interact with the space. However, many visitors, especially older ones, were resistant to this mode of game playing; they wanted assurances of how to act and what to do. Moreover, puzzles require an intellectual focus on the part of the visitor which interferes with a reverie-like absorption of the experience. Can we find new narrative forms which invite intervention without depending on puzzle-solving?

In general, we found that creating and communicating a role for the participant was both the most exciting and difficult task we encountered. In life we change roles continually without even noticing we are doing so, but when we are enter a fabricated situation which requires on-demand role playing, we often react with fear or embarrassment. The interactive environment needs to engage the visitor and elicit a spontaneous desire to play along with the game. When the environment or the kind of game is familiar from some other experience, the task seems easier. For example, the situation in the Airship seemed familiar to most participants, relating to their memories of Star Trek. Because they grasped the basic situation very quickly, explorers could concentrate on the task at hand: how to change the state of the characters in the video. In fact, as one of the authors commented, participants for the most part ignored the text of the video—what the characters were saying—as soon as they realized that it would not help them solve the puzzle. Visitors were very good at discovering the truly decisive elements in a puzzle.

The tasks facing the guides were more subtle and more varied, and visitors had correspondingly more trouble with them. Each guide station offered a different model of intervention. For instance, in Water the guide tried to direct the movements of the explorer using a limited set of icons. Detailed instruction was not allowed. This put quite a strain on both explorer and guide, for they had to interpret a new code or language in order to grasp the direction. In Earth, the information was more direct. Most participants understood that when they heard audio that said, "It is the east, and Juliet is the sun," it meant they must stand on the eastern point of the compass. What was not explicit was the requirement that the participant do so only after the guide made the request. As soon as the explorers figured out that the text might refer to the points of the compass, they rushed eagerly ahead without waiting for further instructions and thus upset the relationship of guide as leader we had planned into the interaction.

The interface for the guide station in the air section was playful but obscure. Each log the guide launched had a specific length which was relational to the length of the video clip for the associated character in the airship. Because the guides did not know what was happening in the space, they had to understand their own environment before they could really help the explorer. While most visitors had fun launching the logs in sequence, they had difficulty translating what they learned to running the lights. The lack of audio separation between the spaces added a serendipity feature to the guide's experience, sometimes adding clarity and sometimes not. In general, we found we had to adjust these interfaces more carefully to the range of capabilities and expectations of the visitors.

Conclusion

While many aspects of the technology and narrative could be improved, the project as a whole was inspiring. A design process based on collaboration produced an extremely rich product, for the individual groups of collaborators focused on concepts congenial and stimulating for them. Variety and surprise resulted; and the richness of the narrative context encourages us to look anew at collaboration as an element in global storytelling environments.

Wheel of Life also suggested a new kind of interface for interactive applications, one that changes and evolves with the actions of the user. This dynamic environment allows the user to learn a set of responses of some complexity through actions in time, easing the pressure on the user and allowing for more subtle and more refined kinds of interactions.

Because our narratives were spatial, new kinds of story-telling became possible. In particular, this work united the fable with theater and game-playing. The merger of different genres of narrative echoes in some way the rich merging of media that characterizes the interactive medium as a whole, and creates the challenge of inventing appropriate types of narration.

Putting the technology to new use also opens up new possibilities and challenges for the technology. How can we develop more persuasive wrap-around media that truly create the environment they describe, and how can we create sensitive and speedy devices that which respond to complex interaction? Solutions to these and other problems will open up the development of interactive transformational environments to uses and sites we have yet to imagine, and could possibly revolutionize our relationship with the technology.

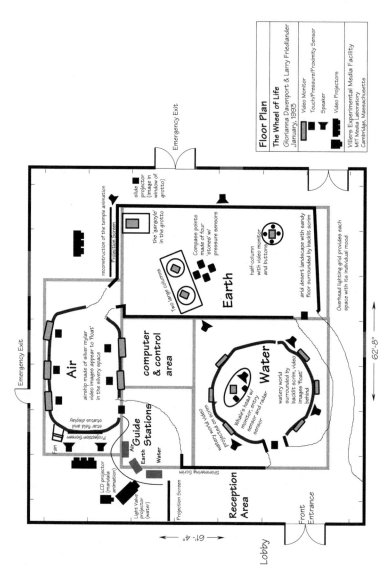

Figure 1.7
Floor Plan: The Wheel of Life.

Acknowledgments

Principal Authors: The piece was codirected by Professors Davenport and Friedlander; Herrick Goldman designed the lighting; Stuart Cody acted as technical supervisor; Greg Tucker was facilities coordinator; David Tamés was production manager. The administrative assistant was Betsy Brown.

Student authors include: Alan Blount, Kevin Brooks, Cris Dolan, Scott Higgins, Gilberte Houbart, David Kung, Mitchell C.H. Liu, Wendy Mac-Neil, Lee Morgenroth, Mike Murtaugh, Gene Rhough, Lucy Tancredi, John Taylor, Wendy Saunders, James Jung-Hoon Seo, Cyrus Shaoul, Carleton Sparrell, and Koichi Yamagata.

Thanks to Zane Vella, who designed the entryway animation, Chris Scovell, who provided carpentry assistance, and Alan Symonds, who lent us the Melange lighting controller. Finally, thanks to Tom Wong, Maureen Costello, and Andy Lippman, who provided us special support when we needed it.

The Wheel of Life was sponsored by: at MIT, the Media Laboratory, the Media Arts and Sciences Section, the Office of the Arts, the Department of Literature, the Department of Theatre Arts, the Media Lab Movies of the Future Consortium, the de Flores Fund, and outside MIT, Bontronics Corporation, Sharp Corporation, Apple Computer, Radiant Technologies, Interactive Media Technologies as well as a number of individual donors.

Photos and line drawings are by David Tamés.

Appendix 1: About the Materials and Technology

How were the materials and technology selected and brought together for the Wheel of Life? As is the case in most artistic endeavors, we acted as expeditiously as possible while keeping an eye on our at first nonexistent budget. The vastness of the Villers Experimental Theatre invites scale; the nature of the experience, moving through worlds, required dramatic theatrical lighting; the nature of the project required an interactive network be put in place for each space.

As technical coordinator, Stuart Cody shared his knowledge of off the shelf house building materials. In Water, PVC piping was used to shape the fishbowl; bent rebar was used to create a solid skeleton for the whale's muslin skin. In Earth, lolly columns were used for the broken column and arch; sifted sand was spread out on the floor. The most difficult structure to build was the wood frame which shaped the scrim around Earth, in part because it had to be hung from non existent points in the ceiling. Alan Blout built the air space in one night using mylar which Tom Wong generously donated and a fan.

Early on in the semester we discovered Herrick Goldman, a talented and experienced theatrical lighting designer, who was working part time in the Theater Arts Department. After his initial introduction, Herrick worked closely with each group to generate a lighting concept which dramatized the space, forwarded the action and which was well integrated in the interactive script. Hanging the lighting grid was the first act of the installation process. The lighting was programmed using a Melange Memory Lighting Controller.

Meanwhile we assembled the necessary hardware to complete the installation. An Apple Macintosh IIfx served as the central software node for each space. The monitor displayed the guide station interface. David Tamés designed a LAN consisting of Ethernet, a Shiva FastPath and Radiant Technology's CNX Common Sense interface boxes connected via PhoneNet to distribute messaging to sequenced sensors for each space and between spaces.

In order to trigger lighting cues, the three guide stations communicated via AppleEvents to a Macintosh IIfx server that in turn controlled the Melange Lighting Controller via MIDI. This Macintosh also controlled via MIDI an Akai PG1000 audio/video switcher that switched the video from several Sony Vdecks in the Water space. An Interactive Media Technology audio/video controller provided distribution and switching between the two videodisc players in the Earth space. The laserdiscs in Air were controlled by the guide station using a four-port serial card from Greenspring Computers.

Each space was equipped with NTSC video monitors, video projectors and sound systems as appropriate. The floor plan and block diagram will provide tech-know-bots with more detail about this aspect of the environment.

Appendix 2: Suggestions for a World, The Wheel of Life Chart of Themes, Correspondences, and Personae

Biology/ Evolution	Psychology	Associated Elements	Passageways	Mode of interaction
Beginning of life in the ocean	**The Instincts** subconscious, intuitive, sensual; dream (the child, the player	**Water** fluid, merging, reflecting *Morph:* the mermaid/man	holes, caves, tunnels, whirlpools	physical, sensual, passive/ receptive
Life on land	**The Will** conflict, ambition, aggression, fear (adolescent, the warrior)	**Earth** solid, explosive, resistant *Morph:* Centaur, the sphinx	bridges, trees, mountains, islands	combat, presentation, attack, defense
Human life	**The Reason** planning, analyzing, strategy (the adult, the philosopher, the scientist)	**Air** movement, power, technology *Morph:* the robot	windows, vehicles, fireplaces, doors	analysis, discernment, creation
Life in the stars	**The Spirit**	**Fire** aspiring, lifting, transformation *Morph:* the angel, the E.T.	the sky	integration, cooperation

Notes

1. The Tibetan Mandala provides a model for such a multileveled schematic space. Mandalas are visual representations of layered complex worlds, whose any one section or symbol may refer to a wide range of interlocking spiritual, emotional, and physical attributes. While the mandala did not impose a story, it offered a model of a complex world formed by separate spaces with resonating physical, psychological and spiritual layers.

2. Brenda Laurel, Tim Oren, and Abbe Don, "Issues in Multimedia Interface Design: Media Integration and Interface Agents," CHI '90 *Proceedings*, ACM, April 1990, pp. 133–139.

3. The name of this workshop was given by Benjamin Bergery.

4. Work on the Fire Area was postponed in the hope that all groups would help with this space at the very end.

5. Some initial exercises, drawn from theater training exercises, sought to demonstrate how a particular sense of a world, whether it is a culture's or an individual's, grows out attentional choices: In other exercises, students created models of worlds governed by specific laws of transformation and developed a chart of symbolic correspondences they could use to design specific areas (see chart in appendix 2).

6. Technically, this would be accomplished by taking a video shot of each visitor using an upside down camera while s / he was waiting to enter the space. This inverted image of the explorer would then be matted and edited into the video introduction in real-time.

7. "Full fathom five thy father lies; / Of his bones are coral made; / These are the pearls that were his eyes; / Nothing of him that doth fade / But doth suffer a sea-change / Into something rich and strange. . . ." Shakespeare, *The Tempest*, I, ii, 482–487.

8. This audio was created by stretching and modulating the spoken text.

9. *Ozymandias*

I met a traveller from an antique land who said
Two vast and trunkless legs of stone stand in the desert.
Near them, on the sand, half sunk
A shattered visage lies whose frown and
wrinkled lip and sneer of cold command tell that its
sculptor well those passions read which yet survive
stamped on these lifeless things
the hand that mocked them and the heart that fed.
And on the pedestal these words appear
Nothings beside remains,
round the decay of that colossal wreck
boundless and bare the lone and level sand stretch far away.

—Percy Bysshe Shelley

10. Sensors were placed under the compass points. These were tied into Earth's Macintosh by means of a CNX Common Sense box with sensing hardware for both the compass and the broken column. Technically, the system needed to sense what the explorer was doing and command media based on that knowledge, while returning this information to the guide. Once the explorer executed the correct sequence, the computer had to send instructions for the second stage of the computer graphic to play on the screen at the end of the space.

11. Shakespeare, *Romeo and Juliet*.

12. The bridge and the fire section were never built, again owing to lack of time, energy, and resources.

13. At MIT January is reserved for IAP (Independent Activities Period). Activities span hours, days or for certain courses the full extent, but in general this period provides time for MIT students and faculty to participate in many granular events. Members of the surrounding community are also welcome to participate in many of the activities.

14. One of many contributions, the mandala animation was created by Zane Vella, using a mandala reproduction, a sequence of images in which Larry danced as if constrained by a wheel and more general images of water, earth, air, fire.

15. Videotapes of the installation.

2

Deconstructing the Humpty Dumpty Myth: Putting It Together to Create Cultural Meaning

Ricki Goldman-Segall

Introduction

Most people would be reluctant to break apart a work of art in order to build their own artifact from the remaining pieces. Imagine tearing up the Mona Lisa, for example, to create our own representation. No, I am not suggesting that we destroy an existing work of art, but I do question the boundaries that separate us from learning lessons from those who have come before us. I question the intellectual framework that does not encourage us to build novel creations in collaboration with those who inspire us. When the image of a famous painting is used in a commercially sold puzzle, for example, the pieces have to go back together in the exact same configuration. From the time of our childhood, we are taught to follow patterns that others have delineated for us rather than use existing artifacts as building blocks to make new constructions. This paradigm changes dramatically in the light of digital technologies. We now have computer applications that let us manipulate a digitized reproduction of the Mona Lisa to make our own electronic rendition. Not only can we change aspects of the image, we can break the whole into components and create something quite unlike the original. In a sense, we now have tools to better understand what the early twentieth century modern artist Marcel Duchamp (whose painting of the Mona Lisa has a mustache over her famous smile) knew—that our tearing and pasting pieces into a collage is a new way of looking at what we thought we understood. It is our interpretation that becomes the work of art.

Multimedia researchers face challenges unknown in traditional scholarship. Using electronic data, shared over distributed networks, researchers can now easily bring together bits and pieces of sound, text, and visual data. Research becomes not only the gathering of data, but also the process of putting discrete chunks of data together in meaningful and persuasive ways. However, these constructions do not remain static. Our collaborators and our "audience" can break them into pieces and use them as building blocks to create their own interpretations and artifacts. In doing so, contrary to putting a puzzle together, researchers are now able to corroborate personal versions and build more valid collaborative portraits of what they and others have grown to understand.

For this volume dedicated to the intersection of culture, interpretation, and technology, I have constructed three overlapping sections. The first addresses the challenges facing multimedia researchers, especially those researchers that focus on interpreting culture—ethnographers. In this section, I discuss how research is changing with the use of electronic technologies. In fact, this section sets the stage for the ethnographic account described in the second section—etchings of an emerging computer culture at a school on Vancouver Island in British Columbia, Canada, called the Bayside Middle School. In this account, you will read how a research study is being constructed with children and adults as collaborators. The children have conducted a multimedia portrait of the growing school culture; a team of ethnographers, led by Ted Riecken of the University of Victoria and myself, are constructing portraits of them and their teachers. Not only do we share our views, but, in the near future, our portrait and theirs will be available on CD-ROM for other researchers to use. How will researchers in distributed places make sense of our ethnographic accounts of video and text to build their own interpretations? In the third section, I will answer this question by describing the use of a *Significance Measure*—a specific feature in an application called *Learning Constellations 2.0*—that enables researchers to e-value-ate what the most significant elements within the data are. Instead of placing chunks back into the same arrangement to reproduce the image, researchers can use tools such as the *Significance Measure* to decide what data are significant. Then they can build their layers of significance. For example, other multimedia researchers could use these tools to formulate their own meanings from our reconstructions of the Bayside Middle School. In fact, Ted and I look forward to the day when we can work with researchers in distributed locations interested in deconstructing our theories as they build theirs.

Challenges Facing Researchers Using Multimedia

What challenges face those of us who are producing qualitative accounts using digital forms of media data? The first challenge is the most obvious. *How do we manage the plethora of raw data that we now have access to?* How do we begin to put the pieces or chunks of various media forms together in ways that make sense for ourselves and others? One approach is to use tools that help us e-value-ate the data. We need to be able to attach weights to the qualities of the data as we see, hear, or read them. Assigning weights will assist our determining which data are significant by seeing the ratings. Thus, the problem of managing multimedia data is not only solved by building more robust databases; the problem is addressed by building tools to (1) visually conceptualize the relationships among the data (Horney, 1994), and (2) assign values to attributes so that we can see what data are important to a given task.

The second challenge facing researchers deals with the problem of how to put the pieces together. *How do we take existing linear streams of any media, chunk them up into pieces, and then put them back together again?* Well, first of all, we don't ever put them back as they were. We build our own versions of what came before. For the typical academic researcher this process may seem to be anathematic and contrary to the integrity of the examined work. But, as Clifford and Marcus (1986; p. 2) maintain, all ethnographic accounts start "not with participant-observation or with cultural texts . . . but with writing, [with] the making of texts." And, to take their point one step further, the making of "texts" is a reconstruction of other texts that takes into account the effect of those texts upon our interpretive and creative processes.

I often refer to the willingness to break linear segments into chunks as overcoming the Humpty Dumpty Myth to establish "collaborative virtual communities" (Goldman-Segall, 1992) From the time of our childhood, we are told not to break things into pieces. We get rewarded for building up structures of blocks and scolded for breaking them into pieces. It is quite common for young children not to want to eat a broken cookie. "The whole is greater than the sum of its parts." DeConstructionism tends to be viewed as a destructive impulse. What I propose is that conducting multimedia research means (1) breaking up linear streams

into pieces—DeConstructionism, (2) analyzing them in new juxtapositions—DeConstructionism, and, (3) working with others to build new
forms of representation—CoConstructionism. In other words, the fundamental principle of working with multimedia data is that we need to be
able to rebuild the pieces to create shared cultural spaces for ourselves
and our audiences. As we assemble, filter through our mental map, and
put chunks of data together with our own interpretation and story to tell,
new creations evolve. However, if we define collaboration in its broadest
sense, we realize that we collaborate with the others' works, and our
readers collaborate with our works. Thus, the products of our reconstructions can be the result of a collaboration with fellow researchers, with the
original "authors" of other works, and with our audience.

To illustrate this new partnership among users, authors, and audience, I
will underscore the work of Claudia Barnett who discusses the relationship
between *communities of viewers* and *communities of players* (1994). The
players are the actors that appear in a multimedia adaptation of playwright
Adrienne Kennedy's 1976 play called *A Movie Star Has to Star in Black and
White*. Barnett is designing a tool called *Storyspace* to bring the community
of viewers to the community of actors.

Movie Star is a mysterious, provocative, yet difficult to read play. . . . Three black-
and-white movies from the forties provide the backdrop, and their stars occupy the
stage with (and for) the characters of this play. That is, Marlon Brando and Bette
Davis exist on stage with Kennedy's creations, Clara and her family, and Davis, Jean
Peters, and Shelley Winters recite Clara's lines for her. Those not familiar with these
movies and these stars (i.e., most students today) may read the play as a general
statement about society and cinema. . . . *Movie Star* cannot be completely understood without clarifying the movie references, which is one task *Storyspace* can
achieve. With this program, film stills and sample dialogues may be included as
writing spaces, as may plot summaries and critiques. (Barnett, 1994)

Another challenge facing the multimedia researcher is *what happens to the
meaning when we break streams into pieces and reconstitute them*. In this act,
we are significantly imposing our point of view and our interpretations onto
the data. I argue that researchers have always done this to a greater or lesser
degree. What makes sound research has less to do with impartiality and
more to do with (1) disclosure of point of view and (2) validation of results
by checking out our theories (and our sources) using diverse types of measures to triangulate the data (Lather, 1991). In fact, one also wants to

increase as many "points of viewing" of the data as possible. In other words, more than one researcher should be viewing the data and adding their points of view. This call for ownership of point of view has seeped into the academic research communities via the new breed of science, philosophy, and feminist scholars who have questioned traditional objectivist foundations upon which events in the world have been described (Kuhn, 1970; Fox Keller, 1985; Lakoff, 1987; Lather, 1991; Turkle and Papert, 1991; and Barrett, 1992;). Lakoff, rather than disputing objectivity, redefines it in his own unique way. He says that objectivity requires:

knowing that one has a point of view . . .
knowing what one's point of view is . . .
being able to assess a situation from other points of view . . .
being able to distinguish concepts that are relatively stable and well defined . . .
from those concepts that vary with human purposes and modes of indirect
understanding (Lakoff, 1987: 301).

Working on multimedia research projects almost always follows Lakoff's definition by involving a team of collaborators with multiple points of view making decisions based upon their respective domains and expertise. Thus, I would pose the fourth and critical challenge in the following way: *where and with whom is the interpretation taking place in a multimedia document?* The video recorder, the editor, the digitizer, the categorizer, the director, the writers, the software designers and developers, and the audience of viewers are all adding their layers of interpretation. They make decisions as subtle as: (1) the angle of the shot; (2) the point at which the segment begins and ends, (3) the framework or application within which it is viewed, (4) the time spent viewing the piece; and (5) the ordering of viewing. A multimedia research team begins to act in ways similar to how small companies or movie production teams function. Every member has a contribution to make as the culture constructing the product grows. Unlike the traditional entertainment model, the audience is not only the recipient of the content through a given medium. As Davenport (1994) points out, a new bridge is constructed across content and tools wherein the audience interacts and contributes to the learning and building of the story. In scholarly research, the multimedia artifact may become an ever-expanding composition authored by multiple viewers. The product may illustrate a range of interpretations.

Cultural Account/Ability: "Welcome to the Bayside Middle School"

Culture is what we create and what we experience, not what we inherit. When our means of communication include electronic media, we create virtual cultures. This is not to say that the virtual culture only lives in cyberspace. Rather, our constructed communities live within and around the relationships we form by moving within an electronic space that connects us with others. Virtual cultures extend, rather than exclude, our physical contact with each other.

In this part of the chapter, the emergence of a computer and video culture in a technologically-rich middle school on Vancouver Island in British Columbia is sketched for you. Educational ethnographers, Ted Riecken and myself, guide you through the physical and social spaces. Ted is a faculty member in the Faculty of Education at the University of Victoria. In the following section, we describe our initiating a multimedia research project in the first year's operation of this new high-tech school called the Bayside Middle School. We also describe how the common culture is growing as young people and adults share perspectives. These young people are also engaged in conducting ethnographic accounts of their new school. Understanding the qualities of their lives in the place they study is at the core of their hypermedia project. They have interviewed members of their immediate school community using video and audio recording, and notetaking; they have visited members of the local community to deepen their understanding of how the construction of the school became a municipal concern; and they have gone on field trips to local sites to gain an understanding of their immediate environment. These experiences were recorded and brought into their HyperCard program they and their teachers created called, "Welcome to the Bayside Middle School." In short, teenagers have begun to use multimedia qualitative research methods to study their school culture.

The problem facing these teenage qualitative researchers using new electronic approaches is that same problem I alluded to in the previous section: How do they know if they have fully captured something significant about their project from the many bits and pieces they gathered? At what point do they know they have finished describing the school? Is time the constraint? Is boredom? Is the technology? Is their project an interesting snapshot of what is happening to this school culture? Obviously, our young ethnographers are faced with the same issues that we adult researchers face. When is our project done? How do we know it is done? How much data do we need before we make conclusions? And what is an interesting portrait we feel we can share with others?

As multimedia ethnographers, young or old, we will always face the polarization of opinions between those who believe that research must be objective, and those who claim that we can only see the world from our own lenses and therefore our empirical reality can only be a subjective and social construction. Epistemologist and educator, Jerome Bruner (1986) maintains that knowledge does not live in the text but the text is loosened in the mind of the reader. We know from our experience of the world that the potential for knowing something is often a result of experiencing representational forms whether they be works of art, music, scientific claims, or cuisine (Eisner, 1993). Yes, building them is better. But there is "knowing" through experiencing the works of others. As alluded to earlier in this chapter, knowing something is the result of an interaction between authors of texts and readers or, we could say, between creators and audiences. Even Geertz (1988) cites a range of anthropological writers to show us how an author's power to persuade us has much to do with her discursive style becoming the vehicle though which her story becomes credible. In multimedia research, readers become authors.

The challenge is to bring in additional voices to create face validity or what is often referred to as member checks. Therefore, in the following description about our research project at the Bayside Middle School, several voices other than my own will be included so that my interpretations of what is happening at the school become more representative of what is going on for children at the Bayside.

The Bayside Middle School: Etchings

Additional Voices: Ted Riecken, Faculty of Education, University of Victoria, and the young people at the Bayside Middle School—Amber Adams, Kelli Dianne Taaffe, John Isles, and Wendy Van Osterhout

The following etchings in text form can be read according to the interest of the reader. We welcome you to read our story, using a linear print medium. We look forward to the day when we will be able to bring you to our school, via an electronic medium, and build a common culture with our readers. Our purpose at this early stage of our longitudinal study is not to present results and conclusions, but to "point to an emotion that is around the corner" as writer Margaret Atwood stated about her method of writing prose (1992). Our intention is to capture the hermeneutical tone of this new culture. To do so, we look around or to the side of the events we record, like one would do when star-gazing. The actions we describe do not yet contain our full meaning. The lurking intention that lives "around the corner" is what we want to bring to light. We gaze around the actions and then describe the school in a way that provides the reader with the context and the atmosphere surrounding events.

Background to the Research at the Bayside Middle School

Ted Riecken: Two years ago I had proposed action research as a model for inquiry at Bayside Middle School because I thought it could fulfill the dual purposes of a staff development/in-service model while allowing the University of Victoria (UVic) research team, including Leslie Francis-Pelton, a researcher in secondary Mathematics Education, and Pierce Sarragher, a researcher in secondary Science Education, to gather data that were of interest to our own research agendas. I believe that action research served those purposes quite nicely, but felt it was time to move on to what seemed to be the next logical stage of the project—looking at what students were doing with the exceptionally rich technological environment they had available to them.

In the fall of 1992, the staff and students of Mount Newton Middle School moved into their new building fully equipped with computer labs and computers in many of the classrooms. The students and staff chose the name Bayside Middle School for their new school. I looked forward to the fall of 1992 as a chance to get into the new setting and do some research about a number of factors related to the use of computers in schools. One of the questions I had in mind was simply: What happens to a group of students when you immerse them in a technologically rich environment? I was interested in looking at what sort of learning opportunities there were, and documenting the kinds of learning that emerge when students and their teachers have access to a wide range of computer based technology.

In November of 1992, I dropped into Ricki Goldman-Segall's presentation at our local Computer Users in Education conference in Vancouver to see what she was doing with video data and computers. Ricki studied with Seymour Papert at MIT. She conducts cultural studies of computer use and uses a combination of computer and video technologies, with ethnographic research methods to gather and analyze data about school cultures. As part of her talk, she presented the audience with rich, personal portraits of the children who were using computers in Boston's Hennigan School, the site of her doctoral research. These portraits were not the simple snippets of ethnographic narrative that one has come to expect from presentations of ethnographic research. They were multimedia portraits that could be viewed from many different perspectives. Just as one picks up an artifact and examines it from different angles, in different lights, and from different frames of mind, one could view Ricki's video ethnographies, and then search, and sort, and sift, and theorize. I sat through the session, half listening, and half thinking of the tremendous potential that Ricki's methodology held for research at Bayside. I don't remember at exactly what point I decided this was "it," but before the session was over, I knew that this was the technique I wanted to use at Bayside. After the session, I asked Ricki if she would be interested in coming to UVic to give a presentation on the latest version of *Learning Constellations,* her multimedia tool for video data analysis. During one of the phone calls in which we were arranging the visit, I asked Ricki if she would be interested in seeing the school. I don't know why, but I was almost surprised when she said she would love to see Bayside. For some reason, I thought that asking her to visit Bayside would be something of an imposition on her time. So, I almost didn't ask!

Ricki: I was overwhelmed with Ted's generosity of spirit when he invited me to work with him and his team at his research site on Vancouver Island. My experience of academic life to date has not provided me with many instances of colleagues wanting to share. But then, Ted is not the typical insular scholar. A tall white male who towers over the children and those of us closer to the earth, Ted has the ability of creating comfortable open spaces around him. His eyes sparkle when he talks about children. When we talk about multimedia ethnography, we build on each other's thoughts and go to places neither of us went to alone. So, how could I not

want to work with him in a school where he has been working with
teachers for over two years?

Journey to Bayside

Ricki: I sat on the ferry from Tsawwassen to Vancouver Island thinking
about the school. Yes, I knew it would be a new building with state-of-the-art
technology. I also knew that the teachers were not "high-tech" specialists;
the teachers had previously taught at the old Mt. Newton Junior High
School. Ted, Leslie, and Pierce from UVic along with technology co-
ordinators from the Educational Technology Center (ETC) had been working with these teachers over the past three years, while the physical manifestation—the school—was still a twinkle in the eyes of the community.

The *Spirit of British Columbia* wove its slow path through Active Pass, a
narrow passage between Pender Island and Galiano Island. A young girl on
a school trip sat beside me, telling me her life story. One forgets how
reflective a young woman of thirteen can be when she encounters an interested stranger. Yes, I would be the "stranger" in the school, the "other."
What would the children of Bayside want to tell me about their lives? How
would I tell their story so others would be able to read, hear, and see what life
is like for the children in a semi-rural Canadian community on an island
jutting out into the Pacific Ocean? Would emerging technologies help me
share with others the texture of life at the Bayside Middle School?
. . .

Later that day, Kelli, a student in the school, uses my portable computer to
write the following about what I have written. (I have decided to make my
notes available to those I am researching. I leave my Powerbook on with my
fieldnotes and reflections open for the children to read and add their comments to.) The layers begin to form . . .
. . .

Kelli writes: I love your work so far. It's so true. The only thing I would
change would be if you called us young adults instead of children. (May 14,
1993)
. . .

As I made the appropriate right and left turns from the ferry dock along
hilly country roads spotted with farmlands, horses, and large evergreens

outlining the sky with wispy dark triangular designs, I thought back to my last research site, the Hennigan School in a Boston inner-city community called Jamaica Plains. I remembered the fear of walking the two blocks from the bus. I remembered the red and black graffiti covering the low gray concrete building where parents would drop off their children for seven hours a day. Schools are schools, I thought to myself as I watched the seagulls following the ferry's waves.

I drove up the long driveway toward a neo-classical Greek style structure standing creamy white amongst a large encircling forest of evergreens. It was a sunny, warm day in a rather gloomy wet Pacific Northwest Spring. Children were meandering outside in spite of the fact that scheduled classes were in session. Some were returning from an outdoor activity with their teachers; others were sitting with pen and paper writing, talking, or relaxing in the sun. After a month of rain and clouds, some fresh air and sunshine was probably a good idea. (I was used to seeing children herded in lines to their classrooms and yelled at to keep quiet until they reached their classrooms.) I asked myself, where are the teachers? Granted, this is not an elementary school, but the mood exhibited by their languid body movements suggested that something different was happening for the young people at the Bayside Middle School. What gave these young people so much comfort and confidence? Did they know or sense the extent to which adults had worked to build a learning environment for them? Did this sense of comfort have to do with the fact that these young people come from a semi-rural community? Is life just slower here and therefore looks more relaxed to my harried city eyes? The thought of getting to know these young people and their teachers seemed as much a challenge to my citified being as did trying to find ways to understand the racially and ethnically diverse school populations in Boston. New places; new challenges.

It is somewhat uncommon for educational researchers to describe what life in our semi-rural communities is like for young persons. (Tom Barone's ethnographic account of the Appalachian community in North Carolina stands out as an exemplar [1983].) Stereotypically, we urbanized researchers have labeled rural communities as being less technologically advanced and definitely we portray them as being less sophisticated. We think it is in the cities where young people and high-tech interact—in their homes, in the schools, and in the malls where children encounter video games and other virtual adventures. To date, when advanced technologies are brought into schools, these schools are mostly in either affluent, "exemplary" communities, or they are in extremely poor urban communities. What has not been studied in depth is the integration of advanced computer related technologies in the semi-rural setting that is not terribly "exceptional" in any way. What can we learn about young people's diverse approaches to designing and using technological tools in what appears, at first glance, to be a homogeneous group of children who are more interested in the outdoors than in computers? What differences will emerge in this study? How do gender differences among semi-rural children affect both the process of becoming computer literate and the products they create?

The school is divided into four main pods: North, South, East, and West. The vice-principal, Kevin Elder, has worked hard to build a sense of solidarity among the members of pods. Each pod in the school has its own computer lab with a computer for each person in the class. Classes within a given pod share common activities and compete in sports activities as a group. As an outsider, I think of the pods as being small schools within the school. A nice transition from the sheltering atmosphere of elementary school; a precursor to high school. Walking into the bright airy corridors with children's art covering every possible blank space along the upper half of the walls, I was again struck by the openness of the physical space. Smells of sweet baking led me to a kitchen-like classroom with teenage girls and boys baking. Girls and boys were also busy in what we used to refer to as Shop or Industrial Arts. I walked into the school office and Ted Riecken, my colleague from the University of Victoria, was there to welcome me to the Bayside.

A Visit to Joe Grewal's Class

Ricki: I hadn't finished drinking my sparkling mineral water when it was time to visit Joe Grewal's class for the afternoon. I sealed and stored the drink into my purse while walking into the room. Needless to say, the first thing I noticed was that Joe, wearing shorts and a sweatshirt, was sitting cross-legged on a table drinking a bottle of sparkling mineral water and eating his sandwich. He was explaining an assignment to the young adults in his class. He later explained that he had just come from gym class and had had no time to eat lunch. I guess he felt that I needed this explanation. After all, how many times have any of us been in a class where the teacher was eating a sandwich? Schools are schools? Maybe not. Maybe this one is more interested in community than regimentation and management, I thought.

Joe's eating a sandwich and beverage is not the only sign that this class is not typical of most classes, even of classes in the same school. Joe's class feels like a community, rather than the typical classroom we think of when talking about schools. Tables are drawn together so that the students can work in groups; they do quite a bit of group work. They sit in clusters of four or five with their desks touching. One feels space rather than clutter. Joe's desk is tucked away in a corner beside huge windows overlooking the forest and outdoor space suggesting that he, too, is permitted to have private thoughts in a public space. Joe's desk does not command authority in the traditional way. The young adults appear to be in charge of their community.

Each classroom has a door to the outdoors which facilitates easy access to outdoor activities. (One day, several children conducted their video interviews on a bench in the sun; another day I witnessed an earthquake drill where children and teachers met outside in a matter of minutes.) Having doors in each classroom contributes to the feeling that the classroom is a home and not a guarded enclosure. Could schools in urban communities have open doors and open playgrounds? Would teachers and children feel safe from violent acts in this type of open architecture? Is the attitude towards safety another difference worth exploring as I watch the growth of this computer culture? How is violence addressed in this kind of setting?

Computers are placed on low tables along the sides of the room. A small adjoining room of about six by ten feet wide runs the length of Joe's classroom. Glass walls from desk level to ceiling give this room a soundproof connection to the activity within the classroom. In this glassed room, several computers and video workstations are available for about five or six people. The HyperCard projects are designed in this room; the lab down the hallway is for learning how to use the computer. The glassed room is for classroom multimedia projects.

The lesson continues. Joe has finished his sandwich. His voice is gentle, warm, and almost inaudible as he speaks to his class.

. . .

Jon and Wendy write: Mr. Grewal does yell a lot and his voice is as gental as a donkey! (May 21, 1993)

. . .

Joe's voice blends into the sounds of the rustling of shoes, paper moving, and the scraping clicks of chairs as the students move from one position to the next. The young people break into their group activities. Joe seems to be everywhere, even when he is not in the classroom. At the same time, his presence does not appear to rule the class. Someone is always moving. The movements in the class are fluid, comfortable, and without fear. No one looks to Joe for approval when they move or talk. Shoulders are low; heads shifting from side to side; arms active, engaged; and even the legs of the students seem to fold in soft angles. Moving and talking are part of the rhythm of the class. In fact, many local activities seem to be going on, even when Joe is giving his instructions for a particular part of the assignment.

As I watch Joe and the young people, I am once again struck by the level of engagement. Jan, Amber, Heather, Kelli who are sitting together at one table find ways of weaving in and out of each other's thoughts. I wonder how much of this has to do with how girls talk to each other, with the presence of computers, or with Joe's teaching style. Does it have to do with the fact that we are not in a city?

. . .

Dear Ricki,

I love your Powerbook computer, it's "way cool." Well, I guess I have to write something about your notes so . . . I found your notes very interesting, the were deep, way deep! They went straight to the heart. Your words were very descriptive. DID YOU oops Did you like our carnival? I did, but they got a little to much cotton candy (but it did get me hyper!!!!!!) anyways, back to my note. Well, I think thats about all, but the rest of it was totally awesome!!!
Love

Kelli Dianne Taaffe
Age 13, on May 21, 1993
At Bayside Middle School

. . .

Ricki,

I really enjoyed your, what should I call it, Story? Anyway I enjoyed it. I liked the constructive critisisum and of course, the good comments. It was neat how you made Mr. Grewal—or "Joe"—acculy sound like a nice man (just kidding). I'm quite a nosy person, so I like to hear about other peoples lives. This could also be helpful towards our Bayside Multimedia project. I don't know what else to write about, so I'll be seeing you soon?

From Amber Adams

May 28,1993

. . .

Over the course of many visits to Joe's class, Ted and I gained some good indicators about the approaches used by the group of boys and girls while they were using the computer. We noticed that boys and girls rarely worked collaboratively in mixed sex groups. Moreover, when examining what they produced, it seems that the projects designed by girls and boys were different in terms of appearance and intent. Kelli and Amber spent more time on the aesthetics of the interface design. It was crucial to them where to place a QuickTime movie on the page. Roger and Darcy were more interested in the way it worked, its functionality. They spent most of their time trying to fill the HyperCard tour through the Bayside Middle School with "surprises." (A trip to the washroom opens a sound file of the toilet flushing.)

The intent of the programs was also different. Kelli and Amber were composing an ethnographic tool for the user to understand the attitudes of their peer informants toward the new school. It was important for them to give voice to what some young people complained about. (For example, several informants complained that they couldn't go "off campus" for their lunch break.) Their project was filled with chunks from the interviews they had conducted. Darcy and Roger seem to be what Turkle and Papert (1991) would call "hard" programmers interested in placing little surprises into their section of the project. Their designs were user-centered, planning how other children would use their interface. The girls seem to be more interested using the tool as a way for them to communicate with each other about what they found out while conducting their survey. Their conversations focused on the process of collecting the data rather than on the code or the structure of the interface. Kelli and Amber's interface design was definitely more aesthetically interesting, using "special effects" to communicate the changing rhythm of their interviews to others. Roger and Darcy's was technically more sophisticated and rigorous. Part of the problem Kelli and Amber experience, as Kelli told us, is that they don't get to work on the "more powerful" computer because Darcy and Roger are always on it. When I asked Kelli if there was anything she thought she could do about this, she became quite shy, for Kelli, and changed the subject.

A Dialogue between Collaborators

Ted: Ricki, in multimedia ethnography, the ethnographer usually determines which actions are captured by the video camera. The raw video footage is thus a record of what interested the ethnographer at the time of the recording. In recording classroom life, the ethnographer engages in a conscious yet instantaneous selection of material for the ethnography.

Ricki: I agree. This leads to the central problem in achieving validity. To build valid interpretations about subtle events, we may need more sophisticated tools for sharing and checking out with others our understanding of what we recorded. Then we can negotiate our interpretations to reach triangulated conclusions. These layers of weighted descriptions will lead us toward more reliable research results.

Ted: It seems to me that text is used by the ethnographer both as a means of collecting data and expressing the meaning that this researcher has ascribed to that data. Until recently, the results of ethnographic study were communicated almost exclusively via text. Isn't this limiting our understanding of what REALLY happened?

Ricki: Yes. There is a classic American case about a young black male teenager who answers the police officer's question, "Did you kill the storekeeper" by saying, "I, I killed the storekeeper." However, what he said was a rhetorical question, "I??? I KILLED the storekeeper???"—indicating that he was insulted and shocked that he could be accused. What got recorded in text was that the young man had admitted guilt. The video report of this interview would have led us to interpret the words quite differently, and may I add, more accurately. This is not to say that the video is a more objective tool for recording data. The same issue that you mention, that is, that a researcher is not only collecting data but is "expressing" it in a construction that is called fieldnotes, occurs in using video as an ethnographic tool. The recordings (video fieldnotes, one might call them) are still constructions of the videographer! Representations are "Forms" as Elliot Eisner would say (1992). Video records are constructed forms created by the videographer.

Ted: In the postmodern world, traditional ethnography may become anachronistic. With its reliance on the written word, traditional ethnography represents an art or craft lingering in a world bursting with opportunities for multimedia expression and communication.

Ricki: When working on a collaborative video analysis team project, writers/recorders and readers/users share multiple views on what was happening for other readers. When electronic journals become pervasive in the culture, the distinction between writer and reader will blur even more dramatically. Interactive documents wherein interpretations can continue to be shared and negotiated on distributed networks will enable users to interact with authors of these documents in a way that the users become part of the interpretation process. The notion of fixed interpretations may be part of our pre-electronic past.

Tools to Organize and Interpret Multimedia "Stories"

In this part of the paper, I will describe the use of a new feature, a *Significance Measure* in an application for organizing, analyzing, and interpreting video, text, and sound chunks of data called *Learning Constellations 2.0 (LC 2)*. To begin this section, I will explain several methods of layering data in *LC 2* that bring the reader of multimedia documents closer to understanding the meaning that the author in the culture is describing. Imagine you are working on the multimedia version of the Bayside data with sound, text and video star chunks to put the pieces together for your own understanding of what happens to children in an emerging technology culture.

Methods of Layering Data

Our team at the University of British Columbia's multimedia ethnographic research lab, MERLin, has added a feature called a *Significance Measure*. This *Significance Measure* enables the researcher to rate the significance of attributes as she is coding her data (Goldman-Segall, 1993). Layers or thickness are added as she and others add their values to raw data. These layered clusters enable teams of researchers "to see" which data are most significant, and for whom, to the total body of data. Using the *Significance Measure* will support the work of those researchers who share the same video (and text) by building "thick," as Geertz would say (1973), descriptions and interpretations.

How does a tool for layering data act as a method of dealing with the central issue inherent in interpreting video, that is, that interpretations of visual information are exceptionally linked to both the perceptions of those who are interpreting the data as well as to the ways in which the data are recorded and presented? Point of view is not intrinsically *bad*, as long as it is disclosed to readers or viewers. I am not proposing that layering can be dealt with in a purely mechanical or technical way. However, I believe that designing tools for layering data provides us with a vehicle for opening a critical discussion about how to build textured and rich descriptions based upon segments of video data.

Over the past eight years, I have been working closely with colleagues, Glorianna Davenport and Seymour Papert, from the MIT Media Lab, and with Kellogg Booth of the Computer Graphics group at UBC in Canada. During this time, I have been developing a theory of how to layer data so that the meaning of a recorded event could be easily communicated and understood in a multimedia documentation. With separate design teams, I have designed two different versions of *Learning Constellations*, which are software applications for annotating, linking, and juxtaposing media forms into multimedia documents (Goldman-Segall, 1990 and 1993). (Monika Marcovici has been the head programmer for this second application.)

In both systems, the researcher can build layered descriptions upon which she and others can e-value-ate the validity of her conclusions in the following ways:

1. Building groupings that are similar (clustering, stacking)
2. Thickening the description with annotations
3. Linking across attributes: slicing through the layers
4. Signifying the meaning by adding weight to the attributes
5. Adding perspectives and "points of viewing": triangulation

6. Juxtaposing video/text/sound in diverse configurations
7. Making fine-grained selections
8. Fine tuning, trimming, narrowing focus, reaching core concepts.

Let me expand upon a few of these ways of layering. One way of layering our understanding occurs during the process of interpretation when multiple users comment upon, or annotate, the same video stream. As they annotate, they thicken the data because each user interprets the same event quite differently. Multimedia designers are now beginning to realize that diverse users manipulate video data differently. The likelihood of conclusions being the same is minuscule.

Having access to multiple forms of representations of research data—video, text, sound—also adds to the building of layers. The days where text was the only legitimate form of data are over. The use of sound, photographs, video or film, or drawings and sketches have become commonplace. However, most applications, such as Microsoft Word, treat researchers as being married to one form—usually to text. It is possible to add a digitized image or a QuickTime movie to a text document, but if the researcher wants to codify this data with the other data, she must resort to using either a text-based or video-based or sound-based application. In *Learning Constellations 2.0 (LC 2)*, all data forms can be codified and linked as equal but different forms.

However, the kind of layering that is more crucial to the researcher is a result of what happens when data are shared. How can members of a research team explore the various significant ratings of colleagues? In other words, can layering enable the researcher to get a sense of seeing the data from other perspectives in order to triangulate interpretations?

In *LC 2*, layering tools have been introduced so that they visually represent the significance of specific video data to the body of the data. As a result, layered frameworks for how to build systems that can weigh specific data are being developed. Consider the following description of the *Significance Measure*.

The Significance Measure

The *Significance Measure* is a tool for researchers to rate the relative significance of a certain topic or participant in a chunk of information (see vertical bar in upper left hand quadrant of figure 2.1). A significance rating is recorded by sliding a button on a colored vertical scale, from an unsaturated color at the very bottom (corresponding to a rating of "0") to a saturated color at the top (corresponding to a rate of "10"). The color matches the color that has been assigned to the category. In this way, the researcher is provided with visual clues in her or his building of significance. Searching for data containing a certain keyword will not only provide a random list of matching data, but will sort the data in a list according to its rating in relation to the criteria in question. In addition, information such as 'the most important themes for a specific contributor, or author' are now possible.

This kind of layering data through sharing perspectives, using a simple tool for rating chunks, is an introduction to more sophisticated tools that, in

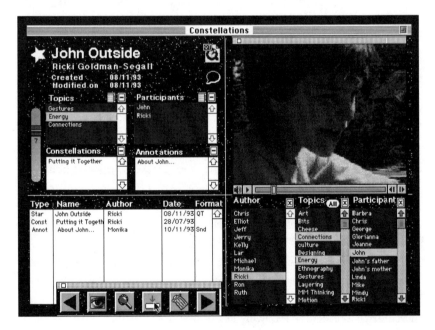

Figure 2.1.
Main page from *Learning Constellations 2.0*. *Significance Measure* icon is the vertical bar in upper left quadrant (directly below the Star Icon). It rates the importance of items in the *Topics, Participants, Constellations,* and *Annotations* windows. Data are displayed in upper right quadrant. The database is in the lower right quadrant. Results of searching through the database are displayed in lower left quadrant. Clicking on an item displays the item and brings up specific data in the upper left quadrant.

the near future, may automatically be able to compare similarities and differences according to attributes. At the present stage, however, the layering of significance is an interpretive approach wherein the researcher places herself inside multiple frameworks and perspectives. It is not meant to replace a conversation but rather to act as a pointer for discussion among colleagues.

We expect that as analysis systems become more automated and sophisticated, large-scale groupings will be possible where researchers will be able to "ask the computer" to find and compute (according to a plethora of attributes) the most significant chunks that relate to a given topic. Layering at this level could be a visual representation of how diverse persons view a given attribute. We also expect that we will be able to design star chunks that will "live" in a three dimensional coordinate system (resembling the galaxy under investigation) where each axis represents another measure. In a possible scenario, the three-dimensional graph could act much like MultiLogo agents—with individual stars reacting to each other in much the same way as do Resnick's (1991) concurrent turtles do. Researchers, using this kind of environment, will be able to create a visual view that expresses the relevance of each attribute.

Learning Constellations 2.0

For your better understanding, let me briefly describe how *Learning Constellations 2.0* works. The main card of *LC 2* is divided into four Quadrants. In the upper left hand Quadrant, the user is able to select the type of data to be displayed (text, video, picture, sound), chunk the data, describe each chunk and rate the significance or importance of that chunk. In the upper right Quadrant, the data are displayed. This area is of particular importance because it works globally with the rest of the computer. If displaying video, this program will automatically launch QuickTime; if text, it will launch the word-processing program of your choice. In other words, you can work in your preferred application and the data remains as a file in that application with pointers in *LC 2* to the data. The lower right Quadrant is where the database is located; any categories selected from the database are displayed in the lower left quadrant.

We could ask how this particular illustration works. A researcher named Ricki is using the system. Her name appears as the creator of that star chunk on the upper left Quadrant under the name of the chunk called "John Outside." This researcher has given values to the various topics which are listed in the same quadrant. Notice how she has given the topic "Energy" a 7.0 in the *Significance Measure*. We also see her relative ordering: "Gesture" first; "Energy" second; and "Connections" third. Those topics which have higher significance to her are listed closer to the top of the list.

Now let us suppose after seeing this star chunk "John Outside," Ricki wants to see the other connections to this chunk. Well, she could just double click on any attribute in the upper left Quadrant describing the star, or she could go to the database in the lower right hand Quadrant and make a selection by clicking on any of the listed attributes that appear in the description of the star chunk. Her search for other links to the topics "Connections" and "Energy" has brought up two other items—(1) a Constellation, or cluster of star chunks (Goldman-Segall, 1990), called "Putting it together," and (2) a sound annotation star called "About John." Double clicking on either would bring up that item or group of items. If she wanted to see how Monika, Elliot, and Ruth had made sense of this chunk, she would do another search in the database. In this way, the user could browse, but not change, her colleagues' chunks and view their ratings. In this way, a researcher has access to other colleagues' ratings.

Putting the Pieces Together

Those of us concerned with the layering of video data will need to pay attention to the problems that have been addressed using other existing tools and methods of video analysis—e.g., *CVideo* (formerly *Videonoter* [Rochelle, Pea, Trigg, 1990], *VANNA* (Harrison and Baecker, 1991), and more recently, Elliot's (1992) video streamer and shot parser. Moreover, we will need to design and implement a mechanism that communicates from the annotations to a visually based database structure where layers of data can be easily accessed, simultaneously taking the user back to the contextual information which supports a general understanding of the meaning of the video event. In other words, we need to begin to address how we analyze video streams and "droplets" of data after we have placed them, accessed them, and linked them. In the testing phase, we will need to study the ways in which individual researchers from a variety of domains learn to know which aspects of their video data are significant to them. Then, we need to implement a system of layered descriptions that would provide them with visual clues.

In the very near future, on-line consumers of research findings will have access to our video snapshots. I won't be able to write about the children of the Bayside Middle School on Vancouver Island without including the relevant video data, for example, of a child telling me: "I don't need to write as much anymore now that I have a computer." On viewing this data with Ted, we came to the conclusion that Sean means that he doesn't have to use a pen and paper to write because he is using the computer as his writing tool. Will the multimedia reader of this data in an article in an electronic journal—such as the *Arachnet Electronic Journal for Virtual Culture*—be persuaded? Will the reader think that Sean is not composing his thoughts, organizing his ideas, or representing them in a form of his choice? Maybe Sean is playing games on the computer instead of "writing." What does Sean really mean when he uses the term *writing*? Do I dare provide my audience with the same data I have access to and encourage readers to partake in the interpretation process? Will the reader want to do this? Certainly, I would want to see the film rushes that Gregory Bateson shot while Margaret Mead was conducting her research. These data would help me think I am getting closer to understanding the events, but is this true? As an ethnographer, I am interested in Mead's filter, I want to see her husband, Gregory Bateson's point of view, and I want to read their daughter Mary Catherine Bateson's reflections of growing up in that culture. Nevertheless, if I could also have access to the data that is both affecting and being affected by the ideas of a colleague, I would be able to better weigh its importance in relation to what I am reporting to others. In fact, a similar situation has happened to me on more than one occasion. Helping students and colleagues analyze their video data has changed my mind about the validity of their written representations. I have found that the video data did not tell the story that the video researcher was reporting as conclusions. In fact, I sensed that these researchers were not listening to, or carefully watching, their own video rushes. They were reporting what they thought had happened or what they had wanted to happen. One researcher told me that he had purposefully selected the video that did not support the premise of his paper in order to be more accurate to the chronology of events that took place. I wondered why he had not tried to build his theory from all his data and negotiated this artifact with his memories of the event in a more congruent method.

I realize that filters are not the sole ownership of the makers of the media while recording the data. Video researchers are surrounded by a dense filter when they view their own data. As editors viewing their own footage and making decisions what to show to others, they are trying to bring to light what they experienced and not only what their "subjects" may have experienced in that place and time. Often, they see what they choose to see; they tell us what they want us to know. However, if researchers open themselves to the challenge of digital data, they will seek disclosure, shedding layers to open their research topic to the affirmation or scrutiny of others. They will become collaborators, sharing data and points of view to build more valid studies (Goldman-Segall, 1993).

In conclusion, layering and adding significance will address the needs of either the individual researcher or multiple researchers sharing data. A team of users will be able, at a glance, to check out how important a given chunk of video or text is to a collaborating colleague. These *significance tools* will substantially support the work of teams of researchers interested in building more sophisticated methodological approaches of managing the multi-grained and intangible nature of this electronic medium. Throughout this paper, I have addressed the theme of creating collaborative virtual communities when conducting multimedia ethnography. Although in its infancy, the use of electronic media points the way for a deeper rigor in scholarship. Eventually, we will share our data and build theories together. Negotiated conclusions will be the products of these endeavors. Maybe all the king's horses and all the king's men can't put Humpty Dumpty together again, in exactly the same configuration, but maybe we will have new versions of Humpty Dumpties to tell us stories we have never dared to consider.

Acknowledgments

This research is supported by the Natural Science and Engineering Research Council (NSERC) of Canada Strategic Research Grant (§5–81457) called

Logging, Annotation and Navigation for HyperMedia Video Analysis Tools. This research is also supported by the Educational Technology Center (ETC) of the British Columbia Ministry of Education.

The person who has confirmed my belief in the need for collaboration while conducting multimedia ethnography is Ted Riecken, a key voice in this chapter. I would also like to thank Leslie Francis-Pelton and Pierce Sarragher for welcoming me as a team member. Kevin Elder, the Vice-Principal, and Joe Grewal, a teacher, and the young people of the Bayside Middle School have given me a renewed sense of respect and admiration for what schools can be like for young people. Mike Hoebel from the Educational Technology Center has supported this research with funds for travel. I thank him and his staff. I would also like to thank the graduate students and research staff who work in MERLin, our Multimedia Ethnographic Research Lab in the Faculty of Education at the University of British Columbia—Monika Marcovici, Lar Halff, and Scott Flinn. They worked diligently on the redesign of *Learning Constellations*. Thanks to the UBC graduate students and University of Victoria faculty who are using LC 2 to analyze their own video data. To friends, Rory Wallace and Silvia McFadyen, thank you for the talks about artists of the early twentieth century. And, to Avner Segall, for his comments and suggestions for how to improve this chapter, I am grateful.

References

Atwood, M. (1992) Television interview of poet and author, Margaret Atwood, by June Callwood, Canadian Broadcasting Corporation (CBC), Canada, October 8.

Barone, T. (1983) "Things of Use and Things of Beauty: The Swain County High School Arts Program." *Deadalus, Journal of American Academy of Arts and Sciences* 112, no. 3: 1–28.

Barnett, C. (1994) "A Movie Star Has to Star in Hypertext: *Storyspace* and the (Re)Interpretation of the Printed Play Script." *Computer Graphics* 28, no. 1 (February).

Barrett, E., ed. (1992) *Sociomedia: Multimedia, Hypermedia, and the Social Construction of Knowledge*. Cambridge, MA: MIT Press.

Bruner, J. (1986) *Actual Minds, Possible Worlds*. Cambridge, MA: Harvard University Press.

Clifford, J., and G. Marcus. (1986) *Writing Culture: the Poetics and Politics of Ethnography*. Berkeley: UC Press.

Davenport, G. (1994) "Bridging across Content and Tools." *Computer Graphics* 28, no. 1 (February).

Eisner, E. (1993) "Forms of Understanding and the Future of Educational Research." *American Education Research Association 1993 General Meeting's Presidential Address*, April 14.

Eisner, E. (1992) *The Enlightened Eye: Qualitative Inquiry and the Enhancement of Educational Practice.* New York: Macmillan.

Elliot, E. (1992) "Multiple Views of Digital Video." Unpublished paper. Cambridge, MA: MIT Media Lab.

Geertz, C. (1973) *The Interpretation of Cultures.* Basic Books: New York.

Geertz, C. (1988) *Works and Lives: Anthropologist as Author.* Palo Alto, CA: Stanford University Press.

Goldman-Segall, R. (1990) *Learning Constellations: A Multimedia Ethnographic Research Environment Using Video Technology to Explore Children's Thinking.* Doctoral dissertation, Massachusetts Institute of Technology, Cambridge.

Goldman-Segall, R. (1992) "Collaborative Virtual Communities: Using *Learning Constellations*, a Multimedia Ethnographic Research Tool. In *Sociomedia: Multimedia, Hypermedia, and the Social Construction of Knowledge*, edited by E. Barrett. Cambridge, MA: MIT Press.

Goldman-Segall, R. (1993) "Interpreting Video Data: Introducing a *Significance Measure* to Layer Descriptions." *Journal for Educational Multimedia and Hypermedia* 2, no. 3: 261—283

Harrison, B. L., and R. M. Baecker. (1991) "Designing Video Annotation and Analysis Systems." *In Proceedings of CHI'91.* ACM, New York.

Horney, M. (1994) "Interactive Data Visualization in Qualitative Research. *Computer Graphics* 28, no. 1 (February).

Kuhn, T. (1970) *The Structure of Scientific Revolutions.* 2d ed. Chicago: University of Chicago Press.

Lather, P. (1991) "Issues of Validity." *Interchange* 17, no. 4: 63—84.

Lakoff, G. (1987) *Women, Fire, and Dangerous Things: What Categories Reveal about the Mind.* Chicago: University of Chicago Press.

Resnick, M. (1991a) "Animal Simulations with *Logo: Massive Parallelism for the Masses." In *From Animals to Animats*, edited by J. A. Meyer and S. Wilson. Cambridge, MA: MIT Press.

Resnick, M. (1991b) "MultiLogo: A Study of Children and Concurrent Thinking." In *Constructionism*, edited by I. Harel and S. Papert. Norwood, New Jersey: Ablex Publishers.

Roschelle, J., R. Pea, and R. Trigg. (1990) "VideoNoter: A Tool for Exploratory Video Analysis." *IRL Technical Report* no. IRL 90–0021, March.

Turkle, S., and S. Papert. (1991) "Epistemological Pluralism and the Reevaluation of the Concrete." In *Constructionism*, edited by I. Harel and S. Papert. Norwood, NJ: Ablex.

3

How to Do Things without Words: The Multicultural Promise of Multimedia

Michael Roy

At the W.E.B. Du Bois Institute for Afro-American Research at Harvard University, we are managing the evolution of our research projects from those prepared and published entirely on paper—with notecards, typewriters, carbon paper, and traditional typesetting—to those prepared and published entirely on computer, with many intermediary steps, and many works that adopt familiar hybrid solutions. The production and publication decisions we make are driven as much by social and intellectual forces as they are by available technology. The aim of the Institute—to produce scholarship and reference works in African-American studies, and to promote intellectual exchange among scholars and students of African-American studies— can clearly be facilitated through the use of emerging technologies. At the crudest level of distinctions, multicultural scholarship and teaching will benefit greatly from multimedia. And yet both terms in this equation— multiculturalism and multimedia—are used in such wide and disparate contexts as to render them nearly meaningless, apart from their identification, in the first case, with things socially progressive, and in the second with computer things on the (for now) cutting edge of technology.

African-American Studies is at heart an interdisciplinary approach to scholarship in the humanities and social sciences. Drawing on the powerful interpretive tools of a range of disciplines—from anthropology to literary theory, from religion to economics—the discipline seeks to document, understand, and critique the fundamental role the concept of race plays and has played in American and world history. However, as Stanley Fish has pointed out, "being interdisciplinary is so very hard to do" (Fish 1994, 231). By this he means that the narrative frames of the various disciplines that self-proclaimed "interdisciplinary" approaches draw on to bring light to its subject are at best unable to make sense of their competing vocabularies, and at worst, entirely at odds with one another. Fish calls into question the utility, and even the possibility, of an anthropologist, for example, talking meaningfully with an economic historian. Looking at these narrative frames as a system, one immediately sees that (taking Fish's view) the largest challenge in interdisciplinary software development is not getting the Macintosh to share files with the PC, but convincing scholars from a broad range of intensely specialized fields that their work might "be compatible" with the work of their colleague in a different department.

Given these fundamental and perhaps unresolvable contradictions that lie at the center of any discussion about "what is African-American Studies" (and similar disputes about what is "true multimedia"), I would like to explore these issues within the context of the complex interplay of intellectual, social, and technical issues that come to bear on a particular project—the development of the African Art History Project at the Du Bois Institute at Harvard—in the hope that this exploration might reveal both the limits and possibilities of technology's ability to enable new forms of scholarship and education.

The African Art History Project is directed by Suzanne Blier, of the Fine Arts Department at Harvard. The project has three goals:

• the collection and presentation of information in support of Blier's ongoing research on the societal roots of creativity
• the production of a large scale multimedia database (with accompanying tools for searching and presenting information) for the more general study and teaching of African cultural history.
• the production of a set of communication tools that will allow the database to interact with other on-going projects in allied fields.

We are producing an application that will run on the campus network at Harvard, while simultaneously designing for extensibility, both onto the Internet, and as a shell application that might be used to support and connect with teaching and scholarship in other disciplines.

In what follows, I will examine some of the tensions that exist as we design the specifications for this application. The underlying assumption is that despite the necessary compromises and shortcomings that accompany any attempt to collect, categorize, and present a sizable number of disparate materials, these new technologies provide powerful benefits to people interested in exploring African cultural history.

The most fundamental tool for the entire application is the image server and its accompanying database. We are working with a collection of over 20,000 images of African art objects, all of which will exist in digital form and will be indexed according to a variety of schemes. At present, the images exist as slides. Physical access to the collection is limited to faculty and teaching fellows, while intellectual access is limited to either prior knowledge ("I know that this slide is somewhere in this drawer because I saw it there last time I taught this course"), or by country, and then by material within country.

The benefits of digitizing and indexing the collection are many, and obvious. Students will be able to work with the same high resolution images that they saw in class as they write their papers and prepare their exams. Faculty will be able to quickly assemble collections of images for display in class and for examination by students as homework, as well as for their own examination in support of their research. Researchers in allied fields—anthropology, economic history, Afro-American Studies, political science—will be able to draw on cultural materials that otherwise might have been neglected for lack of finding aids for the collections.

As a touchstone from which to think about the limits and possibilities of this project, I would like to review Janet Murray's discussion of "the kinds of functionality humanists will increasingly demand from computer-based environments" (Murray 1993, 340) from her essay "Restructuring Space, Time, Story, and Text," and consider the tension between these new abilities and the more traditional forms of scholarship, in this case an essay that appeared in *Transition Magazine*, Eliot Weinberger's "The Camera People."

Murray describes the desired functionality in these terms:

[T]ext and video clips should be capable of being annotated, rearranged, and stored for retrieval in selected form. One should be able to write multimedia essays, incorporating video clips into text. The interconnections in such a system would be dense, and the key to making it workable would be to ensure that users could start with any piece of it—texts, films, or commentary—and access the appropriate parts of any other piece without having to encounter a cumbersome apparatus or to follow rigid pre-formed paths. The invention of a medium to support such explorations is an important task in supporting the development of the next generation of applications in the humanities.

Murray is exactly right to describe developments in multimedia computing as "the invention of a medium," and to describe the arrival of a mature, stable process for creating multimedia essays as taking place sometime in the fairly distant future. While the history of the novel, the essay, and perhaps all forms of analytic or creative behavior teaches us that no form is ever entirely stable, it is clear that (at least within cultural and literary studies) the form of the essay is in crisis.

Consider Eliot Weinberger's brilliant essay "The Camera People" (*Transition 55*, pp. 25–54), which offers both a history and critique of ethnographic filmmaking. Within the course of the essay, Weinberger makes mention of dozens of films, and provides detailed descriptions of particular scenes from these films, intermingled with searing (and hilariously sarcastic) critique, or high praise, depending on the film.

Here is Weinberger describing John Marshall's use of narration in his film *The Hunters*:

> The film is sustained by continual narration. At times the narrator is a crafty insider ("Kaycho water is always brackish this time of year"; the kudus, a kind of antelope, are "more restless than usual"; and so on). At other times, Marshall takes the Voice of God, familiar in most documentaries since the invention of sound, to new heights. Not only does he tell us what the men are thinking—what one critic has wittily called the telepathic fallacy—we even learn the thoughts and feelings of the wounded giraffe. ("She traveled in an open country with a singleness of mind." Later, she is"troubled," "too dazed to care," and "no longer has her predicament clearly in mind.") Worst of all, God has been reading Hemingway:"He found the dung of a kudu. The kudu is a big animal. A kudu would be ample meat to bring home." The machismo of the spoken prose becomes manifest when the final killing of the female giraffe is described in terms of gang-rape: The men "exhausted their spears and spent their strength upon her." (Weinberger, p. 32)

In this text we see at work a skilled rhetorician, carefully crafting an argument through the conventional means of quoting, summarizing, comparing, contrasting. Since the majority of readers do not have immediate access to the films he is talking about, nor have they likely seen all of them, the reader most likely has to take on faith the evidence that Weinberger presents. One can imagine Weinberger deploying to good effect the sorts of functionality Murray describes—inserting video clips, alternative narrations, allowing the soundtrack to be muted or swapped—within the essay.

Simply being able to "quote" from these films, or even ideally include each of them in their entirety, would not be sufficient to achieve the same effects of the traditional essay. Weinberger himself discusses the limits of technology in a critique of Margaret Mead's faith in the ability of the camera to deliver unmediated access to reality. In response to Mead's claim that

if tape recorder, camera, or video is set up and left in the same place, large batches of material can be collected without the intervention of the filmmaker or ethnographer and without the continuous self-consciousness of those who are being observed. The camera or tape recorder that stays in one spot, that is not tuned, wound, refocused, or visibly loaded, does become part of the background scene, and what it records did happen. (Weinberger, 1952, 38)

Weinberger responds:

Leaving aside the obvious moral and political questions of surveillance—white folks, as usual, playing God, albeit an immobile one with a single fixed stare—the value of such information could be nothing more than slight. The simplest human events unfold in a tangle of attendant activities, emotions, motivations, responses, and thoughts. One can imagine a !Kung anthropologist attempting to interpret the practices and effects of the American cash economy from footage obtained with the cameras in the local bank. (Weinberger, 1952, 38)

To hope that multimedia might provide unmediated and complete access to what Weinberger calls the "tangle of attendant activities" is to commit the same sort of ideological and intellectual faux pas that Weinberger so clearly enumerates in the many ethnocentric ethnographic films that he condemns.

And yet reading essays such as Weinberger's forces one to confront the limits of traditional forms of description, analysis, and critique, when these methods are being applied to television, cinema, radio, and the visual arts. In his essay, Weinberger constructs a compelling argument, and yet I am curious how much more compelling the argument might be were Weinberger to have at his disposal the sorts of tools that Murray alludes to towards the end of her essay.

How would one evaluate the validity and force of such an argument? How would one "publish" the essay to a wide audience? How might Weinberger be rewarded for having produced this sort of work? These are three quite interconnected questions that bear directly on the various technical, social, and intellectual forces that shape the development of the African Art History Project.

While the technical requirements of serving high-resolution images over a campus network and linking those images to a highly indexed database is nontrivial, the problem becomes far more technically demanding once one factors in what I am calling the social and intellectual forces that come to bear on this aspect of the application. Many of the images are still under copyright, and therefore access to them must be both controlled and monitored. While there is presently enormous controversy and debate over what counts as "fair use," any application that delivers copyrighted material over a network clearly requires an accounting system, the likes of which are under development throughout universities in the United States and elsewhere. More specific to the intellectual work of the project, and therefore more interesting to us, is the technical requirement that has less to do with staying within the law, and more to do with the specifics of the "content" being pushed around the network.

African art, as is true of all major transhistorical, transcultural categories, is hard to categorize. The history of Africa is the history of shifting political boundaries, suspect "ethnographic" categories, migrations, invasions, periods of wealth, periods of intense intercultural contact, war, and myriad other events. As a result of the multiplicity of conflicting interests—social, political, intellectual—that come to bear on the definition of African history, there is intense debate among African art historians over periodization, vocabularies to describe ethnic groupings, the various boundaries between groups, and significant groupings of geographic territory. As new evidence is uncovered and new theoretical paradigms evolve, old systems of cataloging and indexing cease to be "valid" and (for some) devolve into historical curiosities or offensive racist, ethnographic systems, while for others these old systems are an important fact of the intellectual tradition of African art history, and worthy of preservation and in need of evaluation. As elsewhere within the specification of the application, our commitment to an "open" system (nonproprietary file formats, interchange of data among various operating systems) must be weighed against the economics and intellectual utility of "overindexing."

The tensions between the technical ability to describe in detail the material, period, genre, place, and the history of "miscataloging" must be weighed against the cost of paying someone to perform this indexing. If one accounts for financial matters under "the social," one finds an allied problem when designing a system for indexing. Ideally, if one were indexing a particular Yoruba mask, one would want to apply both the standard museum categories—period, place, provenance, etc.—but also include the annotations of someone knowledgeable about the mask. Who would count as knowledgeable? How could we convince whoever it is we deem qualified to annotate the mask to spend her time writing annotations for our database? Do we develop a system whereby absolutely anyone can append annotations to the database? If one decides that one wants only the annotations of "true experts," how does one filter these annotations from the rest?

While the fundamental tool of the application is an image server and database, we recognize that because the subject area of the database—African art history—can not be as neatly bounded as, say, that of *Perseus*, the aim is to produce nodes of certain periods and places that are representative, and engage the particular sub-field on its own terms, while simultaneously providing points of access to the collection by nonspecialists, and people from allied disciplines.

Recognizing that all databases are ultimately ephemeral, and that the utility of their categories may evaporate long before the platform on which the application runs, we see the greatest future of multimedia computing in the humanities in the direction of projects such as *Who Built America?* (Rosensweig, Brier, Brown, 1993), which combines a rich database of primary and secondary materials, scholarly annotations to these materials, all supporting an argument, which in this case takes the form of a textbook on American labor history during the guilded age. The centrality of place given both text and the argument of the text marks an important shift away from "mere" collections of resources that can then be manipulated by users to perform research, and toward the creation of a vehicle that, while still allowing users to manipulate resources, also makes an explicit argument itself. *Who Built America?* is a database, but it is also a piece of scholarly interpretation, complete with an explicit point of view that one can engage with in nearly the same way that one might have engaged with its print predecessor. One may want to quibble with the degree of rigidity built into its structure and its failure to fully exploit the hypertextual possibilities of using the same resources in support of multiple points of its argument. Yet its recognition of the importance, if not the centrality, of narrative and argumentation mark it as a milestone in the brief history of multimedia computing in the humanities.

We are building into our application the ability to produce what Suzanne Blier has called a narrative out of the results of surveying the imageries and a subsidiary database of secondary literature. Blier will write narratives herself using these tools, and we intend to commission her colleagues to construct their own narratives, drawing on resources from within our database, which of course will grow to include other narratives within its pool of secondary literature. Students will use the same tool to construct reports for classroom use. That students and teachers will be sharing resources and using the same tools to "publish" their work for some raises again the issue of authority and "authorized" versions of the application. When the student hands in her narrative to the professor, how will the professor evaluate the quality of the work? Does the student's narrative become part of the database alongside the professor's? The question of inclusivity raises an allied problem: that of evaluation. Even if software tools existed so that scholars could effortlessly tap into terrabytes of data, extract quickly and accurately exactly the resources that would be most helpful for them, and seamlessly construct some form of hypermedia document, the existing structures of evaluation and reward do not yet contain vocabularies capable of making sense of these documents. Part of this has to do with a latent technophobia among humanists, combined with a certain threat that these new forms of communicating ideas (via computer) pose to people who have earned their status (and their livelihood) on their relative mastery of older forms of communicating ideas (writing on paper.) But partly the slow growth of evaluative terms for these new forms has to do with the problems of interdisciplinary software with which I began this essay. In trying to develop interdisciplinary software, not only do the scholars from the various disciplines and sub-disciplines have trouble talking sensibly between themselves, the resulting documents are orphans, lacking (for the moment) relations with which to compare themselves.

Blier intends to explore using the database and its writing tools what she calls "the social topography of artistic creativity in Africa." Investigating the relationship between social and artistic forms, she hopes to demonstrate a co-relationship between 'creative' periods in a culture's history and periods of what she calls socio-cultural cross-currency. In addition to looking at the cultural production of a particular cultural and historical moment, she will examine archeological site locales, the growth of cities, places of empire expansion, zones of military conflict, trades routes, kinship patterns, language families, forms of political organizations, religious belief clusters, forms of agricultural production, and myriad other types of evidence. Blier hopes to develop a technique for visually mapping these disparate data types in order to model the degree of conservatism or innovation a particular culture displays at a particular moment.

To do this effectively will require that our application learn to "talk" with other applications that contain data that might be of use to Blier's and other researchers' projects. There are a great number of other imagebases, bibliographies, and collections of resources being developed and maintained on the Internet, and that number is bound to increase. The Museum of African Art in Washington, DC, will be making its selective bibliography of secondary materials on African Art available on-line in the near future. Similarly, the University of Pennsylvania has an African Studies Gopher server and Mosaic server that provides regularly updated access to resources for students, scholars, and activists interested in African Studies. In addition to information utilities, we foresee the ability to access other applications similar to ours. For Blier's project, for example, it would be fascinating to examine the contents of *Perseus*, along the matrix of Blier's questions about creativity. This level of interoperability—various databases and electronic books that are hyperlinked both internally and among themselves—is the goal of an open systems approach to application development. And yet we are probably still years away from this sort of rich computing environment, as we wait for the social and intellectual structures of the academy to catch up with the abilities of today's computer networks. One can point to the accelerating growth of the Internet, the rash of Mosaic home pages, to projects such as *Who Built America?, Perseus, A la recontre de Phillipe*, as the future of multimedia computing in the Humanities. And yet in many ways these examples are still orphans waiting for their families to grow up around them.

It is my hope that the African Art History Project—and other projects with similar interdisciplinary perspectives on the study of the Humanities and

Social Sciences—will ensure that the conversation on and about the Information Superhighway will register voices that were not heard at the birth of our existing forms of mainstream media: television, radio, and film. Of course there is no *necessary* connection between multimedia and multiculturalism. Nonetheless, as a tool for what Cornel West has called "cultural work," multimedia scholarship and teaching may prove capable of bridging the ever-widening chasm between the hyper-specialized world of the Academy, and the generation of students accustomed to the depth, pace and production values of MTV and Nintendo.

Works Cited

Crane, Gregory, ed. (1992). *Perseus: Interactive Sources and Studies on Ancient Greece*, Yale University Press.

Fish, Stanley. (1994). "Being Interdisciplinary Is So Very Hard to Do," in *There's No Such Thing As Free Speech and It's A Good Thing, Too*, Oxford University Press, pp. 231–242.

Murray, Janet. (1993). "Restructuring Space, Time, Story, and Text," in *Sociomedia* edited by Edward Barrett, MIT Press.

Rosensweig, Brier, Brown. (1993). *Who Built America?* Voyager.

Weinberger, Eliot. (1952). "The Camera People," *Transition Magazine*, no. 55, Oxford University Press.

4

The Virtual Curator: Multimedia Technologies and the Roles of Museums

Colin Beardon and Suzette Worden

Introduction

Multimedia and interactive displays are fast becoming a vital part of the educational environment in the "progressive" museum (Hoffos 1992). To date most developments have attempted to enhance exhibitions or to make information more accessible within the traditional concept of a museum, with high investment and advanced technology being essential to the application (Hoptman 1992). There are, however, alternative ways of interpreting the role of the museum which can also take advantage of the potential of multimedia technology. The possibilities of reproduction mean that the museum need no longer be centered around the experience of unique objects but can exist as a distributed system. We argue that if we discard its need for unique objects and, in addition, re-order its internal power relations, the museum can begin to function as a powerful metaphor for the organization of knowledges.

This paper builds on work carried out on a project that aims to provide educational software for design history. The project operates within a particular educational context and explores the potential of interactive multimedia computing to develop an active, rather than passive role for the student. This means providing a creative role which stresses the power the student can have as an author rather than as an operator who simply retrieves information or selects between predetermined routes. We take seriously Sherry Turkle's criticism that,

Educators emphasize the computer's nature as a teaching machine or an analytical engine, but give insufficient attention to and even deny the computer's "second nature" as an evocative subject, an expressive medium that people use for self-projection and self-reflection. (Turkle 1990, 145)

The concern of the design historian is to understand the historical significance and meaning of mass-produced consumer goods and associated prototypes which come within the category of craft or the decorative arts. Design history involves researching and interpreting the social context within which these artifacts have been designed, produced and consumed. Historiographically the subject has been informed by interdisciplinary work drawing upon discussions of both the arts and technology. Debates within cultural theory, feminism and material culture have also influenced its development, challenging the process of design history as well as broadening its potential subject matter. Of particular note are the methods for reading objects and representations that have emerged from structuralism, semiotics and post-structuralism, and the necessity, as an historian, to understand one's location with respect to dominating organizational structures. As Elspeth Probyn states

Location describes epistemological maneuvers whereby categories of knowledge are established and fixed into sequences. It is also a process which determines what we experience as knowledge and what we know as experience. In its hierarchical movement, location insists on a taxonomy of experience. One doesn't have to scratch the surface very deeply to find that class, race, and gender have a lot to do with whose experiences are on top. (Probyn 1990, 184)

These issues are also part of feminist accounts which place stress upon technology's social construction. Technology is not seen as a set of neutral artefacts, so the effects of society on technology as well as the effects of technology on society need examination (Wajcman 1991, ix).

By its nature the subject matter of design history is both visual and textual and it is about both objects and representations. Multimedia technology can enable students to confront issues surrounding the relationship between object, text and image in new ways. Because of its immediacy, the separation of form and content within a multimedia presentation is by no means clear. In producing and reviewing an electronic publication the subject content and the computer interface design can become indivisible.

The project to provide software for design history explores the "sophisticated" use of available technology, which means assessing its use not in providing the complete answer to one isolated problem but in providing assistance to students in their achievement of more complex and socially defined tasks. From this perspective the primary role of the technology is as a means of communication; it also has potential as a means of empowerment for both individual exploration and collaborative group work.

The project was established as a collaborative venture principally involving a design historian and a computer specialist. From the outset the project adopted the traditions of work-oriented design developed in Scandinavia (Ehn 1988; Kyng 1991). This decision implied the adoption of a number of viewpoints: seeing the computer primarily as a communications medium rather than as a processor of data (Andersen 1990); aiming to enhance the tacit, or craft-based, knowledge of those working with technology rather than to replace it by rule-based formal knowledge (Rosenbrock1989); studying closely the professional language that people use in the course of their work and building computer systems that in essence speak the same language (Nygaard 1984).

The most fundamental implication of this initial decision was, however, the need to confront the issue of power. Both the historian and the computer specialist were forced to consider the often unnoticed assumptions of their own discipline, and to see how subject-based structures of knowledge serve to control the distribution of resources and the outcome of events. This applies not just to the specialisms of design history and systems design, but also to wider disciplines such as history, education and computing and more material institutions such as museums, universities and the computing profession.

Nor was this the only dimension of power to be confronted. Collaboration within education should involve not only technologists and teachers but also those who learn. As an integral part of the research, course units were developed and offered to undergraduate students. Issues that were raised by these units included: the dangers of early alienation; the value of a broad experience of possible applications; the advantages of students setting their own agenda; and the need for authors to develop a critical viewpoint on both their own work and that of others.

When assembling the range of multimedia that we would like students to experience we became acutely aware of the lack of any significant authoring role in any of the products. Users were routinely allowed to select which information they could access next and were occasionally given the opportunity to copy sections for their personal collection; however the maximum participation allowed by most products could be achieved sitting in an armchair using a TV remote control. The fruitful development of multimedia systems within our objectives relies upon empowering the users in ways not generally realized in today's products.

Current Multimedia Systems

In the wider context, design historians have to negotiate with museums as institutions: they are consumers of its output and can, in many instances, contribute to its development. An examination of museum-related multimedia systems in Britain reveals three types of activity. In the first, the computer is seen as an efficient administrator of the (unquestioned) function of the museum. The anticipated advantages are greater integration and efficiency and direct cost benefits. The computer is seen as containing information that is neutral and independent of the use to which it may be put. This view is epitomized in a recent U.K. report on multimedia in museums and its recommendations to "integrate the cataloguing and interpretation of all materials. . . . Integrate curatorial, educational and collection management roles" (Arts Council 1992, 3).

Access to this monolithic system should not be open to everyone. The museum curator is seen as a key specialist who has responsibility to control access to the data. "The need for editorial control remains a priority" (Arts Council 1992, 9–10).

In the second type of multimedia system, a museum or gallery attempts to provide an attractive and informative catalogue or guide to their collection that is accessible by any visitor. One of the earliest of these in the U.K. was located in the Design Museum (London) and one of the more recent is the MicroGallery at the National Gallery (London). Acting principally as a guide to the objects in the museum, these systems may also introduce extra-contextual material. In the distributed video system in the Imperial War Museum (London) this becomes the principal function of the system.

The third type of system is where a museum is "electronically published" and made available for distribution to colleges, libraries and homes. This type of system may take various forms; for example one set of products attempts to recreate the experience of a particular museum (e.g., the Smithsonian) or an imaginary museum (e.g., Apple's Virtual Museum). Other products attempt to create new museums by representing and linking "the knowledge" within a particular domain. For example, there is a project run by ICOGRADA (the International Council of Graphic Design Associations) to create a set of photo-CD products about significant designers each to a standard format. Finally, we find global approaches to the electronic distribution of knowledge, for example the HyperCard stack entitled "Culture" (Cultural Resources 1989).

All the systems we examined seemed to be influenced by the dominant concept of the market. On the one hand we have museum directors trying to make their institution more efficient and competitive, while on the other we see the necessity for packageable and easy-to-use commodities. Whichever direction we look in we seem to find design decisions being taken that are aimed more towards the market than towards the integrity of the system. To meet our project objectives we had to stand outside these current traditions of multimedia development and the institutional process of system design and to do that we first had to clarify our theoretical position.

Multimedia System Paradigms

We identify three paradigms of system architecture which we call the database paradigm, the hypertext paradigm and the communications paradigm. Each paradigm involves a different set of values, a different epistemology, a different methodology and results in a very different product.

The database paradigm adopts the view that the world consists of objects and events which can be perfectly described by a set of special phrases called "facts." These facts can be collected and stored and theoretically anyone can gain access to them. The view is summarized by the belief in "All information in all places at all times" (Godfrey and Parkhill, 1980).

From such a positivist viewpoint different facts about the world are produced by different disciplines. Each such discipline enjoys a uniquely privileged position with respect to knowledge within its specialist area and each has its own concepts and methods of measurement (Laufer 1991).

Within this paradigm the role of information technology is primarily to facilitate the accumulation and retrieval of facts. This requires that we legitimize the integration of facts from different sources into a single system of knowledge and this was achieved by refining the distinction between "data" and "information." On the one hand facts are universal because they are all in the same format (as data), while on the other they are meaningful only within their specific discipline (as information). This dualism is, however, bought at a price. While a database can be accessed by universal operations, an information base will, by definition, be ordered with some purpose in mind and can only be accessed through a classification system that embodies that order.

To many people public collections of information (such as libraries and museums) are organized in the most practical way to allow users access and it is considered esoteric to suggest that such a collection is biased. However, not every profession is so confident of its facts. The legal profession is probably the first to recognize the principle that data are only meaningful in the context of their collection and that it is illegitimate to use them for any undeclared purpose. A basic principle of computer privacy legislation is that subjects should be told how data are to be used before they are collected from them and that, once collected, data should only be used for that purpose. The realization that two professions disagree over the status of facts raises serious questions about the database paradigm.

Mark Poster makes it clear that the hypertext paradigm denies the positivist's belief that the world can be described by a set of facts.

"No set of phrases about the world contains the truth of the world and, to make matters more complex, the world itself contains, among other things, texts." (Poster 1990, 81).

Laufer argues that around 1950 positivist epistemology was replaced by the "science of systems" (Laufer 1991), a new epistemology based upon networks, i.e. nodes and links represented by circles and arrows.

The role of information technology within the systems paradigm is embodied in the concept of hypertext. George Landow traces the intellectual origins of hypertext to *Of Grammatology* (Derrida 1967) which he describes as "the art and science of linking" (Landow 1992, 30). In contrast to positivism (which has meta-narratives and progress), hypertext lacks any sense of direction because there is no fixed starting point and no end. "One of the fundamental characteristics of hypertext is that it is composed of bodies of linked texts that have no primary axis or organisation" (Landow 1992, 11–12).

From the hypertext viewpoint knowledge is infinite: we can never know the whole extent of it but only have a perspective on it. To implement pure hypertext is impossible because we would have to do two things: decide what is the unit we make into a node, and represent the infinity of links that connect this node to all other nodes. This is impossible: life is in real-time and we are forced to be selective, we decide that this much constitutes one node and only these links are worth representing. In this sense the concept of hypertext obscures the real decisions that are taken and which are, by default, resolved in favor of those with the power and resources to act effectively. As Poster comments, "The fact that it is technically possible for information to be available to everyone at little cost in no way ensures that it will be" (Poster 1990, 72).

The need to consciously allocate resources within the infinity of the hypertext paradigm has implications for computer-mediated discourses. Michel Foucault describes the process of selection among discourses and its relationship to the exercise of power:

"There can be no possible exercise of power without a certain economy of discourses of truth. . . . We are subjected to the production of truth through power and we cannot exercise power except through the production of truth" (Foucault 1980, 93).

The weakness of the hypertext paradigm is that it is too general and does not address the reality of knowledge production and dissemination and its relationship to systems of power in society.

Within the communication paradigm the computer is seen not as a depository or processor of knowledge, or even as a virtual world in which users act, but as a medium by means of which humans communicate knowledges. There are many forms that this communication can take: one-to-another, one-to-many, one-to-oneself, interactive, simultaneous, etc. Crucially, there is no room within this paradigm for the computer itself to have any power to act or to embody any human properties such as intelligence or thought. The term "human-computer-interaction" is avoided because the act of communication does not take place between humans and computers but between one human and another via a computer.

The role of language in the communication paradigm is critical. The medium should not impose a uniform structure of knowledge upon users but should enable humans to exchange knowledges in ways that are natural to them. If we want users to create texts in which the meaning is open, then the language of communication must not force closure. Ludwig Wittgenstein (1953) was concerned that language is not seen as a closed meaning system in which each word has a predefined meaning and the meaning of texts is made up from the meanings of the component words. He argued not only that meaning must remain open to the extent that new meanings are created by new uses of words, but also the way that language works to convey meaning cannot be understood irrespective of the practical task that the participants are involved in. Hence his concern with "language games" in which meanings generated within a language can only be seen in the context of some practical activity.

Extending this to a design method for multimedia requires that we study the user's professional language and incorporate it, as far as possible, as the language of the system (Andersen 1990). We situate ourselves broadly within this tradition, but find that it has hitherto been concerned primarily with work tasks that have relatively clearly defined objectives. We see a need to review the concept of task within the specific context we find ourselves: that of design history and education.

Power, Subjectivity, and Institutions

If our ultimate aim is to improve the critical abilities of students with respect to their subject (design history) it is important that we locate the project with respect to an analysis of power and, particularly, institutional power. For students to be active and to be empowered, their historical investigations must have meaning in the present. Through a sense of the past, groups and individuals create social meanings for themselves. These issues have relevance both from the point of view of the author, and within a collective responsibility.

Michel Foucault is an important influence. His writings on the nature and historical specificity of the role of authorship opened a debate that has been extended within feminist theory to recognize the political role of subjectivity and authorship and the importance of being the makers of history. Relationships between creativity, subjectivity and identity are crucial. Feminists, speaking from the margins, seek to escape the marginalizing effects of universal theory. As Nancy Harstock writes,

Rather than getting rid of subjectivity or notions of the subject, as Foucault does and substituting his notion of the individual as an effect of power relations, we need to engage in the historical, political, and theoretical process of constituting ourselves as subjects as well as objects of history. We need to recognise that we can be the makers of history as well as the objects of those who have made history. (Harstock 1990, 170–171)

Instead of being spoken-for, it is vital to constitute ourselves as subjects to question universal claims. On one level the task is a deconstructive one: that of noting the fissures, shifts of meaning, the endless referring to the other. The task is also to create by denying neutrality and emphasizing the power dimensions of difference. As Christine Battersby writes, the feminist critic "examines what is involved in writing as a woman: as a person confronting the paradigms of male individuality and female otherness, defining herself in terms of those paradigms . . . and resisting them" (Battersby 1989, 148).

Linda Nicholson also focuses on discourse, not as structures susceptible to abstract formalization but as human interaction—"a discourse that recognizes itself as historically situated, as motivated by values and, thus, political interests, and as a human practice without transcendent justification" (Nicholson 1992, 65).

As we move toward a position that includes a significant component of subjectivity, are we in danger of lapsing into relativism?

If one conceptualises discourse not as a structure but as a process of interaction, the issue of relativism must take on a different meaning. . . . To think about discourse as a communicative process is not to endorse or reject relativism but to reconceptualize relativism as communicative breakdown, a real-life possibility whose outcome can never be stipulated in advance. (Nicholson 1992, 68)

Within this quotation there is a shift from the terminology of Foucault to that of Habermas and this is significant. Habermas introduced a terminology of historical and social practice based upon three terms: praxis, politik and technik which we translate as lifeworld, institution and system (Habermas 1984). These concepts refer to three essential modes of interaction with the world and we find them useful in talking about the role of subjectivity and authorship, the role of institutions and power, and the belief in universal knowledge.

The world of systems is the world of objects that is "out there" and, we assume, behaves in a consistent manner. We interact with this world through technical knowledges which allow us to describe regular patterns of behavior and to predict the future outcome of events. The technical world can successfully be acted upon through rule-governed technical action.

Lifeworlds are the worlds of the subject rather than the object. They are essentially phenomenological in that they embody a viewpoint upon the world from which subjective reality is actively created. Other people are not objects to be acted upon, but rather subjects to be interacted with through language. Within our lifeworlds we are involved in practical action aimed in part at communication and agreement.

Institutions can be of many kinds: marriage, museums, education, historical societies, standards for human-computer interfaces. The world of institutions is the world in which resources are redisposed. Resources in this sense may be objective (e.g., material objects, computer terminals, formal knowledges) or subjective (e.g., understandings, languages, emotional energy). Institutional action involves shifting resources around, and through institutional action the possibilities for action by other subjects can be constrained or expanded. Recognition of institutions provides us with a richer language in which we can avoid universality without resorting to relativism.

Within this framework, we can see that the use of information technology has traditionally been interpreted as a form of technical action; hence the contents of computer systems are often seen as containing knowledge about objects. We argue that this is not their major mode and that the use of information technology is primarily a form of institutional action, i.e. it is really about the allocation of resources. We find this view is shared, for example, by those who recognise the "social shaping" role of new technology. "New information systems embody partial choices, inclusions and exclusions: they enable the generation and dissemination of information which—to a greater or lesser extent—constitutes a picture of what organisational reality is taken to be" (Owen, Bloomfield, and Coombs 1993).

It is also found in Nicholson's conclusion that, "Finally, our best safeguard may ultimately lie not with the kinds of discourse we rule acceptable or not but with the more practical issue of who is able to take part in discourse—that is, with the question of access "to the means of communication" (Nicholson 1992, p. 67).

From this perspective it is impossible to separate out the role of technology from the institutional roles of museums and the discipline of design history, each of which establishes a discourse and instinctively uses technology instrumentally to control resources. If students are going to develop an ability to critically view their subject, then any technology developed from an established institutional viewpoint will limit the resources that they can bring to bear and will limit their access to the "means of communication."

The Virtual Curator: Exercising Control in the Virtual Museum

The practical task we set ourselves was to devise a piece of computer software that enables the user to be as free as possible from the preconceptions of traditional institutions. The author should be in control of all aspects of the collection of information and its arrangement and be able to make statements in the form of exhibitions or other displays. The starting point is the idea of the museum. The central processes are those of collection, selection, order and arrangement which in themselves give meaning, but the appearance of their product as universal total knowledge is questioned. As Eilean Hooper-Greenhill has stated, it is a "mistake to assume that there is only one form of reality for museums" (Hooper-Greenhill 1992).

By embracing information technology the aura of the object is destroyed but, more importantly, if this is placed alongside the aim of recreating the museum as an institution, a more radical position becomes possible. This is achieved by reorganizing the power structure between the curator and visitor, by opening up the store room. The strength of the museum metaphor lies in seeing the museum as the mediating institution between design historians and their audience. The museum is the archive and it is also the means of communication and presentation. The design historian needs to control, rather than be controlled by the museum.

The first challenge of the project was to set up the formal procedures needed to make this process possible but there was the additional challenge of considering what might be the basis of a special aesthetic for interactive media. As Peter Bogh Andersen states, interactive media needs a suitable aesthetic which will sever its links with other traditions and make it into a medium in its own right (Andersen 1992). A consideration of the museum develops this because it deals in the organization of images, objects, texts and sequential media. Additionally, the museum offers an opportunity for non-linear readings. The relationships the viewer has with the museum not only combines various media but is creative in another sense. Ludmilla Jordanova writes, "In order to gain knowledge from museums, viewers, whether they are aware of it or not, both reify the objects they examine, treating them as decontextualised commodities, and identify with them, allowing them to generate memories, associations, fantasies" (Jordanova 1989, 25).

The museum display can promote "facts" and "values" simultaneously. The way that a viewer acquires knowledge within the museum context acknowledges these contradictory facets.

Working from these premises, a prototype system called the "virtual curator" was developed. The name was chosen to deliberately contrast with the "virtual museum" which aims to provide access to a museum in as naturalistic a manner as the technology makes possible (Garvey and Wallace 1992). The differences between the two systems are marked. The virtual curator does not attempt to excel in technological sophistication for its main aim is to develop certain ideas concerning what systems should be built, how they should be built and how they should be used. The underlying metaphor is not that of a pre-classified exhibition in which the user can passively select one of a limited number of paths: such approaches seem to encourage what Groot (1992) has called a "tourist" approach. Rather we aim to encourage Groot's "travellers" by opening up the institution of the museum and allowing users to construct an exhibition or display from a store room of objects. We also allow them to add objects to the store room if they so wish. As a challenge to the power structure found in traditional museums, the organizational structure of separating curator from visitor is broken down.

A Description of the Virtual Curator

We start our explanation of the system with the store which is a darkened space containing a number of objects. We want to simulate a sense of exploration and discovery and feel that this is not easy within the rectangular borders of the monitor. We adopt an approach developed by Andersen

Figure 4.1
The store room showing an object.

(1992) which involves simulating a torch beam that follows the cursor, illuminating objects as it goes (figure 4.1). The penumbra allows some features of nearby objects to be revealed. The user goes in search of objects and nothing is revealed unless actively sought.

The first and most fundamental principle of the store room is that it contains all objects known to the system and they are all first-class objects. Technically this means that any object can be manipulated by the various operators we shall describe later. Philosophically it means that we do not follow the division of sources of information between primary (the object itself), secondary (facts about the object) and tertiary (interpretations of the object) that is normally upheld within the culture of museums. The system does not deal in physical objects and deliberately does not try to simulate the experience of confronting a physical object. The virtual curator deals only with images and it makes a virtue of this: every image has the same status as every other image.

The store contains a "collection" of images which may be of objects, documents and pattern books as well as notice boards, posters, display cabinets, plinths, etc. Objects are placed randomly in the store, which is conceived as a two-dimensional grid. It is only possible to refer to another object indirectly by means of its grid location. The document in figure 4.2 is an object in the store which has been selected for closer inspection. Though it is a document it has exactly the same status as the object in figure 4.1.

Figure 4.2
Close-up of another object in the store room.

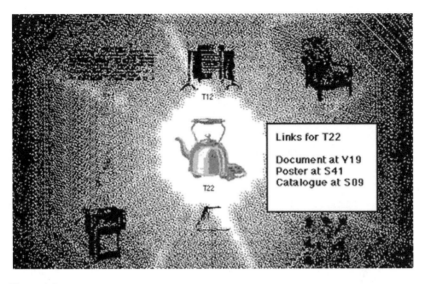

Figure 4.3
User-entered link.

A second essential feature of the virtual curator is that there is no pre-classification of objects. There is, for example, no preexisting link between the image of the kettle in figure 4.1 (which is located at grid position T22) and the document which appears to refer to that kettle (which is to be found at grid position V19). If a user wishes to make a personal link between these two objects she or he may do so. In constructing an exhibition it is important to be able to record the results of research, and this involves making links between objects. It is also important from an educational point of view for students to show the process whereby their visual statements are constructed and for their tutor to be able to interrogate these constructions and discuss them with the student. Figure 4.3 shows a user-link between these two objects.

The user is set the task of making a visual statement or exhibition and the generic name for the place where exhibitions are created is the stage. The stage can take many forms and all objects in the store can be copied and displayed as many times as required on the stage. One form of statement is the two-dimensional graphic poster. To create one of these a blank poster is first selected from the store, objects are then copied from the store and pasted onto the poster along with any user-supplied text that is required. Figure 4.4 shows a poster that incorporates the kettle image from figure 4.1. The completed poster is copied back into the store room and then behaves just like any other object.

Another way of displaying objects is in a display cabinet. Display cabinets also appear in the store and can be selected and then filled with objects from the store. In constructing a cabinet there may be a need for labels and these too are selected from the store room and constructed. A cabinet display is shown in figure 4.5 and it too, when completed, can be copied back into the store room.

It is also possible for the stage to simulate a three-dimensional space such as a room. A background is presented which can be read as three walls of a bare room seen from the central point of the fourth wall. Objects can be placed into this "room" and, if required, they will behave similar to real objects in three-dimensional space. For example, objects can be made to

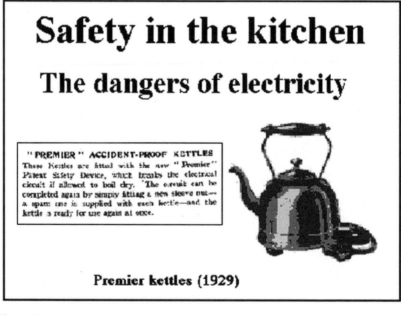

Figure 4.4
User constructed poster.

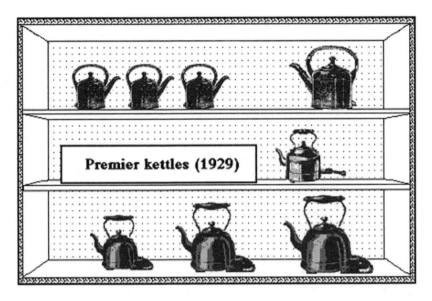

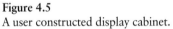

Figure 4.5
A user constructed display cabinet.

appear to scale, or only appropriate locations are permitted for objects that expect to be fixed to the walls or ceiling (e.g., light fittings).

Another kind of object that is found in the store is a book of fabric samples and this behaves very much like its real world counterpart (figure 4.6). The pages can be turned, a copy of the current page can become an object, or a particular fabric can be chosen and subsequently used to cover certain objects such as a chair, carpet or wall (figure 4.7).

Of particular note is the fact that other visual statements, such as a completed notice board or cabinet, are already objects in the store and can now be copied and placed in the room (figure 4.8). In theory this process can be repeated recursively, so that we could get an object in a cabinet which appears on a poster that is in another cabinet within a room. A student using this facility is able to create combinations of image and text which can be viewed on the screen or printed.

There are three basic sets of operations that an author can carry out within the system:

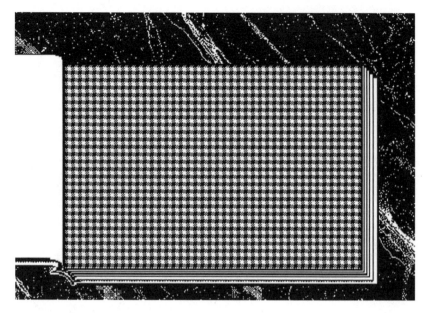

Figure 4.6
Examining the book of fabric samples.

a) within the store, objects can be added, examined and copied and personalized links can be made between them;
b) objects can be copied between the store and the stage; and
c) within the stage, objects can be rearranged and resized.

For the person reading a statement, both the store and the stage may be
explored and any object may be interrogated (i.e., seen enlarged) and any
links to other objects within the store may be viewed.

Using the Virtual Curator

The virtual curator is, in essence, the architecture of an authoring system for
design historians who wish to make largely visual statements. It is envisaged
that it be used in the context of design history education and that students be
set projects using it. It is not supposed to be a fully self-supporting module.
It is an environment that relates to the activities of design historians but takes
advantage of the computer's functionality when appropriate to do so. What

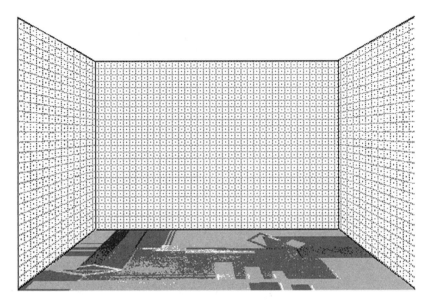

Figure 4.7
The room with fabrics copied to walls and floor.

has been described here is a bare skeleton upon which other facilities can be built. For example: a user may wish to develop sequences of statements, as in the case of an animation or a series of tableaux; or a user may wish to add sound or film material to the store.

Current developments within information technology and multimedia are important for design history students in that they will affect the means by which they receive information and also offer possibilities for creating their own statements; their education must equip them with the critical ability to assess and use these possibilities. The Virtual Curator is therefore offered both as a text to be analyzed and as a creative tool for the production of statements. Its innovative role lies in both these areas, but the primary aim is to offer a way of exploring the process of design history. It is self-reflective and emphasizes the historical specificity of the student's own means of ordering knowledges as well as the ordering structures they inherit from the discipline itself.

Figure 4.8
An exhibition on safety in the home.

The Virtual Curator is designed to be introduced as part of a group discussion at the beginning of a course. A seminar based course with approximately ten students is ideal. A "collection" introduced in the store varies according to the interests and subject expertise of either tutor or students. This highlights the desirability of being able to replace objects in the store room.

The unclassified store room de-naturalizes classification and makes users explain their expectations of classification. Any move in customizing the store room raises issues about the relationship of the "content" of the course to the thematic aims and what kinds of representations are most suitable. For example, the aim of object analysis, decoding images and exploring their internal characteristics becomes feasible with certain representations but a de-centered approach looking at cultural determinants creates the need for other kinds of material.

The way the Virtual Curator uses the technology tests the potential of information technology within the discipline. The use of multimedia raises questions about how different media are interpreted and what happens when they are brought into close contact. The presentation of the museum as an abstract concept allows students to discuss the concepts of classification and access, form and content, acquisition and display, fact and interpretation, and relative media values, that could be reapplied to their experiences within the wider, traditional museum world.

An understanding of the shared or personal experience of these issues should become apparent. This recognizes the way artifacts have a complex presence that is subject to multiple interpretations and is a recognition of the role of the reader in interpretation.

The Virtual Curator is also offered as a creative medium, whereby students and tutors can use any of the presentation formats to provide an interpretation of their historical material, for group discussion or for final presentation. The course at Brighton already recognizes alternative presentations, including video, exhibitions and tape/slide presentations, as organizational methods to complement the traditional essay. Assessment criteria already exist which have been built upon to take into account the demands of non-linear work.

Working with the Virtual Curator as a creative medium highlights the relative skills necessary for presenting representations of objects and other kinds of information, particularly in using predominantly visual as opposed to a text based "language." Noting the way that visual statements can remain open and can be re-interpreted, the presentation is not final and leads to further discussion, thus emphasizing its role as a means of communication and its place in the "social" world. Exploration of the various ways of presenting information enable the user to confront issues about the kind of control they, as author, can have over the resultant meaning and how far it is possible to represent the place they speak from. The integrity of the final statement also needs examination in terms of the way that its total meaning has been constructed out of previously discrete representations.

Conclusions

Collaborative design has created a context within which it has been possible to start questioning propositions about both technology and design history. It requires the abandonment of formal procedures for the design of systems and sees technology as supporting processes rather than resulting in products.

If education is partly about challenging existing institutions then the traditional museum should not remain as the sole model for educational software within historical research. This view of education learns much from feminism, particularly the ability to both read and resist. It is also informed by an understanding of institutional action in terms of the allocation of resources. The Virtual Curator provides an active way into the subject of design history that is not constrained by existing institutional priorities.

By asserting the creative potential opened up by the software, the use of the Virtual Curator in an educational context becomes an open means of communication. Such a viewpoint is counter to the universalizing tendencies of the database or hypertext paradigms.

References

Andersen, P. B. (1990) *A Theory of Computer Semiotics.* Cambridge University Press, Cambridge.

Andersen, P. B. (1992) "Vector Spaces as the Basic Components of Interactive Systems: Towards a Computer Semiotics." *Hypermedia* 4, no. 1, 53–76.

Arts Council (1992) *Very Spaghetti.* Arts Council, London.

Battersby, C. (1989) *Gender and Genius: Towards a Feminist Aesthetics.* The Women's Press, London.

Cultural Resources (1989) *Culture^a 1.0: the Hypermedia Guide to Western Civilisation.* Cultural Resources, Cranford, NJ.

Ehn, P. (1988) *Work-Oriented Design of Computer Artifacts.* Arbetslivscentrum, Stockholm.

Foucault, M. (1980) Two lectures. In C. Gordon et al., eds. *Power/Knowledge: Selected Interviews and Other Writings, 1972–1977.* Pantheon, New York.

Garvey, G., and B. Wallace (1992) "From 'Le Musée Imaginaire' to Walls without Museums." *Computer Graphics* 26, no. 2, pp.391–392.

Godfrey, D., and D. Parkhill (1980) *Gutenberg Two.* Porcépic, Toronto.

Groot, P. (1992) "On Redesigning the Museumplein as a Dream Area." *Mediamatic* 6, no. 2, pp. 45–55.

Grudin, J. (1991) "Systematic Sources of Suboptimal Interface Design in Large Product Development Organizations." *Human-Computer Interaction* 6, 147–196.

Habermas, J. (1984) *The Theory of Communicative Action (I)—Reason and the Rationalisation of Society.* Boston.

Harstock, N. (1990) "Foucault on Power: A Theory for Women?" In L. Nicholson, ed., *Feminism/Postmodernism*, Routledge, London, pp.157–175.

Hoffos, S. (1992) "Multimedia and the Interactive Display." *Library and Information Research Report 87*, British Library, London.

Hooper-Greenhill, E (1992) *Museums and the Shaping of Knowledge*, Routledge, London.

Hoptman, G. (1992) "The Virtual Museum and Related Epistemological Concerns." In E. Edward Barrett, ed., *Sociomedia: Multimedia, Hypermedia and the Social Construction of Knowledge*. MIT Press, Cambridge, Mass. pp. 141–59.

Jordanova, L (1989) "Objects of Knowledge: A Historical Perspective on Museums" In P. Vergo ed., *The New Museology*, Reaktion Books, London, pp. 22–40.

Kyng, M (1991) Designing for Cooperation: Cooperating in Design 34, 12, 64–73.

Landow, G. P. (1992) *Hypertext: the Convergence of Contemporary Critical Theory and Technology*. The Johns Hopkins University Press, Baltimore.

Laufer, R. (1991) *The History of Computers: an Epistemological Point of View.* In J. Berleur, A. Clements, R. Sizer, and D. Whitehouse, eds., *The Information Society: evolving landscapes*. Captus/Springer Verlag, Toronto/New York.

Nicholson, L. (1992) "Feminism and the Politics of Postmodernism." *Boundary 2*, pp. 53–69.

Nygaard, K. (1984) Profession oriented languages. Keynote speech, Medical Informatics Congress Europe 1984, Brussels.

Owen, J., B. Bloomfield, and R. Coombs. (1993) "Information Technology in Health Care: Tension and Change in the UK National Health Service." In J. Berleur, C. Beardon, and R. Laufer, eds. *Facing the Challenge of Risk and Vulnerability in an Information Society*. Elsevier Science Publishers (North-Holland), Amsterdam (forthcoming).

Poster, M. (1990) *The Mode of Information: Poststructuralism and Social Context*. Polity Press, Cambridge.

Probyn, Elspeth (1990) "Travels in the Postmodern: Making Sense of the Local" In L. Nicholson, ed., *Feminism/Postmodernism*, Routledge, London, pp.176–189.

Rosenbrock, H. (1989) *Designing Human-Centred Technology: A Cross-disciplinary Project in Computer-aided manufacturing*, Springer-Verlag, Berlin/Heidelberg/New York.

Turkle, S. (1990) "Style as Substance in Educational Computing." In J. Berleur, A. Clements, R. Sizer, and D. Whitehouse, eds., *The Information Society: Evolving Landscapes*. Captus/Springer Verlag, Toronto/New York, pp.145–60.

Wajcman, Judy (1991) *Feminism Confronts Technology*. Polity, Cambridge.

Wittgenstein, L. (1953) *Philosophical Investigations*. Blackwell, Oxford.

Notes

1. The project is carried out in the Rediffusion Simulation Research Centre, Faculty of Art, Design and Humanities, University of Brighton.

2. To remedy this situation we wrote a piece of software that questioned and explored the relationship between authors and users. This took an object the students were familiar with (their course prospectus plus a collection of quotations and graphics that related to the text) and enabled them to both explore and add comments. The significance of the technically simple software was that material entered by students appeared in the same format as any of the "authorities" that were initially included.

3. Grudin (1991) argues that it is particularly difficult to involve end users in the design process within a system of product-based development.

4. This principle is embodied, for example, in the U.K. Data Protection Act and the US Privacy Act of 1974.

5. The concepts as we have developed them are loosely based on Habermas's work. No claims are made that these are accurate interpretations of that work.

6. Arts Council (1992, 23) reported that visitors and students asked: Why is it here? How was it made? and Why was it made? Curators asked When was it made? What size and medium? Who owned it before us?

5

Multimedia Production: Nonlinear Storytelling Using Digital Technologies

Marie Redmond and Niall Sweeney

Introduction

The availability of digital technologies offers new tools and methodologies to artists and creators working in all media. Computers have now developed from their traditional role as numerical processors with text-based interfaces, to become high-speed processors, capable of storing and displaying color images linked to sound and text. Interface design has also evolved from a cumbersome text-based entry facility to an intuitive and visual interaction. As the technical feats involved in storing and displaying huge digital files in real time disappear, the challenge facing interactive storytellers is how to use these new nonlinear techniques effectively to enhance their stories and reach new audiences.

Multimedia production is still a relatively new field, and just as there are many types of multimedia applications, there will be styles and methodologies of production developed to accommodate the different requirements of these applications. This paper describes the production techniques developed for and used in developing a narrative-based multimedia presentation system for The National Gallery of Ireland. The production process is suitable for a narrative-based application which aims to engage and educate the viewer for a reasonable period of time. This style of production would not suit a reference type point of information system where the user requires a quick response time to a specific inquiry; an example of such an application would be a travel inquiry system.

The paper concentrates on the overall design and content objectives of multimedia production rather than on the technical issues and dependencies.

The overall objective for this production was to use digital technology to enhance existing non-digital facilities and create a title which would reach a far wider audience, presenting information in a way that was both visually appealing and educational. The objective was to avoid using technology for the sake of technology; this has to be a concern for multimedia producers and audiences as they anticipate the imminent proliferation of multimedia titles and applications.

The National Gallery of Ireland

The National Gallery houses Ireland's collection of both Irish and European paintings in a splendid Georgian purpose-built gallery. Technology has been obviously absent from the gallery; its insensitive introduction could disturb the atmosphere that the Gallery strives to create for its visitors. The experience of visiting the Gallery is of entering a bygone era of Georgian splendor where visitors can view paintings in the context of the architecture prevalent in the lives of most of the artists' whose works are on display.

The Gallery, sponsored by IBM, put together an exhibition of its European paintings called Master European Paintings which toured four cities in the United States: San Francisco, Chicago, Boston, and New York. When the paintings were returning to their permanent home in Dublin, IBM sponsored a multimedia presentation to mark the occasion and to permanently record the exhibition and its success.

The introduction of technology into the ambiance of the gallery had to be clearly thought out and planned. Given that the sponsor was a major supplier of computer hardware, many of the technical questions were answered. The primary requirement of the hardware was to be able to reproduce images of the paintings to the highest quality possible. The delivery platform had to be IBM and wherever possible IBM tools and software were used in the production process.

We designed cabinets to enclose the computers so that only the fronts of the monitors offering touch screen interaction were visible to the visitors. The cabinets were designed so that they were the antithesis of all prevalent shapes in a large Georgian room; they were modern and curved in contrast to the symmetric angular shapes of the architecture. We discussed many designs and colors for the cabinets including the possibility of duplicating the pedestals used in the gallery for displaying sculpture. The idea was to place the monitor on a pedestal and hide the rest of the hardware behind screens. We rejected this idea because of the size of the monitors and the general unattractiveness of a large gray plastic box. The only part of the monitor unit that viewers of the multimedia needed to see was the actual screen. We enclosed the monitor unit within a cabinet, leaving only the screen exposed. The cabinet shape was modern announcing the arrival of something new and different in the Gallery.

Conceptualization

The important decisions to be made before developing the multimedia software or designing the cabinets to enclose the computer systems were:

what information should be stored and displayed,
where the multimedia systems were located in relation to the paintings,
what audience the presentation was directed at,
how the information was presented.

Defining the scope of the presentation was the first major task. The introduction of multimedia should in no way interfere with or interrupt the viewing of original paintings as they were displayed in the exhibition. There were three parts to the exhibition: the paintings and how they were arranged, an illustrated catalog, and the multimedia presentation; another factor is how these three different viewing experiences relate to each other. The paintings were the focus of attention for visitors and the experience of visiting the exhibition could be enhanced by referencing the catalog or by viewing the multimedia presentation. The connection between viewing the paintings and interacting with the multimedia presentation only became evident after following up visitors' comments. Many visitors remarked on how the multimedia presentation had increased their interest in the paintings and the painters and especially how it made them pay more attention to details in the paintings.

One of the most difficult tasks in planning a multimedia production is defining clearly the contents of the digital presentation and often this can consist of placing limits on the information that will be included. Given the nature of the technology, it is easy to be carried away with the lack of space restrictions, or cost implications. This can, however, be a serious mistake and could detract from the overall impact of the presentation. The work must be based on a story or a narrative and given the nonlinear nature of the technologies and tools being used it is too easy to wander away from the basic narrative and include extraneous or loosely associated but not necessarily relevant information.

One of the lessons we learned early on in multimedia production, was exactly how easy it is to wander off on sidetracks and to include details not relevant to the main narrative being developed. This has implications for viewers as they can lose the theme of the work and it can also cause navigation problems, again detracting from the overall impact of viewing the work. A viewer must feel satisfied after viewing the work for a short time or for the entire length of the production; this is an absolute requirement for developing a nonlinear multimedia production and one of the main benefits of presenting information in this manner.

Linear Viewing of Nonlinear Information

The experience of viewing a multimedia presentation is a linear event; however the information contained in the presentation is not written or stored in a linear manner. The main challenge in multimedia production is how to write and develop information in a nonlinear form for linear viewing. It is the narrative that connects the linear and nonlinear forms of the presentation; this must be present and valid when creating and viewing the information.

Levels of Interactivity

Selecting the level of interactivity appropriate to the title is one of the most difficult tasks: the temptation is to include many instances of opportunity for the user to change subject matter and direction. There is no magic formula or time period for incorporating choices for changing viewing direction. The objective has to be to include options for the user to select topics or change direction so that the choices seem natural and are almost transparent to the flow of the narrative.

In Master European Paintings, we built the choices for topic selection and interactivity around each painting and within each painting selection we included subtopics. The level of interactivity was built around these changing topics about a particular painting or selecting a different painting or artists. We did not build in choices for interactivity within these subtopics; the viewer was presented with the option of stopping any sequence of audio and associated image display as soon as an option was selected (see figure 5.1). Other options were then presented when the sequence had finished or on interruption, allowing the viewer to select another subject.

The Team

There were three groups within the overall project team: subject experts, design, and programming. The subject expertise was provided by two members of the Gallery staff. The multimedia team consisted of two groups: design and programming. The design group, which was lead by an information designer, provided skills in audio, video, scripting, graphic design, and

Figure 5.1
Screen for one of the main paintings.

cognitive psychology. The programming group included three programmers experienced in both graphical user interface and object-oriented programming. The overall technical design was conceived of as a powerful, flexible set of software tools implementing the interface design and also capable of running on standard software platforms such as Windows; the programming language used was C + +.

Selection of Subject Matter

Working with the Gallery staff, we clearly identified the information to be included in the multimedia presentation. It would not duplicate the information contained in the catalog and would instead develop stories about the paintings and the artists which would benefit from the use of digital technologies. There were forty four paintings of which ten were considered major works. We described the major paintings in greater detail than the minor works and developed themes about each of these paintings and their artists. We wrote shorter scripts about the other thirty four paintings and artists, again avoiding any duplication with texts from the catalog.

Working with such experienced subject experts as the staff of a gallery is almost a dream project for a multimedia production team. Both teams had similar expectations and standards for the project and we were equal in our sensitivity to visual aesthetics and attention to detail.

When we attempted our first multimedia project, we struggled to understand where to start. What did we need first? Was it a script, a storyboard, a collection of images and sounds, texts? We researched a subject and produced written texts about the subject including ideas for collecting images and sounds. We attempted to draw a traditional storyboard which was both hierarchical and nonlinear; it was almost impossible to place this on paper because of the limitations of two dimensional space. We used software applications as storyboarding tools. These tools worked to a certain degree but what we needed was an overall design or architecture of the information content and flow. We introduced the concept of information design into the production process.

Information Design

Information design is the creative process of specifying the information contained in a presentation, detailing the navigation paths, and developing the user interface. The process consists of three components: writing the scripts, designing the interface, and producing the storyboard.

The first step is to produce a representation on paper of the types of information that will be included in the presentation and how they relate to each other. Hierarchical flow charting does not work for this type of information mapping. Multimedia has four elements or four dimensions:

x co-ordinates,
y co-ordinates,
time,
links between assets.

The positioning in two-dimensional space over time is essentially linear and can be represented with a time-based editor; showing all the links between the subjects and themes in a single comprehensive display is not possible using a two-dimensional representation. A linking tool such as Hypercard could be used for specifying individual links but this will not provide an overall picture of all the links as any one asset can be linked to a number of assets and be itself both the source and destination of a link. Before attempting to illustrate the links between the subjects and the themes in a two-dimensional representation, the complete range of themes and subthemes must be known.

The Master European Paintings exhibition has a finite and well defined range of subjects and themes: forty four paintings and their artists. Again, this is a crucial step in the planning and conceptualization: clearly defining the subject matter and level of detail on each theme. We distinguished between the main and minor themes and defined the number of subthemes available on any subject. A limit of six subthemes or subheadings was placed on any one painting.

The decision to place the emphasis on presenting information about the ten major paintings, was the key factor in the information design. Figure 5.2 shows the overall information design architecture which consists of three concentric circles. The outer circle contains the information on the ten main paintings, the

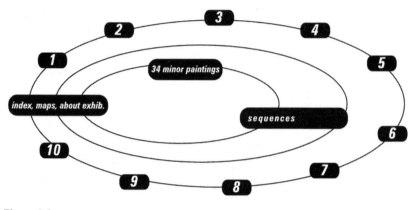

Figure 5.2
Overall information design.

middle circle contains the links between all the paintings and themes, and the inner circle contains the information on the thirty four minor paintings.

The ten main paintings are all linked together and the initial screen for each of these paintings also works as a rotating idle screen. The Map, Index, and Buttons are linked to all the paintings, major and minor. The thirty four paintings are linked to the major paintings and not to each other. This forms the basis of the information presentation and navigation system used for the production.

We decided in the planning of Master European Paintings that very little text would be displayed on screen; the emphasis would be on audio rather than on text. It is our conviction that people do not want to read large amounts of text on a computer screen; this is far more enjoyable and effectively communicated in a printed form. Visitors to art galleries are looking for a visual experience rather than an opportunity to read about an exhibition; the catalog is available for reading either before or after visiting the exhibition. The only texts that appear in Master European Paintings are words offering different options, some related facts which would disrupt the flow of the spoken word, for example, dates, names, and dimensions, and some informational messages (see figure 5.3).

Figure 5.3
Main screen showing themes and ribbon panel.

Scripting for Nonlinear Material

Two distinct styles of writing are required for the spoken and written word. The selection of words and the elimination of unnecessary phrases is vital in scripts that will be heard rather than read. One method of writing a multimedia script is to first write the script as if it will be read and then edit the style to include shorter more succinct sentences containing minimal extra verbiage. Reading texts aloud and recording the reading for review and revision is a good test of how the script works as a spoken text.

It is vital that the skills of professional voice-overs are used in multimedia productions. Multimedia production requires high quality sound and images at least comparable to television. We recorded the voice-over in two sessions: the final edited audio recording lasted ninety minutes. This time is not an indication of the length of the production; it is simply a measurement of the audio available in the title. We used digital audio facilities and edited the sound sequences noting all timings of individual segments on the storyboard.

Multimedia production has one element in common with television production: the starting point for both is a script from which a storyboard is developed. Producing a storyboard for interactive material, is, however, more complex than its television equivalent. In television, the issue of building in interactivity is absent and only two media are used: sound and moving images. Multimedia offers the producer two additional media: written texts and still images. People watch television from a distance of approximately ten feet while multimedia is viewed from as close as one foot which introduces the possibility of viewers reading texts.

The single biggest difference between television and multimedia is the introduction of interactivity; television is a linear medium and multimedia is, with the inclusion of interactivity, a nonlinear medium. Television programs have a fixed length: 30 minutes, one hour, ninety minutes or however long the program makers allocate to the subject. With the introduction of interactivity, a multimedia production is as long as it is viewed and each viewer selects individual viewing times.

Interface Design

Several overall design decisions were made before starting the individual screen designs. The paintings were the centerpiece for each screen. All other colors appearing on a screen were background to the painting; for example, the subject selection panel was shown in a dark gray with buttons defined as a simple black oval. The painting title was shown in foreground with the name of the artist and the subthemes appearing in middleground. Options, such as zooming, or instructions were subdued as this introduced the viewer slowly and intuitively to the functionality available for changing direction and subject. A design grid similar to magazine design grids was developed showing the possible positioning of the images and buttons together with font and color specifications (see figure 5.4).

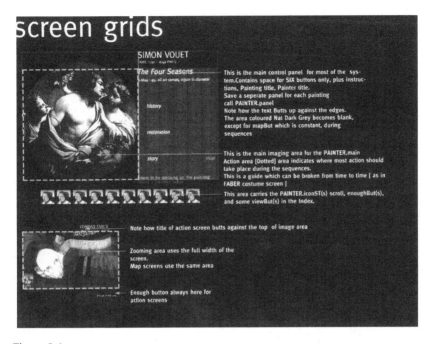

Figure 5.4
Screen grid.

Ribbon Panel

A panel appeared at the bottom of each screen containing representations of the ten main paintings in de-saturated color (see figure 5.3). The viewer could move between paintings without a sense of "flipping pages" or changing topic or theme while maintaining both a sense of narrative and the relationship between the multimedia presentation and the exhibition.

The principles of the interface are derived from the script. In written texts, headings are used to highlight subjects and changes of subjects. There are no headings or titles accompanying the spoken word; this would interrupt the flow of the reading and be disruptive for the listener. The idea of headings translates into the interface where options or buttons are labeled with the theme of the subject; these button labels are in fact functioning as headings and subheadings.

Storyboarding

One of the hardest methodologies to understand and develop is the idea of storyboarding for interactivity. When creating a storyboard for a linear production, such as television, a visual image of each scene contained in the script is created and the accompanying text is married to the image together with instructions for gathering the image. This method of linear storyboarding does not work for multimedia because the axis for a multimedia production is not the length of the production or any fixed time.

Multimedia, however, has a time dimension; the difference is that it is a variable and is different for each viewer. When a viewer interacts with a multimedia production, the length of the production is the length of time spent interacting with the presentation. The difficulty in storyboarding for interactivity is the conflict of creating a nonlinear information set which will be viewed as a personalized linear production by each viewer. Each viewer tailors their own production and this varies in length and detail of subject matter but it is always a linear viewing in that it has a beginning and an end.

We developed our own version of storyboarding which also became the functional specification for the technical implementation of the design and display of the multimedia assets on the chosen hardware platform. This document was created by the design team and handed over to the programmers to implement. It represented the transition from design to implementation. A sample page of our storyboarding technique is shown in figure 5.5.

All the images were captured and stored as bitmaps as were the texts that appeared on the screens. The storyboard has four columns for the linked assets. From left to right, the columns are for script, images, text, and video. The individual assets were stored in files and given logical filenames using the artists name as the root for the filename.

In the left hand column, the script is printed and words are highlighted where transitions are made between images. The transition is boxed, and this is similar to how words are highlighted to indicate that they are hot spots. The timings of the transitions are also indicated in the script. Each audio file is timed from beginning to end and the transition timings were prototyped using a multimedia authoring tool. This allows rough timings to be specified but they have to be fine tuned to suit the speed of the hardware and the size of the file being retrieved and displayed.

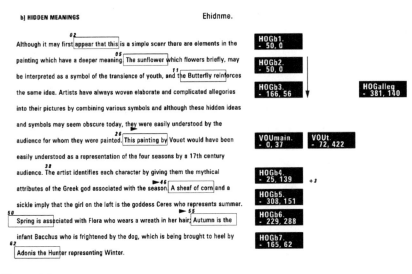

Figure 5.5
Sample storyboard.

The second column contains the names of the image files that are to be called in at the transitions specified. The box contains the filename and the co-ordinates where the image is to be displayed on the screen. The number of boxes in the second column corresponds to the number of transitions indicated in the script column. The text column contains the names of the files containing the bitmaps of the words and their screen co-ordinates. The text and image files when related appear at the same time and for the same duration.

The final, fourth, column contains the name of any digitized video sequence and its screen co-ordinates.

Transition from Design to Implementation

The design and programming teams worked closely when planning and defining the scope and content of the project. The overall software design was conceived and the architecture was developed from analyzing the project requirements; methodologies were based on object-oriented theory.

Object-oriented techniques and methodologies are particularly suited to multimedia production.

When the initial screen designs were produced, the programmers created screen templates for each screen type being implemented using the output from the design software which in this project was Adobe Photoshop. The software for storing, retrieving, and displaying the paintings and associated assets was written in the C + + programming language.

The design team collected and generated all the assets adopting a suitable naming convention defined with the assistance of the programming team for the text, image, video and text files. All text and still image files were generated as bitmaps; bit mapped text files produced the highest quality possible using anti-aliased text strings. The assets were handed over to the programming team together with the in-house storyboard (see figure 5.5) which contained details of the asset positions in two-dimensional space and their associated timings and links. The storyboards were then implemented in the programming language. The two teams worked closely together at the implementation phase; the designers verified the accuracy of the implementation and refined asset selections and positions.

Conclusion

Creative and technical people can work together productively to complement each other's work and skills. In multimedia production, the synergy between the creative and the programming teams helps to advance the individual limits of both teams. The programmers can see their efforts enhanced with the addition of an appropriate and visual interface to their programming; the creative team appreciate the programming techniques which implement their ideas in an exact and appropriate style.

Viewers of the multimedia presentation appreciated the simplicity of the interface design and the ease with which they could interact with the presentation. While the exhibition was open, there were queues at the multimedia systems. Most visitors stayed at the systems for as long as an hour unless there were long queues. The general feedback from visitors was that the multimedia presentation enhanced their visit to the exhibition and increased their interest in the paintings and the artists.

We collected comments from all the viewers and asked them to fill in a questionnaire. No one had any difficulty using the system; younger viewers loved the interaction and especially loved the concept of being able to "touch" a painting: something they can never attempt in a gallery! The emphasis that we placed on the importance of the visual aesthetics of the interface and the simplicity of use was appreciated by visitors to the exhibition. We proved that a gallery is a natural application for multimedia presentations if they are clearly conceived and well designed.

6

The Shakespeare Interactive Archive: New Directions in Electronic Scholarship on Text and Performance

Peter S. Donaldson

An Interactive Archive for Shakespeare Studies

The history of the use of the computer as a partner in the study of Shakespeare in performance begins with Larry Friedlander's *Shakespeare Project*, completed at Stanford in 1989. Friedlander's work included the *Theater Game,* an animation program in which students could move "actors" around on a stage to try out different options for costuming, blocking and interpreting a scene, as well as a *Performance* study program, in which students could work with alternative filmed performances of three scenes recorded on video laserdisc.[1] Users could play these scenes sequentially or in a segmented mode, comparing each "beat" of the performance to its alternative; they could access the corresponding text of the play or the edited screenplay, and could take notes of their own and integrate them with moving image "quotations" from the scenes to create multimedia essays. The *Shakespeare Project* was primarily an educational application, and was limited both in the amount of video included and in restrictions on its use due to copyright, but it made a fundamental contribution, initiating new ways of thinking about the relationships between the text(s) and performances of a play. The *Shakespeare Project* treated words and moving images as aspects of a unified multimedia hypertext, components of a densely linked, navigable, and reconfigurable environment.

Such an innovation held great promise for scholarship as well as teaching. Since the late 1970s, films, videotapes, and filmed performances of Shakespeare had played an increasing role in the teaching of Shakespeare, and had provided subject matter for an extensive body of criticism and interpretation devoted to the transposition of these Elizabethan and Jacobean plays into contemporary media. An increasing flow of scholarly books and articles, conference sessions and panels bore witness to a shift toward performance studies as a central concern of the field: specific theatrical productions, films and television versions of Shakespeare were now studied in their own right, and also (in a departure from past practice) as guides to the potential meanings of the plays themselves. As Shakespeareans began to think of the "original" text (itself increasingly seen as multiple and shifting) as a script awaiting realization on the stage, as the site of an exceptionally various and often contestatory proliferation of "reproductions" in many different cultures and in several media, modern films and theatrical productions assumed a new importance.

The media available to support this shift in interest were cumbersome and inadequate, however. In researching and illustrating my book *Shakespearean Films/Shakespearean Directors* (1990), for example, I used slow-winding videotape, prepared frame enlargements from 16 and 35mm film with the help of slot-load projectors, micro lens and bellows, Steenbeck editing tables, manual rewind machines—with such tools one could begin to study performance options, the significance of textual cuts, and the implications of the collision of cultural and aesthetic assumptions involved in the translation of Renaissance stagecraft to modern media. But with interactive multimedia, there is a qualitative difference: a shift from the *preparation of illustrative materials* to the *exploration of a virtual research environment*. In such an environment, of which *The Shakespeare Project* offered a tantalizing sample, access is rapid, and the various elements of performance—text, image, sound and movement—are brought into close conjunction for careful study.

The textual and visual materials relevant to the study of Shakespeare in performance are, of course, immense in quantity and broad in their cultural diversity. There are four hundred years of editions, translations, commentaries, promptbooks, and theatrical records. There is a vast body of art work including oil paintings, watercolors, engravings, book illustrations. For many productions in the last hundred years there is a photographic record. The recent filmography prepared by Kenneth Rothwell and Annabelle H. Melzer, *Shakespeare on Screen* (New York: Neal-Schuman, 1990), lists over 700 items, from early silent films to Brazilian television versions of *Othello*.

In addition to extensive listings of American and British films, there are strong traditions of Shakespearean film adaptation in Russia and Japan, including several of the films held in the highest critical regard.

The materials that exist for Shakespeare constitute the largest potential multimedia archive for any author in any language. The task of using the computer to begin to link these materials together to form a virtual electronic environment for teaching and research is the challenge that led to the formation of the Shakespeare Interactive Archive at MIT in 1991. This endeavor is codirected by me, Larry Friedlander and Janet H. Murray, Director of MIT's Laboratory for Advanced Technology in the Humanities (LATH). Stuart A. Malone serves as Head Programmer. The group is based principally at MIT (Larry Friedlander has spent the Fall terms of 1992 and 1993 at MIT as Visiting Professor of Literature and Media Arts) but, as our activities expand, we have formed active collaborative relationships with scholars at others universities, including Michael Warren (U.C. Santa Cruz), who is working with me on a digitized facsimile edition of *Hamlet*, Alan Young (Acadia University, Nova Scotia), who is collaborating with us in assembling a large collection of digitized images of art work and book illustrations relevant to *Hamlet*, Kenneth Rothwell and Thomas Simone (University of Vermont), who are working on educational applications of the Archive, and Bernice Kliman (Nassau Community College), who is working on editorial as well as educational aspects of the project. The goal of the group's work is to develop all aspects of the relationship between Shakespeare study and emerging electronic technologies, including educational programs, new forms of electronic publishing for scholarly, educational and general use, and the creation of an electronic archive.

In 1992, major funding was secured from the National Endowment for the Humanities[2] for two initial projects, a *Classroom Presentation System* and a *Prototype Research Archive*. These projects are closely related, and embody a number of decisions we made in order to progress toward our more expansive long term goals. Our design choices included the following:

1. We decided to create links at an *extremely fine-grained standard*—approximately every line or two of text—so that once the appropriate disc is loaded, one need only highlight a passage of text and choose from a video menu to watch a performance—or, in many cases, one of several alternative performances—of the exact passage selected. The project uses

industrial standard Pioneer 8000 players. These players are an expensive component of the system, but they allow precise frame access ($\frac{1}{30}$ second) to both CAV (industrial standard) discs and the less expensive CLV (commercial standard) format in which most Shakespeare films are published.

2. Though the Archive project will eventually extend to material transferred to laserdisc from tape and other media, we began by making the *fullest possible use of the current list of commercially available laserdisc performances.* This list includes more than twenty-five titles, including many of the major Shakespeare films such as Laurence Olivier's *Hamlet* and Richard III as well as the Granada Television production of *King Lear* with Olivier in the title role, Orson Welles's *Othello* and *Macbeth,* Zeffirelli's *Taming of the Shrew, Romeo and Juliet,* and *Hamlet,* and Kenneth Branagh's *Henry V.* Two of Akira Kurosawa's Shakespeare adaptations, *Throne of Blood (Macbeth)* and Ran (*King Lear*) are also available and have been linked to text. This approach has several advantages. It allows us to link *complete* performances without the expense of tape-to-disc transfer, and it will allow us to distribute the Archive software to other universities for use with discs that can be separately purchased. Such distribution will be the first step toward a modular electronic archive, in which the MIT interface and links to various materials can be used at other sites. We envision a tiered system of access, in which some materials will be available over the information highway of the future, others, such as videodiscs and collections of texts and images on CD-ROM may be "plugged into" the archive system at specific sites, while still other materials for which we have created links will be available for on-site use at collaborating research and rare book libraries.

3. Both projects emphasize the development of *dynamic, fully interactive tools*, enabling teacher, students, and researchers not merely to *access* linked film and text, and to make choices among them according to their interests, but also to *reconfigure* them for presentation in their own multimedia "essays." In the Archive environment, materials may be searched, displayed, excerpted for temporary storage in electronic "notebooks" and subsequently repositioned in more formal essay and presentation formats. Our major programming effort is aimed at the development of *authoring software* and an *electronic workspace* that will make it possible to work with many large documents—texts, films, etc.—in simple and intuitive ways, eliminating as much as possible the pull-down menus, stacks of overlaid "cards" and other infelicities of currently available systems.

4. In designing the prototype Archive, we also decided that for one play, *Hamlet*, we would provide more extensive features to serve as a model for subsequent work on other plays. For the *Hamlet* archive we plan to link electronic texts of the early editions (First Quarto, 1603; Second Quarto, 1604/5; First Folio, 1623), to provide digitized photofacsimile reproductions of the pages of these early texts as well as character-based transcriptions, and to include an extensive collection of artwork and production photographs, all linked to appropriate passages in the text when possible. In addition, the *Hamlet* films would be accompanied by extensive commentaries on film, performance and interpretive issues and interactive lexica of film and performance terminology. They would also be *searchable* for visual patterns as well as verbal ones: figures of film style (close-ups, camera movement, and distance) as well as performance choices (blocking, shifts of attention and focus) would be indexed and linked to the text. A number of these additional features would also be created for the Zeffirelli *Romeo and Juliet*, along with software specifically designed for educational use of the system.

Constructing the Archive: Initial Steps

By 1993, we had created text-video links for fifteen films including the Olivier and Zeffirelli productions of *Hamlet* as well as a suite of *working tools* and *prototype interfaces*. We had enough to use the system regularly in classroom teaching, both as a presentation medium and for use in workstations at which students could write their own multimedia essays. We were also able to explore the emerging environment in extensive and interesting enough ways to begin to use the system for interpretive research and scholarly presentation.

Figures 6.1, 6.2, and 6.3 illustrate the most important of the *working tools:*

Figure 6.1 is the basic *text-video linking tool*, used to create the thousands of links between electronic text and videodiscs on which the system is based. Once created, a similar tool, slightly simpler in design, is used to access video in the classroom or at a workstation. The user can search the text in the familiar word processing mode, highlight text, and then, by using the *follow link* function, call up the corresponding video instantaneously.

Figure 6.2 is a film style linking tool and search program. So far we have created interactive stylistic indexes to Zeffirelli's *Hamlet* and *Romeo and*

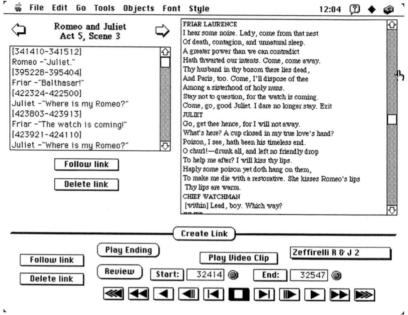

Figure 6.1

Juliet and Olivier's *Hamlet*. There are well over 1000 electronic index cards for the Zeffirelli *Hamlet*, each with several categories of film style, all of which can be searched. We have found this an extremely useful tool that enables us to think about patterns of verbal repetition and rhetoric in the playtext and the details of the filmmaker's art as aspects of a single, complex presentation.

Figure 6.3 is one version of the stacks we use to create multimedia essays. Video can be "quoted," integrated into text on scrolling cards, and cards can be linked one to another to create multimedia hypertext discussions.

As we currently use these tools, they exist in distinct card-based stacks, and one must activate each stack in turn to use them. In the more integrated environment we are building, text-video links, visual searches, various texts and commentaries, and tools for composition and presentation will all be available in a single multifunction workspace.

Figures 6.4 and 6.5 illustrate an early *prototype* of such an environment, still card-based, in which an electronic "notebook" can be used to store text

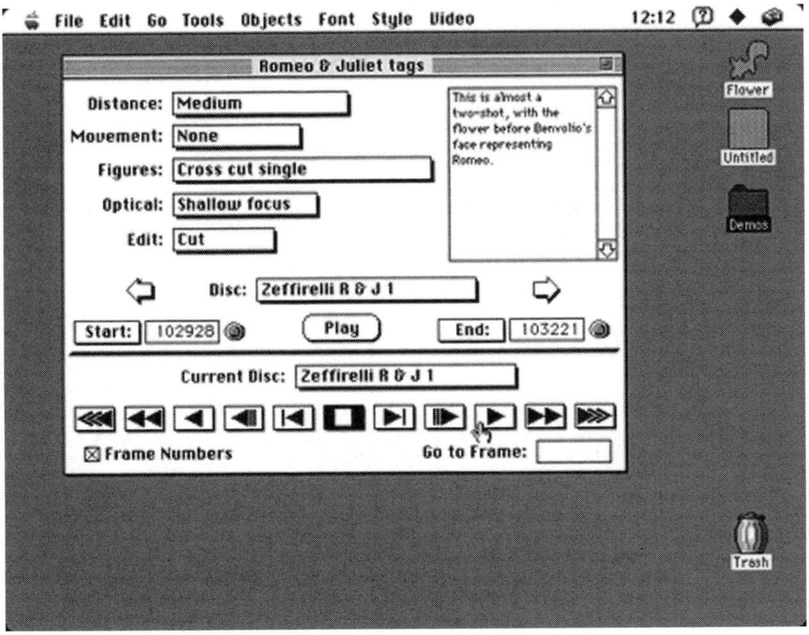

Figure 6.2

and video clips (now represented by frame-icons instead of a string of frame numbers) for transfer to a presentation outline.

In the following section, examples of our current *presentation interface* will be discussed in detail.

Educational and Scholarly Use

Our educational use of the system has been exceptionally rewarding, especially in small seminar setting in which students can have ample time on one of the two workstations devoted to the Archive. Even with our relatively rough prototype tools, students at MIT require very little introduction to the system. We have encouraged students to explore and invent ways to use the Archive software, and after one term's use, several trends in their work are apparent. As expected, students become closely attentive to the details of performance as interpretation of text. One student "paper" for example, dealt with differences between Helena Bonham-Carter and Jean Simmons as

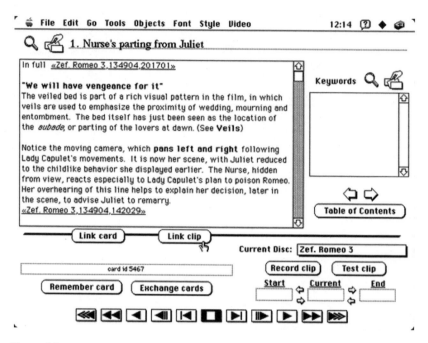

Figure 6.3

Ophelia, attending to such elusive aspects of the generation of meaning as the quality and implication of a smile and the implications of close-up versus long shot presentation. Another student chose what, in a paper on the text alone might be a relatively conventional verbal and thematic topic—"nature" in *Hamlet*. But because the student could carefully check what happened in both films each time "nature" appeared in the text, the multimedia essay that resulted became in part an exploration of the *mis*representation of the Shakespearean meanings of "nature" in these films, and a meditation on the reasons for the relative neglect of the rich possibilities suggested by the text.

When we added electronic transcriptions of the early printed editions of *King Lear, Hamlet* and *Romeo and Juliet* to the workstation software, the effect was surprising, exceeding my fondest hopes that the system might increase interest in matters strictly textual. I had attempted, in the past, with mixed success, to interest my students in variant readings, and in the contemporary theories (associated with Honigmann, Michael Warren, Steven

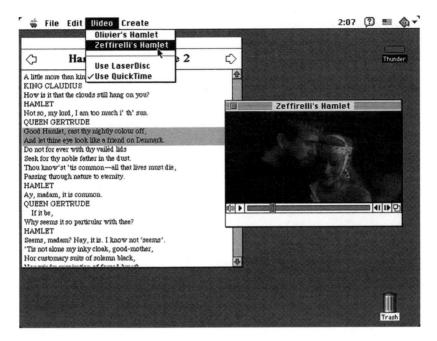

Figure 6.4

Urkowitz, Gary Taylor, Stanley Wells and others, and now perhaps dominant, at least for *King Lear*) that such variants can sometimes derive from authorial "second thoughts" or wholescale revision. Whatever the final consensus regarding such theories, I believed it was important for students, even at the undergraduate level, to be familiar with the debate concerning the authority of these early texts relative to the conflated editions of *Hamlet*, *Lear*, and other plays that have been prepared since the early 18th century. What I found was that students using the electronic archive needed no coaxing—soon they were citing particular texts (quartos, folio, Bevington, Arden, Oxford) and finding the differences as interesting as the performance choices they were analyzing in their essays. The medium facilitates such "horizontal" readings and fosters the sense that a variety of such "readings"—those of early texts, contemporary performances and our own belated interpretations—can coexist and enrich the experience of a play without fragmenting it.

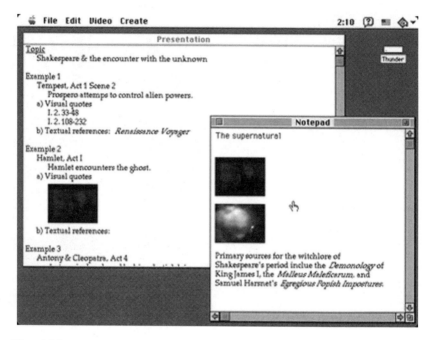

Figure 6.5

The system was also ready for use as a vehicle for scholarly work. In the Spring of 1993, I used our prototype *Hamlet* Archive to research and "write" a multimedia essay on *Hamlet* for presentation at the plenary session of the Shakespeare Association of America's annual meeting in Atlanta in April. The presentation, entitled "Ghostly Texts and Virtual Performances: Old Hamlet in New Media," focused on a brief passage—the appearance of the ghost to Hamlet in Act One and attempted to relate the interpretive choices made in two film versions of the play—Olivier's 1947 production, and Franco Zeffirelli's 1989 film starring Mel Gibson and Glenn Close—to variations among the three principal early printed editions (First Quarto, 1603; Second Quarto, 1604/5; First Folio, 1623). Using a Macintosh Quadra 800 in conjunction with a video projector and sound system and two Pioneer 8000 industrial videodisc players, the presentation contained over one hundred computer-accessed references to primary and secondary texts, digitized photographs of pages of early editions, still photographs, and excerpts from the two principal films as well as comparative video material from Zefirelli's earlier *Romeo and Juliet* film (1968).

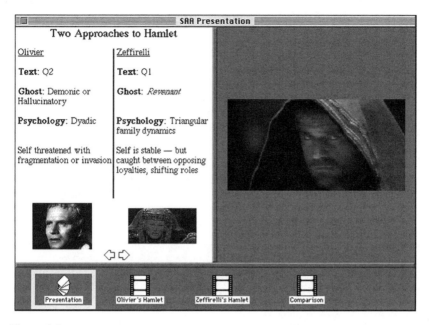

Figure 6.6
Screen 1.

The remainder of this paper offers an informal account of this first attempt to use the Archive to create a new form, the multimedia interpretive essay. I will not attempt to recapitulate the argument of that essay in its entirety, but will discuss a number of the presentation screens[3] in detail in order to explain the current state of the research and presentation workspace, and to give a "backstage view" of its use.

Screen 1. Two Approaches to Hamlet

Our first screen outlined a *multilevelled comparison* between the two films anchored by a *salient sequence* from each which played in the right hand window when the appropriate icon was clicked. In "Ghostly Texts" I tried to illustrate some advantages of multimedia presentation by deploying, in turn, several modes of analysis not usually brought together, including discussion of:

1. The relationship between the two films and the *early printed editions* of the play. In the case of Olivier, passages existing only in the Second Quarto are given special prominence, while the relationship between Zeffirelli's

interpretation and the First Quarto, often thought to be an actor's remembered version, is a more general one, perhaps merely a resonance between the performance choices appropriate to film and theater that aim at a popular audience.

2. The echoes, in each film, of the *divergent theories concerning the status of ghosts* in the Early Modern period. Most treatises in the Reformed or Protestant tradition held that no ghost could actually be a spirit returned from the dead, and that all such appearances were either hallucinations or demonic illusions. Some Catholic texts, on the other hand, though nearly equally suspicious of ghosts, held that it was possible for the ghost of a family member to return, perhaps to reveal the facts concerning his wrongful death. It is surprising how closely and with what extensive detail the two films reflect these centuries-old traditions. Later cards in the sequence contained extensive citations from primary texts such as King James's *Daemonologie* and secondary materials such as Eleanor Prosser's *Hamlet and Revenge* and David Ward's recent speculations concerning Shakespeare's revision of *Hamlet* in 1603 following James's accession to the throne and his assumption of the role of patron to Shakespeare's company.

3. The central psychological issue or conflict. Olivier's conception of *Hamlet* was explicitly influenced by Freudian psychoanalysis, and the film is full of portentous "symbols," romantic interactions between Gertrude and Hamlet and oscillations from elation to guilt and self-destructiveness on the part of the main character. Yet, when analysed carefully, a case can be made that the Zeffirelli film actually is more attentive to the triangular rivalries within the family on which Freud based his theories than the Olivier film, in which fears of merger with the father are more prominent.

4. For each film, signal differences in cinematic style correlate with the textual, discursive and psychological issues that differentiate the interpretations. *Salient sequences*[4] activated by clicking on the filmic icons select moments in which each director's approach to the play can be discerned in miniature. The Olivier sequence shows a high angle track-in "through" Hamlet's head to the imagined scene of his father's murder, while the ghost describes that event. This way of suggesting that the ghost's words have become Hamlet's thoughts so completely that there is almost a fusion of personalities is repeated elsewhere in the film, and defines a major problem for Olivier's Hamlet—how to hold his own against the powerful "possession" of the ghost. For Zeffirelli, the sequence chosen is a tense and anxious exchange of glances involving the three principals—Gertrude, Hamlet and Claudius—over the body of the dead king. The style—and the psychology—of Zeffirelli's *Hamlet* is triangular, involving rapid, intimately observed shifts of energy, affection, resentment and jealousy in the family. The idea of the

salient sequence in the analysis of film adaptation is similar to the notion of a "signature shot" in film analysis—for example Hitchcock's cross-cut tracking shots—except that the attempt is made to select material relevant not only to the director's style, but to as many aspects of the work of adaptation as possible. The salient sequence can be a continuous video citation or a collage of short sequences from different parts of the film, brought together for analytic purposes. The salient sequence is also an effective teaching tool: in my seminars, students are often given the task of constructing such sequences as a starting point for discussion of a director's approach to a Shakespeare play.

Screen 2. "So oft it chances": Q2 (1603) and F 1(1623) in digitized photofacsimile.

In this card, the digitized images of original pages which appear as reduced icons on the left expand to fill the right hand window when clicked. For this feature, we worked with 35mm Kodachrome transparencies of Folger Library copies which were then scanned to PhotoCD format and then color

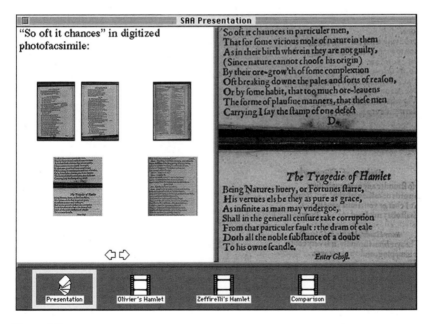

Figure 6.7
Screen 2.

corrected using Adobe Photoshop. The same conceptual point—that the famous speech in which Hamlet speaks of a fatal, undermining fault or flaw that can undermine a kingdom or an individual personality exists only in one text—might be made using normal word processing fonts, but we are learning that digitized photographs of texts can be very important components of the virtual archive we are building. We included digitized facsimile as an experiment, and found that it was extremely effective and led to extensive discussion. This medium of presentation is strongest when it does not merely cite or refer to material, but evokes or instantiates it, moving among representations of culturally situated, contextualized data, in this case from images of the book (one of seven extant copies) to moving images of the text as performed.

Digital images are, of course, far more memory-consuming than their alphanumeric counterparts, yet we plan to include full sets of digitized photographs of pages of Q1, Q2 and F1 in the Archive and are collaborating with Michael Warren, the noted textual scholar and editor of The *Complete King Lear* (Berkeley: University of California Press, 1989) on a complete digital facsimile edition of *Hamlet* for separate publication on CD-ROM. In the completed system, it will be possible to access video, alternate e-texts, facsimile pages and other materials from any line of text.

Our experiences with digital facsimiles suggest that some notions of "information" encountered in theoretical accounts of hypertext may be inadequate to deal with the processes of cultural simulation and reproduction possible in multimedia hypertext or "hypermedia." It is true, of course, that digitized photographs, like digitized video, alphanumeric text or any other computer generated representation, are "nothing but bits," having been reduced to the binary code of the raster grid. But—paradoxically—the fact of reduction to a common medium can lead to more, not less interest in the detailed cultural contexts and the highly particularized material form in which historical and literary information is transmitted. Facsimile editions of Shakespeare's early texts have been prepared since 1806 in the medium of print, since 1864 in lithograph copies and since 1866 in various photomechanical media such as collotype, photo offset and photozincography. In the electronic age, facsimiles will be digital, full color, permanent records of the originals. But our use of them will shift away from photographic notions of exact replication as we learn to construct dense, contextualized simulations of the histories of dramatic texts as they move from manuscript or book to recorded performance.

In parallel with such developments, the role of scholarly editing of Shakespeare may be expected to shift as well. Instead of attempting to establish a single authoritative text in one medium editors will become guides to the evidence provided by several media, helping the "reader" through the web of relationships among texts, interpretations and performance options that constitute the complex life of a play as it moves through historical time.

Screen 6. Focus Shifts from King's "Fault" to Hamlet's

This card illustrates the use of several modes of multimedia analysis: video cross-reference, finely detailed analysis of performance, and the integration of textual and visual argument. Hamlet's speech, "So oft it chances in particular men," begins as a criticism of the king's drinking habits, becomes a more general reflection on the international reputation of the Danish people, and then modulates into a meditation on Hamlet's own faults and insecurities. Yet this last set of implications can vary greatly in performance. In Zeffirelli's treatment of the scene, the focus remains on the king and his faults, while in Olivier's treatment, the king is eventually forgotten, and Hamlet's feelings of guilt and inferiority are emphasized. The film clips included here make these points by looking closely at the texture of visual allusion and at the details of blocking, framing and the shifting emotional tone of Olivier's delivery. The cannon which is heard on the ramparts and seen in the courtyard below signals the king's revels, but it is also, as we establish through video quotation of earlier sequences almost a symbol or icon of the king and all that Hamlet dislikes about him. As Olivier turns his back to the cannon (Screen 6A) and eventually obscures it completely, his focus turns inward, to his own guilt.

Analysis of the textual decisions supports this pattern: working with an already guilt-laden Q2 passage, Olivier cuts two lines ("As in their birth, wherein they are not guilty/For nature cannot choose his origin") which could tend to modify or alleviate the self-condemnation Olivier wants Hamlet to display at this point (Screen 6B). The text-display option—in which material used is bolded and material cut reduced to grey—is a preliminary version of more elaborate and partly automated schemes for text comparison

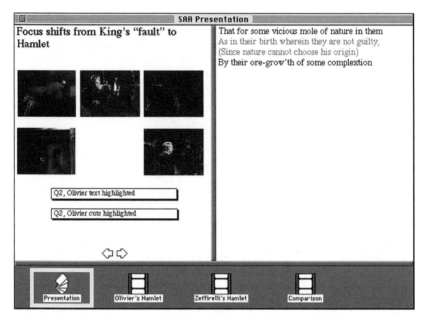

Figure 6.8
Screen 6A.

under development. It has always been possible, with some effort, to compare the text of a play to a published screenplay or promptbook, or to compare readings from the several early editions of a given play. What we are trying to do is to make such comparisons *dynamic*, so that the effect of cuts, additions and variations can be experienced as alternatives more easily, and *available on demand* by clicking on a text-option button or menu choice. In class, or in a formal presentation, it is often helpful to show such differences in two forms: with text used bolded and then with text cut bolded. We are striving for the dynamic impression of language transmuting from one version, text or production to the next, attempting to establish habits of hearing differences as well as similarities in closely related texts in a more intimate and meaningful way than the medium of print permits.

Screen 13. Angels and Ministers of Grace

This screen illustrates the use of the system to effect simultaneous, or near simultaneous, comparisons between significant moments in two performances.

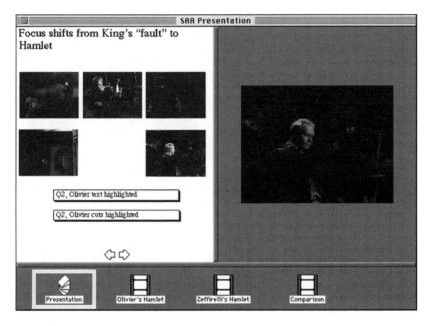

Figure 6.9
Screen 6B.

At the moment of the advent of the ghost, Hamlet exclaims, "Angels and ministers of grace defend us!" In Zeffirelli, Hamlet's companions are thrown back to the wall by the sight of the ghost, while Hamlet, in contrast, walks firmly toward the ghost, crosses himself, and holds his position despite his evident apprehension. In Olivier's interpretation, it is Hamlet who is thrown back, into the arms of his companions. This detail of performance is an instance of a recurring pattern in the film: Hamlet is often thrown back, suffers physical and emotional collapse followed by recovery. In fact, at the end of the scene from which this excerpt was taken he loses consciousness and falls, overcome by the revelations of the ghost. The interplay between Hamlet's vulnerability and his ability to recoup and transcend his "weakness" is one of the central features of Olivier's interpretation of the character. Each of these clips takes only several seconds to run, but they sum up salient aspects and key differences between the two *Hamlets*.

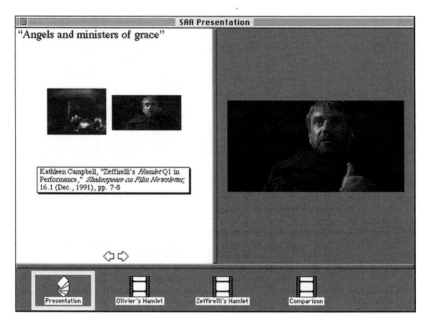

Figure 6.10
Screen 13A.

Screen 15: The "Mind's Eye" in Q2 and Screen 16: Olivier and the "Mind's Eye"

These two screen suggests some of the interesting ways in which an interactive research environment can lead to enhanced understanding of the relationship between film and playtext. Sometimes that relationship is one in which visual images replace or substitute for textual cuts. In this case, Olivier does not use the lines in which Bernardo warns him that following the ghost may lead him to the summit of the cliff, where the influence of the place alone may suggest self-destruction, putting "thoughts of desperation" into his "brain." Though the lines are not used, a visual equivalent occurs in Olivier's striking interpretation of the "To be or not to be" speech. Here, Hamlet sits at the edge of the castle parapet, with the surf below. A high angle track-in seems to enter his head and even for a fraction of a second to suggest, in an indistinct and convoluted image, that we pass through his skull before the focus clarifies and we share Hamlet's despairing view of the rocks beneath.

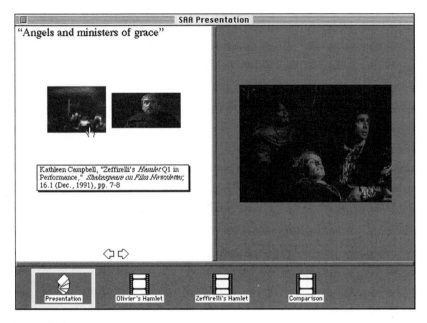

Figure 6.11
Screen 13B.

This idiosyncratic treatment is a visual equivalent of Bernardo's lines, even to the fleeting suggestion of a glimpse of the brain itself. In addition, the high angle tracking shot to the head of a seated figure has been used before to suggest that the ghost's discourse is invasive, taking over Hamlet's thoughts. Its repetition here, even though the ghost is not present in the scene, implies that—just as in Bernardo's warning—it is, ultimately, the ghost of Hamlet's father who has turned Hamlet toward thoughts of self-destruction. This is a striking interpretive move on Olivier's part, and moves his *Hamlet* closer to readings of the play in which the ghost is a dubious, even demonic presence. The sequence, no doubt, is effective without our knowing how it is constructed by the "rhyming" of figures of film style, and the weaving together of textual and visual representations. But understanding how these effects are created is valuable in its own right, and in this case I think we understand more clearly that the ghost has played a role in driving Hamlet to the "edge" when we are able to represent the structure of the sequence in multimedia terms.

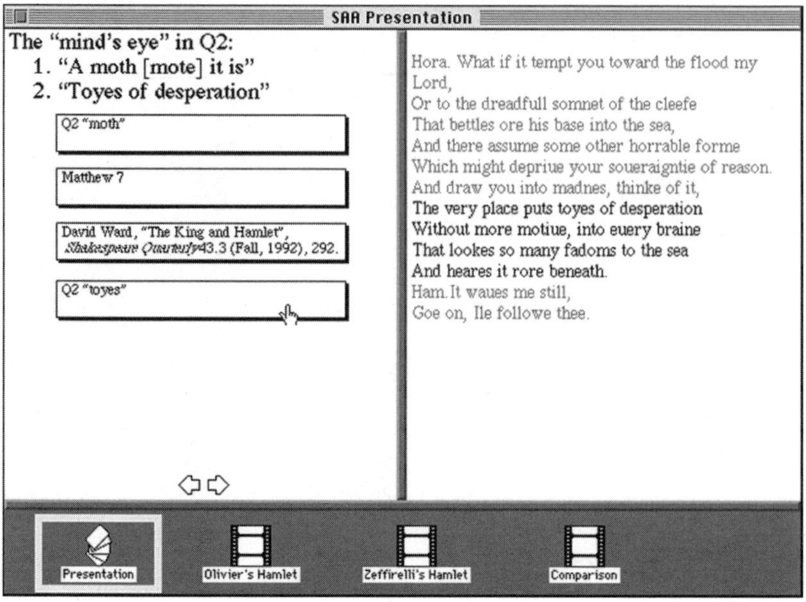

Figure 6.12
Screen 15.

On another level, these two cards illustrate something of the research and interpretive methods possible with an interactive system. In constructing this portion of the argument, I began with the shot that seems to move through Hamlet's head, and wondered if there was a source for the fleeting "brain" image. Calling up the corresponding text for the scene yielded no results, but searching the text for key words—"mind," "brain," "sight," etc, and then looking at the corrsponding video for those instances began to yield a rich pattern to explore, eventually leading back to David Ward's interesting analysis of the Q2-only passages in Hamlet, and their special use of the idea of the "mind's eye." In the current state of the system, I could also have used a film style search index to find the conjunction of "track-in," "high angle," and "one figure in frame" to locate earlier instances of this stylistic figure. As with any research environment, including a library, the environment facili-tates certain kinds of search, enriches certain kinds of connections. It is possible that one could make some of the connections among shots, among texts about "minds," "brains" and "thoughts" without using visual and

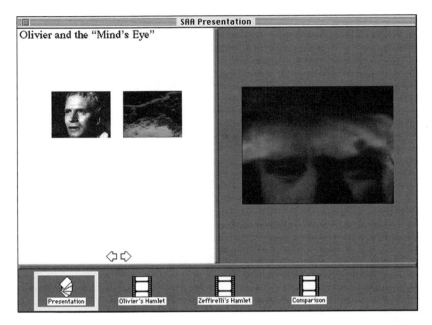

Figure 6.13
Screen 16.

verbal searches—but the availability of search programs and the finegrained linking of text to image means that such an exploration can be greatly enhanced.

Using the Shakespeare Interactive Archive for Research: Some General Observations

The Shakespeare Interactive Archive is one kind of *multimedia hypertext.*[5] Materials originally produced in dissimilar media are digitized and linked together to form a new "text," which can be "read" on the workstation screen, searched, excerpted and rearranged for presentation. Some of the implications of linking texts, pictures and moving images together in this way are becoming clear, but it would be a mistake to imagine that we can specify in advance all the changes in research methods and modes of interpretation that may result. The following observations are therefore preliminary and somewhat tentative in nature.

1. The electronic archive enhances the *close analysis of visual material, especially film and video*. Fine-grained visual citations make it possible to examine closely the details of performance and film style through which an interpretation is constructed in a filmed performance and also facilitate comparisons *between* one filmed performance and another. For some time, theorists have been referring to films, television narratives, and a wide range of cultural performances as "texts." When such materials are digitized and indexed, they become texts in a more literal sense. Recorded in a stable medium, they can be quickly accessed and cited with the ease with which we now locate and excerpt materials in a well-indexed book. Such "textualization" makes it possible to "read" performances against the grain, to discover patterns of meaning and implication that escape sequential viewing and that may exceed the conscious intentions of performers, directors and filmmakers. Such reading is of course practiced by interpreters of film and video already, but electronic tools are far more rapid and precise than videotape or the cumbersome editing tables and analytic projectors now used for the serious study of film.

2. A multimedia hypertext system promotes simultaneous awareness of the spoken word in a performance and the text or texts that correspond to what is spoken. Because this is so, we become sensitized to subtle variations in textual editing and in the ways in which performances enact their texts. We can begin to "hear" the effect of textual excisions and to experience visual aspects of theatrical and filmed performance as translations, in some instances, of verbal imagery cut from the text.

3. A related phenomenon is the enactment effect that occurs when a passage of text is used as a cue for a corresponding moment of performance—the written words seem to evoke the performance. The impression can be magical, dissonant, or even disconcerting, but whatever form it takes, it is different from studying scripts and films in isolation from one another, and is likely to change how we think about their connection. The enactment effect thrusts upon our attention the possibilty of a close, mutually evocative relationship involving the printed word, the moving image, and our own processes of reaction and reflection. And it does so not in theoretical terms but as an experience.

It is important to distinguish the enactment effect from the more immersive illusions of virtual reality, and even from the pleasures of the hypertext web or labyrinth, as described in recent literature. Traveling from print to performance simply by touching a button can suggest an almost magically evocative relationship between these media, but using the system also reminds us that each medium is partial, one mode among many of conveying related experiences. Hypermedia study simulates the process by which written words become performance, and helps us to discern the artistic strategies and creative decisions that have gone into the work of Shakespearean production and adaptation. We can get very close to performances—close enough to "read" them at an almost microscopic level of detail. But our experience is analytic, segmented, intermittent.

4. Multimedia hypertext reconfigures the relationship between an authoritative cultural *source* (a Shakespeare play) and its belated, aesthetically and culturally divergent contemporary *versions*, changing the ways we think about such matters as "the original text" and its reproduction in "authoritative" versions and productions. Much that has been written about hypertext assumes that the computer will be an ally of the contemporary literary theories that unseat the "author," spread meaning out into a web of traces and associations, and change the relation between cultural center and margin. As we begin to produce interpretations in hypermedia form, some of these assumptions are confirmed: the ability to discern patterns in a popular film that are as subtle, intricate, and meaningful as those found in academic criticism of the text can effect a kind of decentering.

But there is a contrary effect as well: computer access to historically and culturally distant materials can have a bridging or unifying function. The "enactment effect" referred to above can work to make us feel that, despite the great differences between, for example, the Peter Brook film of *King Lear* (1970) and the Russian language version directed by Gregorii Kozintsev (1972), the words that the mad Lear utters in recognition of Gloucester on the heath are closer to one another and more indebted to the creative activity of the author than the separate experiences of viewing each film and reading the text might suggest. Multimedia can make us aware of difference, and can enable us to talk about it with great precision; but it can also span time and promote a sense of family resemblance within variation. The advent of multimedia hypertext will alter discussions of the centrality of the author, the status of multiple interpretations, and the cultural specificity of literary experience, but it is likely that, rather than resolving such issues, multimedia will strengthen the case for continuity as well as divergence, and perhaps reframe the false oppositions that sustain the current debate.

Future Directions for Electronic Shakespeare

We envision a digital future for Shakespeare, in which the multimedia resources of major libraries can be used with the tools we are creating, and in which new editorial forms will develop in electronic media. Digital facsimile editions, reading editions in which variant editions appear dynamically within the line, scholarly editions in which video "footnotes" recognize important innovations in performance just as current editions acknowledge important trends in critical thought—all these are active projects of the Shakespeare Interactive Archive group, and some will be ready for publication in the near future.

It would be a mistake, however, to assume that electronic forms will or should replace the printed book. The coming decade will be a period of experimentation and development, of attempts to ascertain, as only use and familiarity can do, which of the many and fascinating potentialities of interactive hypertext will prove most useful. Our work to date has increased our respect for the computer, but has also made us aware, with each medium that we transfer to digital form, of aspects of that medium that cannot be represented or reduced. The computer cannot replace the theater, the library, or the face-to-face interaction of teacher and student.

The longer-range future of multimedia research will include the use of fully automated visual search programs and intelligent agents, so that the power of the computer to process large amounts of information and to find patterns within it will enter into a fuller partnership with the human capacity for intuitive modes of understanding. How would such a partnership work? The computer might, for example, "notice" that a user has selected a series of briskly edited exchanges between two characters shot in close-up, and "ask" if the user wants to see other examples of the same pattern. Such complex functions, "intelligent" interactions, are possible now, though their use to further the understanding of complex cultural phenomena like language use, theatrical performance, or the art of filmmaking has yet to begin. It is our belief that the questions humanists ask about such materials are more interesting and important than the kinds of questions the computer is usually set to work on, and that the partnership we envision can enrich the world of computer research as well as the humanities.

Notes

1. Scenes included the Banquet Scene in *Macbeth* in the Roman Polanski and Orson Welles films, the Nunnery Scene in *Hamlet* in the Tony Richardson and Grigorii Kozintsev films, and Gloucester and Lear on the heath, as rendered by Kozintsev and Peter Brook.

2. Matching funds have been provided by Apple Computer, James Levitan, and Joel and Theodor Bernstein.

3. The SAA presentation consisted of twenty five screens of which five are discussed below.

4. The term was suggested by the "salient stills" constructed from video at the MIT Media Laboratory. A salient still is a digitally manipulated collage that compresses information found in various parts of a moving picture.

5. I prefer this term to "hypermedia" for several reasons. Hypertextuality is too new and too important an idea to risk the elision of the "text" part of hypertext; and it is worth keeping both "multi-" and "hyper-" to refer to the media of which such a hypertext is made. Multimedia is less than ideal because in fact the several media come together to create *one* new medium for which we don't have a good single name. In addition, as Nicholas Negroponte points out in *Wired*, no. 1.5 (1993), multimedia can refer to forms like *son et images* concerts that bear little relation to interactive multimedia on videodisc and CD-ROM. Nevertheless, the term suggests some of the ways in which a "single" event or phenomenon—such as a scene of a Shakespeare play—can take different forms, textual, visual and aural, as well as the ways the computer can link, access and "transcode" the multiple forms of that event.

7

The Pedagogy of Cyberfiction: Teaching a Course on Reading and Writing Interactive Narrative

Janet H. Murray

Since 1992 I have been giving a course at MIT called "21.765: Structure and Interpretation of Nonlinear and Interactive Narrative."[1] I set out in this course to help establish the conventions and building blocks of an art form that is only emerging. The course therefore presents the problem of how to teach students to write in a genre that they will have to invent for themselves.

The course title is a play on MIT's groundbreaking introductory course in computer science: "6.001. Structure and Interpretation of Computer Programs," which does not seek to teach students a particular programming language but instead to acquaint them with the structure of thought that underlies software engineering in any programming language.[2] Taught largely through problem sets, a recurrent theme of the course is "powerful" ideas: elegant abstractions that were also practical strategies for making things.

There are several dramatic highlights in 6.001, including at least one class in which instructors traditionally don wizard's hats. At one point, the instructor demonstrates that there is no difference between data and procedures, a dizzying leap for those who come (as I did) schooled in more traditionally structured programming languages. They illustrate this radical change in thinking by displaying the yin/yang symbol. Another climactic moment comes at the end of the term when the instructor explains how the lisp programming language could be installed on a register machine, the simplest, dumbest kind of computer. At the end of that lecture it becomes clear how abstract objects which seem to made of pure thought can in fact be built on top of very simple wiring. For me, and I think for many who take the course, the moment is thrilling, like being offered a glimpse of the link between mind and brain.

I could have named my course, "Reading and Writing Interactive Fiction," since in form it is very much like courses in "Reading and Writing the Essay," or "Reading and Writing the Short Story." But in thinking about a course which would teach students to create art in a medium which did not yet exist, I was drawn to the model of 6.001. I felt a strong kinship with the attitude of that course: a fascination with the medium itself, with the joy of thinking in terms of essential structures rather than particular instantiations of a form, with the exhilaration of discovering the secrets by which human beings build enticing objects, and with the tantalizing sense that the way in which we represent our knowledge of the world tells us something about the workings of the brain itself. I wanted to address pure structure, to engender the procedural thinking necessary for literary creation in this emerging medium, and—this is the interpretation part—to explore with my students what new truths about the human condition have been waiting to be addressed in this new art form.

Nonlinearity in Traditional Media

Because electronic fiction models are sketchy and as yet take little advantage of the procedural power of the computer, I turned to books and films that are clear predecessors of electronic interactive stories. The selections here are all linear in form: they are books or stories with ordinary progression from first page to last, films that run from opening credits to closing credits. Yet all of them are straining to escape that linearity through nonlinear story elements and even deconstruction of the medium they inhabit. There is a wide latitude for selection here. The books I usually teach are

- Laurence Sterne, *The Life and Opinions of Tristram Shandy* (1759–67) (Books I and II only)
- Emily Brontë, *Wuthering Heights* (1847)
- Milorad Pavic, *Dictionary of the Khasars* (1988)
- Jorge Luis Borges, "The Garden of Forking Paths" from *Ficciones* (1941)
- Alan Lightman, *Einstein's Dreams* (1993), excerpt, "19 April 1905," pp. 18–22. (Lightman).

In addition we view

Duck Amuck (1951), animated cartoon, produced by Warner Brothers, Chuck Jones, director.
Groundhog Day (1993), feature-length film, Harold Ramis, director; Danny Rubin and Harold Ramis, writers
"Parallels" episode of *Star Trek: The Next Generation* (1993), Brannon Braga, writer; Robert Wiemer, director.

It is easy to come up with alternatives to this list,[3] and it is certainly not meant to be canonical. But these selections are useful in giving students examples of ambitious writing in nonlinear modes[4] and in providing them with a vocabulary for thinking about the formal elements of nonlinear fiction.

Tristram Shandy was written in a rage of experimental energy, parodying the forms of the novel just as they were coalescing. For the purposes of the course I read only the first two books.[5] The content of the story, which the students often have trouble relating to, is of considerably less interest to us than the form, which yields a rich vocabulary for considering the story-telling techniques for electronic fiction.

Taking a problem-set approach, I assign the students to come up with a list of nonlinear elements in the narrative and to attempt to categorize them. Then for an in-class exercise I divide them into groups and have them develop a list of Sterne's essential narrative components and an algorithm for assembling them that would produce *Tristram Shandy*. There is of course no right answer to this exercise, and we discover that there are many ways to think about the components of narrative. The most important value of the exercise is that it moves them right away into the role of author.

Of course, the most obvious literary device in *Tristram Shandy* is the *digression*. There are many kinds of digressions, even in just the first two books. Students usually begin by describing them negatively as irritating *interruptions* of the narrative. Their sense of interruption introduces the key perception that narrative pleasure depends upon the experience of *antici-pation and reward*; this is what yields the "what's next" response that keeps us reading. We then discuss how our sense of anticipation comes from working within a set of conventions, which leads to a discussion of a variety of *literary conventions*, both rhetorical and structural. We examine known

conventions of high literature like the novel of courtship and the bildungs-
roman and we discuss how a set of expectations (love, growth) provides for
anticipation and reward while leaving enough room for individual variation
to create the pleasure of surprise. Students often point out that their problem
with "getting into" *Tristram Shandy* is that they can't figure out what the
conventions are. After reading for awhile, though, it becomes clear that the
digressions *are* the narrative, and so they are no longer experienced as
interruptions but as coherent narrative units with their own interest and
integrity.

Sterne is very helpful in providing a virtual catalog of digressions, including *interpolated stories* which are unrelated to the main narrative, *nested stories*
which are complete in themselves but told in the middle of *frame narratives*. We
also note Sterne's *nested digressions*, both narrative and essay-like, building up a
deep tree that almost always returns to the original point of departure; and his
interpolated documents (such as Tristram's mother's marriage settlement or a
French discourse on infant baptism) that serve as a kind of primary source
material and invite the reader to play the role of the scholar/detective. Sterne
provides a term of his own which is useful in thinking about any nonlinear
structure: the *progressive digression*, which actually advances story and character while seeming to take the reader far afield. Tristram's example of a
progressive digression is the story of Aunt Dinah's elopement which inter-
rupts his explicit detailing of Toby's character, and yet itself sheds a great
deal of light on Toby's character (volume I, chapter 22).

In addition to gaining the benefit of these examples, we observe the
techniques by which Sterne *anchors* us in the fiction, while simultaneously
rocking the boat. For example we notice the *weaving* together of several
narrative levels, as when Trim's reading of the sermon is interspersed with his
asides and the reactions and by-play of his audience (II,17). Another device
is the *marker* which can be an object, a phrase, or a gesture, which helps us
to keep our place in the interrupted narrative, such as an interrupted gesture
with a pipe, resumed several chapters later (I,21; II,6). Because these an-
choring devices are clear, we can take pleasure in the disruptions of the
conventional narrative, secure in the knowledge of which expectations will
be fulfilled. The reader soon catches on to the conventions of the uncon-
ventional narrative. We figure out that there will be many digressions but the
key narrative will continue; that what Tristram claims he is telling us (his life) is

just a joke framing his telling of the life of his father and uncle; and we begin to take pleasure in expecting interruption.

This discussion of the discontinuities in Sterne's work and in how they are irritating or pleasurable is always helpful as a landmark in later discussions of student writing. It allows us to ask if we have set up a clear set of alternate conventions to orient the reader/interactor.[6]

We also note what kinds of distortions of linearity are not confusing at all, but clearly meant to be enjoyed as playful tweakings of the conventions of fiction-making itself. The most obvious of these devices is the *complex time scheme*. We could identify several levels of time which Sterne refers to and playfully mixes up: historical time (as in specific battles, the publication date of the several sections of narrative, which was issued two books at a time), narrative time (which involves the events happening to the characters in the story), writing time (which refers to the fictional Tristram's attempts to write his life while living it, leaving him doomed to remain always behind), and reading time (which Sterne sometimes conflates with narrative time, as when he tells us that we have been reading for an hour and a half so it is time that Obadiah returned with Dr. Slop (II,8). In addition to all of these "objective" measures is the non-chronological, unevenly paced telling of the story. Sterne shows us effects before telling us the causes. He takes forever just to get his hero born. But these distortions of time are made enjoyable by the clear temporal structure that underlies the narrative. Things may be slowed up elaborately, but they do progress. The novel as a whole may end four years before Tristram is born, but it does contain a complete account of his birth and christening.

This merging of time into a *simulated synchronicity* turns out to be at the heart of several of the narratives we read and explore. It points to a general impulse of nonlinear fiction: to deny mortality by replacing a *mimetic structure* with *tableaux*. Instead of a beginning/middle/end we have a mosaic. Instead of a focus on action, we have a snapshot of the mind itself. Sterne's novel is based in part on Locke's theory of the mind. The new art form of the novel is coinciding with a new understanding of the mind, just as the experimental art of the early twentieth century coincided with Freud's work. For Sterne, as for Lawrence or Virginia Woolf, the novel seemed to offer the possibility of fixing on paper not just the content but the workings of the mind. The electronic medium offers the same promise in our own time, coinciding with new understanding of cognitive processes and the multiplicity of intelligence. The electronic medium also holds the extra excitement that it threatens to disrupt the distinction between writing about the mind and creating a mind. If we make a neural net that functions like a person, is it a model or another consciousness? These unresolvable questions add a special charge in the literary medium and suggest that the subject matter of the new form will reflect this tension.

Along with Sterne working in a new expressive medium comes a self-consciousness about the power of making a virtual world. Sterne's fascination with his own creative power overflows into *metacomments* which seek to concretize the narrative by describing it metaphorically. Tristram compares the narrative at various points to a *journey*, a *conversation*, and a *play*, all of which are useful metaphors for electronic fiction as well. Tristram's journey is full of pleasant detours, or it has a clear sense of "home" despite its vast extent. His conversation is meant to make the reader active in the narrative, allowing for imagined exchanges and for directions on how the reader should skip certain passages or reread others. His stage references establish continuity with exits, entrances, changes of scene, linking the novel with its emerging form to a world of more established conventions. We note how film conventions lay a similar role for nonlinear fiction, providing models of the manipulation of viewer distance, point of view, and cross-cutting as a way of weaving parallel narrative strands.

We also notice Sterne's battle with the boundaries of print itself—his black pages, rows of ***'s, diagrams of his plot twists, directions to the reader on what to skip and what to reread. This exuberance and impatience with art is partly the result of intoxication with the freedom offered by the new form of the novel, especially the serial pseudo-autobiographical novel form he is inventing which promises (or threatens) to let the author record his life and publish it almost simultaneously.[7] Sterne responds with giddy energy to the promise of a new medium which can mimic life with a detail not possible before.[8] His situation is therefore analogous to that of the writer approaching the electronic medium today. His strategy of making his engagement with the medium explicit is a good model for experimentation in general. In fact we later see him quoted in Michael Joyce's *Afternoon* (1987), the "granddaddy" of electronic fiction in Robert Coover's phrase.

To help students to see the general pattern of calling into questions the formal conventions by which we establish a new medium, I offer an example in a very different idiom. The Daffy Duck cartoon *Duck Amuck* pits the pencil of a sadistic animator (revealed in the last frames to be Bugs Bunny) against an exasperated Daffy as the backdrop is redrawn from farm scene to igloo, Daffy is dressed and redressed, distorted and even erased, the sound is divorced from the picture so that guitars behave like machine guns, and the screen is allowed to go blank (a white blankness very like the black pages of *Tristram Shandy*.) Just when the viewer feels all the elements of cartooning have been displayed and subverted, Daffy is revealed to be in a film strip and is faced with two versions of himself from adjoining frames. Thus both animation and filmmaking itself are deconstructed. Most impressively, when the "camera" pulls back to show Bugs Bunny at the drawing table, the illusion is miraculously reinstated: a world which is not going to be erased is imposed between the creator and the creation, allowing us to renew our belief in the very conventions we have just seen blown apart. Only a medium which is very confident of itself could present this kind of madcap subversion.

Writers of electronic fiction in the 1990s, although not yet at the same stage of stabilized technique as Sterne and Jones, often experience the same exhilaration and self-consciousness about their emerging conventions. They also have the same opportunity to invite the reader/interactor to join in the pleasure of manipulating the elements of the genre. Stuart Moulthrop has described the fun John McDaid has incorporating simulated computer scripts and system messages which he places into his fiction *Uncle Buddy's Phantom Funhouse* as if they were peeks into the mechanism (Moulthrop 1990).

For interactive fiction the pleasure of such formal playfulness is augmented by the mystery of the computer itself, its presence as, in Sherry Turkle's phrase, a "second self." Because we all carry an animist notion of the computer as an extension of human consciousness, the thrill of bearing its workings is a particularly potent aesthetic resource.

The Labyrinth

One major metaphor for electronic fiction (which Sterne also plays with) is the labyrinth. Again it is useful to introduce this concept through both print and visual media. Therefore in addition to reading Borges's "Garden of the Forking Paths," and a short selection from Alan Lightman's "Einstein's Dreams," students choose either the movie *Groundhog Day* (in which a TV weatherman played by Bill Murray is forced to relive a miserable Groundhog Day until he gets it right) or the "Parallels" episode of *Star Trek: The Next Generation*. In the *Star Trek* episode crew member Worf gets caught in a quantum fissure which leads him through multiple variants of his life, culminating in a striking sequence in which Enterprise starships from thousands of alternate realities are stranded together, unable to get back to their home universes. All of these stories deal with the common human sense of multiple possible lives stemming from different choices, the experience Borges describes as a "swarming" sensation. In the print narratives the subject is multiplicity itself. The particular story elements are sparse and meant to illustrate the concept of realized alternate destinies, calling into question the limits of the human condition by asking us to think of life as determined and yet infinite at the same time. The film and TV show are useful adjuncts to these stories because they take the philosophical notion of branching worlds for granted, concentrating instead on richly detailed, formulaic stories with many more variants than Borges and Lightman provide. Thematically, all the stories are related in the questions they raise about moral responsibility and individual choice.

As a kind of a problem set assignment for the week, I divide the students into groups and assign them to map the story elements in *Groundhog Day* or in "Parallels." This assignment can be made for paper or for HyperCard. Since they are asked to start learning HyperCard the first week and will need to be proficient in simple HyperCard authoring by the time their first fiction writing assignment is due (around week six), this is a good opportunity to allow the experienced students to tutor the novices in the context of a real task. The advantage of asking them to build a map of these stories on the computer is that they can see immediately that the computer offers a space in which all of the narrative paths hinted at in the linear films could be realized. Interestingly enough, students generally come up with very linear representations at first. It usually takes the class discussion to open up methods of moving around in their HyperCard stacks in patterns other than the order of scenes in the film.

Among the questions we consider in class is whether it is an advantage to have an infinitely extendible medium in which to represent the infinite alternatives posited in the stories. What advantage comes from showing only selections? What is the principle of selection? The vividness of the two popular narratives are also useful in discussing how we might make an electronic version of either one. Where would we place the reader/interactor with respect to the story? Would we allow readers to make iterative journeys through the narrative maze? Would we allow interactors to influence the outcome of the story?

In discussing labyrinths we distinguish between those that are coherent and those that are purposely more tangled. The coherent labyrinths are like the one Theseus discovered or the ones in English gardens: they have a single solution, a path in and path out. They can be solved. There is fiction written in this mode, most notably *Zork* (Blank) and its descendants. These game board labyrinths are puzzles, with a solution and a clear topography. The pleasure is in solving them, in learning the secret. Often the game includes dangers, just as Theseus's labyrinth led to the minotaur and murder at the center. Other labyrinths, like the ones created by users of the Storyspace authoring system like Michael Joyce and Stuart Moulthrop are web-like in structure, multi-threaded, and have no single path. The pleasure here is not in solving but in dwelling in a seemingly inexhaustible resonant environment, luxuriating in a prolonged state of enticement and disorientation.

The secrets or the danger at the heart of the labyrinth can be a useful way of talking about what is gained by writing plots which disrupt linearity and embed the story in layers of frames. We are drawn into the labyrinth in search of a secret, a revelation. But often the secret is something we are afraid of. Worf finds that his self-conscious relationship with Lieutenant Troi becomes a marriage in other quantum realities; in *Afternoon*, the narrator's son may or may not have been killed in an automobile accident. Being lost prevents us from finding out truth which we are afraid of. The labyrinth keeps us in the realm of what frightens and fascinates us, delaying head-on confrontation with an irreducible, single reality: i.e. with death itself. To be lost in the labyrinth is to be in a tantalizing state of attachment and evasion.

But there are two potential heroes in computer-based labyrinths, the protagonist and the reader. In the classical labyrinth story of Theseus, Ariadne, and the Minotaur the hero finds his way, and by confronting the terrifying beast at the center gains victory and marriage. This may or may not happen to the protagonist(s). In interactive labyrinths structured as games, such as the Nintendo genre, the interactor is the protagonist and is set the task of succeeding at a quest. In the art fictions, like *Afternoon* or *Victory Garden*, the reader is within the maze, wandering through a web of evocative tableaux. It is up to the author to decide how easy it is to reach the center. But it is up to the reader to decide whether or not she wants to go there. There can be a tension between avoidance and goal-centeredness, and the reader and author could each be on either side of this tension.

Acts of violence seem to be intrinsic to the form. It is useful to contrast the acts of violence at the end of the Borges story (when Yu Tsun commits murder as an impersonal semiotic act, an attempt to send a coded message by killing a man whose last name fits like a crossword answer into the spy protagonist's message) and in the climactic scene of the *Star Trek* episode (when Commander Riker must destroy a desperate alternate self on an alternate Starship Enterprise in order to mend a fissure which has conjoined all alternate realities). One is ironically meaningless, the other is suicidal but straightforwardly heroic. But both of them raise the question of moral choice in a universe of possibilities. The murders in each case are not only of other people but of possible alternate lives. Linear fiction has struggled to represent this basic human sense of choice and foreclosure of possibility, but computer fiction will be able to address it with a concreteness not possible before, by allowing writers to construct many alternate lives for their characters and allowing readers (or interactors who are both readers and protagonists) to traverse these realities, enacting choices, suffering happenstance, experiencing the finiteness of life and the infinity of imagination anew.[9]

Schemas for Constructing Plots

The next segment of the course deals in more detail with codifying plot elements and with ways of presenting a story outside of simple chronological sequence. Since we are looking for examples of formal properties and are not going to spend as much time as is usual in a literature class on content, I again offer the students a choice of text. Some of the class reads *Wuthering Heights* and some of the class reads *Dictionary of the Khasars*. Either before or after this class we read Propp's *Morphology of the Folktale*.

We read *Wuthering Heights* in the Norton Critical Edition with Sanger and Daley's chart on the time scheme of the novel. I ask students to make their own charts to represent either the nonlinear time scheme or the repetitive story elements of the novel. Sometimes students make HyperCard stacks linking repeated elements (such as the weather or window scenes) from different sections of the novel. *Wuthering Heights* is an excellent example of how to tell a story non-chronologically but coherently. Discussion centers on what is gained by the chronological juxtapositions that Brontë arranges. We also talk about her nested narrators and about the differences in point of view, both in attitude and in access to information, that each narrator provides. Many students will later pick up on this structure to create stories told from multiple points of view. The parallel elements of the novel, in which the second generation story reads like a repetition with variation on the story of the first generation characters, provide another source of rich material for talking about permutations of formalized story elements. In addition, *Wuthering Heights* is like many electronic fictions, heavily spatialized, with separate sets of incidents happening at the Heights or at the Grange.

Students are usually more enthusiastic about the Pavic novel which creates its own mythos, detailing the history of an imaginary people now disappeared from a Yugoslavia-like country. The story is told through a set of three alphabetically arranged "dictionaries" (actually they are more like encyclopedias), which are written from the Moslem, Christian, and Jewish points of view, and whose entries are cross-referenced. The reader is given the task of constructing the time sequence and making sense of a series of parallel characters and actions. The story is actually quite schematically created, with groups of triplet characters and careful parallels across cultures and across time. But it is told in a highly disjointed manner that makes it hard to reconstruct the patterns of relationships and events. It is a labyrinth in that it offers a prolonged sense of enticement and disorientation. My students are often intrigued sometimes to the point of speechless bliss by the intricacies of the presentation. Although I do not find the story compelling because of its odd emotional detachment, my students' response has made clear to made how intricacy in itself is beautiful and can seem like profundity of understanding. They have also helped me to understand the novel, by creating lucid diagrams that make clear the parallels among the different stories.

The dictionary format raises many interesting questions about the structure of narrative. Pavic encourages the reader to choose their own reading paths, and insists that there is no set order in which to read the story. He is successful in breaking down mimesis in that when I ask the students for a summary of major plot events they are generally at a loss. But *Khasars* certainly does not eliminate beginning-middle-end. For one thing, Pavic puts the earliest characters first alphabetically and the key twentieth century events into an appendix. Secondly, many of the entries tell short interpolated stories like folk tales. We therefore have a juxtaposition of the simplest form of narrative with a form of anti-narrative. Pavic's provocative design raises questions of what we seek for when we want closure in a story; of whether you can read a book without reading every part of it.

The story also raises questions of intratextuality, of the interconnected web of meaning which lies within a densely imagined work of fiction. The novel has a set of symbols next to entries which make an explicit linking structure and which are clearly well suited to translation to the computer. The links are interesting, however, in their incompleteness. The real links are the *inexplicit* ones, the ones the reader must ferret out for themselves, and which point to reincarnations (for instance, two characters in different time periods have the same demonic deformity), mysterious timetravel, and other secret parallels. This is a phenomenon we notice again with the interactive fictions we read; they have links but not necessarily the ones we are looking for. Such frustration makes us wonder whether a wholly, explicitly linked narrative is possible or desirable. We generally talk at this point about novels like *Ulysses* or *Madame Bovary*, dense with intertextual references or with intricately woven repeating patterns of language and image. We would all like to study such texts on a computer. But would we want to read them this way as our primary aesthetic interaction with them? At what point does connecting all the fragments obscure the pattern of the whole?

The *Dictionary of the Khasars* offers a good opportunity for students to practice and demonstrate their computer skills, since it poses the question of whether it would be better represented on the computer than in its current book form. As a hypertext arrangement it is very simple and straightforward. It is also satisfyingly navigable because there are three structures which are organized in a clear way, by alphabet. The links jump around these fixed structures. Interestingly, no student has yet copied this arrangement when it comes time for their original projects. Perhaps the alphabetical arrangement, which is after all only a search algorithm, makes sense as a presentational form only for books. There is no reason to present things on the computer in alphabetical order, since it will do the searching for you. It would make more sense to rearrange the elements of the book by time scheme or according to parallels of incident or character. In fact what thinking about the *Khasars* electronically makes clear is that alphabetizing is actually a *randomizing* strategy; rather than a principle of organization it is a principle of disorganization.

The sense of *encyclopedic* coverage is one of the principal pleasures of cyberspace in general and of electronic fiction in particular. The Khasars offers a good example of what such a fiction would represent. Like *Tristram Shandy* it puts the reader in the role of the scholar/detective, providing what looks like primary source material rather than a constructed story. It relishes details of the culture it creates and is highly elaborated and inter-referential. Students step into an alternate world with its own rules of magic, very concrete and very different from our world. I see this novel as an excellent model for the kinds of aesthetic pleasure that the new media will be particularly suited in bringing us: the pleasure of immersion, or moving through a wholly realized, enticing, other world; the rapturous pleasures of the labyrinth, the delight in purposefully getting lost in a space that folds back upon itself.

Pavic suggests the pleasures of traversing through the text when he playfully offers the reader several possible reading strategies:

> Thus, the reader can use the book as he sees fit. . . . He can . . . read the way he eats; he can use his right eye as a fork, his left as a knife and toss the bones over his shoulder. . . . Then he may move through the book as through a forest from one marker to the next, orienting himself by observing the stars, the moon, and the cross. Another time he will read it like the buzzard that flies only on Thursdays, and here again he can rearrange it in an infinite number of ways, like a Rubik cube. No chronology will be observed here, nor is one necessary. Hence, each reader will put together the book for himself . . . and, as with a mirror, he will get out of this dictionary as much as he puts into it. . . . (12–13)

In the passage of fourteen lines that mark the difference between the "male" and "female" versions of the book, Pavic even hints that not reading a text can be as powerful as reading it (pp. 293–294). This is perhaps the most radical position one could take in empowering the reader. However, the reader's sense of agency is only in how he experiences the book. We cannot change what happen within the book which would take Pavic's sense of reader control to a very different level. Therefore one of the things we discuss in class is how we could situate a reader in the world of the *Khasars* with the power to *interact* with the characters, to affect the events, to restructure the labyrinth itself instead of merely choosing a path through it.

Finally it is worth noting that like earlier labyrinths, both *Wuthering Heights* and *Dictionary of the Khasars* are about a loss that cannot be assimilated. Although I cannot make this argument in full in the context of the present discussion, I would suggest that the dense layering of the narrative represents a refusal to let go of a great loss. In *Wuthering Heights* Catherine's unresolved, self-mutilating abandonment of Heathcliff, and Heathcliff's fixation on the dead Catherine are at the very center of the story. In *Dictionary of the Khasars*, the loss of this imaginary people stands in for the many losses of history, the massacres and holocausts that consumed the dead.

The Khasars also follow the cult of sleep. . . . They believe that the people who inhabit every man's past lie as though enslaved and cursed in his memory; they can take no other step than the one they once took, can meet no one but the people they once met, cannot even grow old. The only freedom allowed ancestors, allowed entire bygone nations of fathers and mothers retained in memories is occasional respite in dreams. There, in our dreams, these figures from our memories acquire some measure of freedom; they move around a little, meet a new face, change partners in their hates and loves, and assume a small illusion of life. Hence sleep occupies a prominent place in the Khasar faith, because in dreams the past, forever captured within itself, gains freedom and new promise. (255–256)

The Khasar cult of dreams is the central metaphor of the novel. Pavic sees dreaming as a collective writing of a sacred book that is identical with the lost Adam, the paradisical presence that human beings keep trying to reconstruct. The attempt to reconstruct a complete redemptive narrative is linked to a failed Moslem/Jewish love story that turns into a murder. Just as the fragmentary nature of the narrative is in some ways a representation of the author's despair at constructing a satisfying world, the final inevitable murder reads like a prophecy of the disintegration of Pavic's nation into incoherency and slaughter. However Pavic's attitude is not prophetic anger but resignation; the labyrinth is perhaps finally a retreat from both past and impending calamity.

Both of these story-rich novels work well with Vladimir Propp's *Morphology of the Folktale* (1928), which is taught either the preceding or following week. Propp was a Russian formalist who provided us with a system of notation for representing story elements in Russian folktales. Although he was not writing from the point of view of constructing narrative, but of analyzing an existing group of stories which were all variants on recognizable actions (e.g. hero leaves, hero is tested, villain is defeated, etc.), his system can be used for generative purposes.[10] The students enjoy reading Propp and usually experience a sense of potential mastery from seeing stories described in such a clear formalism.[11] As their problem-set assignment, I ask them to construct similar systems for use with narratives we have been reading in the course, and for examples of genre fiction (like westerns or detective stories) or highly formulaic narrative (such as TV sitcoms). In fact Propp's own morphemes, developed for these remote Russian fairy tales, prove to be general enough that they describe many of the genres the students come up with. This leads us to a discussion of myth and archetype and of whether there are constants in human experience, at least in western culture, which make for universal plot elements.

In addition to characterizing plot elements, Propp offers some rules for combining them. For instance he thinks his elements must always appear in a fixed order, that the presence of some elements (e.g., a fight in an open field) implies the presence of another element later (e.g., a victory in an open field) (p. 109). We work in class on thinking up such procedural rules for other narrative genres. I do not expect students to be able to instantiate all the schemas we come up with—some would take extensive programming efforts, some would make appropriate research projects in artificial intelligence. The purpose of the classwork is to play with these narrative as composed of discrete generalizable elements and clear protocols for combining them.

Finally, we again look at this narrative space as potentially interactive, and we ask where we would place the reader/interactor. Some students are interested in building the potential for "customized" stories. The reader would still be only a reader but the computer would produce variants of stories based on individual preferences and tastes. One student created a story which could be read in a violent or less violent form. The version was assembled on the computer without asking the reader directly, but in response to whether the reader clicked on a flower or a bomb on the title page.[12] The same student made a final project in which he wrote a story which was made up of two parts which could be read as three different stories, either one separately or both together. The story depended on two different points of view, and one of the POV characters was mad. Reading the narrative of the madman you thought you were in a form of pseudo-medieval fantasy literature. Reading the narrative of his intended victim you realize you are in contemporary L.A. The final project was three story variants and the program written to assemble them.

In general, though we are often eager to begin working with electronic texts, I find the time spent with books and films is extremely helpful in giving students a vocabulary for thinking about story elements and the formal properties of successful fiction. It also allows students to approach examples of interactive fiction from a broad perspective, understanding the tradition on which they draw (such as Sterne and Borges) and aware that there is a choice of aesthetics and strategies to bring to the medium, a choice wider than has been currently instantiated by the range of fiction available.

Reading Electronic Fiction

With this background in nonlinear print and film narrative, we turn to existing electronic texts for two weeks, including both published fictions and fictions by students from previous years of the course. We start with the postmodern school of fiction, Michael Joyce, Stuart Moulthrop, and Jay David Bolter (who with Joyce and John Smith designed the authoring system Storyspace). For this group of authors[13] "hypertext" means a particular subgenre of electronic fiction for which they have a widely circulated if not clearly defined aesthetic. Moulthrop states it this way:

Seen from the viewpoint of textual theory, hypertext systems appear as the practical implementation of a conceptual movement that . . . rejects authoritarian, "logocentric" hierarchies of language, whose modes of operation are linear and deductive, and seeks instead systems of discourse that admit a plurality of meanings where the operative modes are hypothesis and interpretive play and hierarchies are contingent and local. (Moulthrop)

George Landow has carefully charted the ways in which hypertext can be seen as the instantiation of poststructuralist literary theory, the ideal text looked for by the French literary theorist Roland Barthes when he wrote:

In this ideal text, the networks are many and interact without any one of them being able to surpass the rest; this text is a galaxy of signifiers, not a structure of signified;

it has no beginning; it is reversible; we gain access to it by several entrances, none of which can be authoritatively declared to be the main one; the codes it mobilizes extend as far as the eye can reach, they are indeterminable . . .; the systems of meaning can take over this absolutely plural text, but their number is never closed, based as it is on the infinity of language.[14]

Michael Joyce is characteristically more playful, but the love of elusiveness shines through both form and content in this typical critical passage:

Lately I have been writing—much too obscurely—about the simple idea of contours in hypertext. Contours are the shape of what we think we see as we see it but which we know we have seen only after they are gone and new contours of our own shape themselves over the virtual armature, the liminal form, the retinal photogene (after-image) of what they have left us. They are, in short, the essential communication between the writer who was and the writer who will be. (Joyce 1992)

For all their rhapsodic theory, the practice of this group is quite simple in computational terms. Their chief pleasure is the defeat of linear expectations. Joyce has talked eloquently about words that "yield," a concept that Moulthrop echoes and celebrates. Joyce and Bolter's software system, Storyspace, facilitates this yielding by allowing the writer to create separate lexias and to link the lexia itself (it can be thought of as a notecard) or words on the card to another card.

The first acknowledged work of literary significance in this format is Joyce's *Afternoon*. I agree with Robert Coover (1993) that the current best such work is *Victory Garden* (1992) by Stuart Moulthrop. In addition to one or both of these we also usually read one contrasting narrative created not in Storyspace but in HyperCard, Clark Humphrey's *Perfect Couple* (1991). I often tell students to spend a certain amount of time with each of the three stories and then to pick the one they like best and spend the bulk of their time with that. Most students respond positively to *Victory Garden* but the class usually divides over those who hate *Afternoon* and love *Perfect Couple* and those who feel the opposite. In fact *Afternoon* represents an extreme in refusal to tell a story. It begins with the grabber statement "I want to say I may have seen my son die today." But like Tristram Shandy telling about his life it never answers the question of whether the son was in an accident and is alive or not. Instead it traces the angst of a divorced father, his relationship with his lover, his ex-wife, her current partner, and the associated doing of some computer hackers. Mostly it deals with separation anxiety, with the uncertain moment before being severed from contact with someone you desperately love. Despite Joyce's attempt to embed a feminist critique within the story, it is still full of a kind of male egotism and objectification of women which makes it unreadable for some female students. Students who love it are thrilled with the leaps of language, the sheer verbal inventiveness and the swirl of the story from one enticing fragment to another. Students who dislike it are annoyed at the repetitious return to cards they have already read several times and with the lack of information on where branches are leading. On the other hand, those students who dislike *Perfect Couple*, which has labeled branches, find the branching overspecified, giving too little room for surprise (e.g. "For what happens next click here," "For his work at becoming a better employee click here," "For a day in their life at this point, click here").

At this point I offer the students the option of composing their own stories with Storyspace instead of HyperCard. Storyspace has a very simple interface for reading hypertext which allows you to go forward or to click on words to branch. Some words have specific branching points (although how relevant a word is to the card to which it leads depends on the writer and on the reader's alertness), but most of them are linked by default to a single other card. So if you click on a word and it leads you to another card you cannot tell how tight the link is meant to be. If you want to see the all links explicitly you can, either by highlighting the linked words (if the author like Moulthrop has allowed it) or by clicking at an icon and getting a cryptic list to choose among. The list has the name of the link (which does not seem helpful in most cases) and its destination.

What students (and other readers presumably) object to here, when they do object, is that they don't know where they are going or on what basis they are meant to choose. This blind navigating tends to mitigate against the democratic aspirations of the postmodern hypertext group. Instead of feeling empowered by experiencing an undetermined text, students often feel tyrannized by a pre-determined set of often frustrating and incoherent paths.

Storyspace has some excellent built-in functionalities for writing hypertext, particularly in its ways of spacializing text. It offers three different views of the text including tree diagram, outline, and a somewhat confusing "Storyspace" view which is, however, good at showing the links among spaces. It also lets the author set up paths, automatic links between large groups of spaces, and guard fields which bar the reader from being offered a particular link until they have read a particular other card. But the interface is very difficult to learn and does not use standard Macintosh (or Windows) conventions, so that it is not intuitive to use. It is a measure of the meager resources humanists command that such useful functionality has not yet been combined with a sophisticated well-designed interface. Because of its limitations and steep learning curve I do not require students to use Storyspace. I do make it available for those who would like to use it and some students have used it enthusiastically. In my experience it is used by verbally hyper-fluent students whose superfluity of invention exuberantly spills over into many interlinked, digressively structured cards.

Stuart Moulthrop has added more explicit structure to his Storyspace narrative, *Victory Garden*. He provides a map, which though not completely representative of the structure of the story is a good rough guide to where you are and what the main sections (corresponding to chapters) are. He also makes clear the paths through the story, which are largely thematic in nature. His aim is encyclopedic. It is a snapshot of a small community, a college-centered group of friends and colleagues during the heightened period of the Gulf War. There are multiple story lines, multiple points of view, and variant endings for key sequences. The spatial organization is not of a physical place but of the narrative labyrinth itself. The title alludes to Borges' garden of forking narratives. *Victory Garden* is also so large that one must use care in assigning it. I divide students up into the three sections of the map and tell them to read for at least five hours being sure to cover the section assigned and any other parts they are led to or feel like exploring. Students will still have very different reading experiences and come to class with varying knowledge of the whole.

Moulthrop's *Garden* is a satisfying story, especially for a college audience since it is based on campus, and it makes good use of the garden metaphor as an organizing device. By dividing the narrative into separately addressable named sequences Moulthrop provides a sense of orientation, gives the reader real choices, and also allows the reader to gauge how much of the narrative has been read, a crucial factor in reader comfort which we take for granted in books and television, and (to a lesser extent) in films and plays, but which we enjoy only at the explicit direction of the author in computer-based narratives.

In discussing interactive fiction we can address for the first time appropriate sizes and shapes of the lexias, of the units of narration. The screen dictates a unit smaller than the page. Even with larger screens it seems as if the computer environment makes us too impatient or too eye-weary to read lots of print at a time. We review the different ways writers have shaped their screenfuls or lexia, including poetry, pseudo-animation of text, quotations (which are used as boundaries by Joyce and Moulthrop), and units of narration similar to a scene in a film. In long stretches of dialogue or extended scenes, the screen-unit can punctuate the action creating a series of small focused moments. This rhythm of narration could lead us closer to a sitcom writing style, in which we need a laugh (or a sob) every 20 seconds. Or it could lead us to a *Finnegans Wake* aesthetic in which every word leads out into rivulets of association and a single card is an inexhaustible well of meaning and countermeaning, association and counterassociation. It is a good idea to bring in print examples of short narrative segments, from literature or journalism, during this part of the term in order to broaden the range of discussion of what is possible.

In general my object is to introduce the existing fictions so that we can appreciate their strengths but not be constrained by their approaches. However impressive these fictions may be, they should not become prescriptive and narrow the range of students' invention.

Electronic Genre Fiction Games[15]

There is a long tradition of electronic games that occupy the boundary between fiction and pinball. Anthony Niesz, Norman Holland (Niesz and Holland) and Pinsky (Pinsky; Pinsky and Campbell) were among the first to recognize the literary potential of this format. The form was pioneered at MIT in the dungeons and dragons game *Zork*, which quickly became a staple of networked systems and grew to collaborative Multi-User Dungeon systems (MUDs). The essence of a *Zork*-like game is a gameboard architecture which the user navigates with spatial commands (north, south, east, west). The rooms of the game contain items to be picked up, villains to fight, rewards to discover, and most often some kind of riddle to solve in order to pass on. MUDs allow users to make up their own rooms and riddles and to converse with fellow users (usually in persona). It is a kind of remote role-playing simulation and is most popular with young teenagers. Game architecture does incorporate genre writing in many cases, not just of fantasy formulas, but also detective stories, sci fi adventures, etc. There are authoring systems available that allow students to write their own, and I provide these if there is sufficient interest (often students have their own). Although the command structure is maddeningly limited (go north, kill troll, etc.) there is a convention of including books within the game and students can be very inventive in writing mock-fairy tale epics (the movie *The Princess Bride* is frequently their model) and in creating labyrinthine architectures. Zork-like adventures can also be easily created in HyperCard. Of course, I ask the authors to provide me with a key to all the riddles, or grading would be maddening!

The MUDs or MOOs (object-oriented MUDs, which make it easier to create your own characters and spaces) preserve the collaborative fantasy element of dungeons and dragons and have even been seen as model communities (Rheingold). Like *Eliza* at their best they offer a chance for the interactor to be a collaborator. If students have experience with these systems I incorporate their experiences in our discussions but we have not yet included MUDs participation as part of the coursework. This is partly because it can become obsessive and time-consuming, partly because students are shy about their participation. It would be interesting, however, to include a MOO as part of a course such as this and consider participation as part of the writing requirement.

Another model that straddles the world of game and fiction is the simulation or microworld. The most developed of these is SimCity (Wright).[16] The promise of a manipulable world that the user can effect, which has its own rules but does not present the interactor with a narrow set of outcomes is particularly enticing, and points the way to emerging forms of narrative including the promised world of virtual reality. The creation is not a series of plot events but a set of objects and the rules by which they behave. Some games are a mixture of gameboard and microworld. For example, one of the early Infocom games, *Deadline* (Blank) had appealing microworld aspects in that characters came and went at particular times in the story regardless of what the detective did, and a murder might or might not happen depending on whether the detective's interventions came in time. The pleasure of engaging such a world is its combination of solidity and plasticity: we want to know that it has its own rules and relationships, and we want to be able to affect what happens within it.

Another emerging form of game is the database tied to interactive video segments. The popular interactive CD-ROM, *Sherlock Holmes* is structured as a detective investigation. Snippets of interactive video motivate the user to search through lists of names and places until a chain of events is established. The denouement is not the apprehension of the criminal, who may never even appear on-screen. Instead it is answering multiple choice questions posed by a "judge" to see if you've correctly solved the case. Clearly genre fiction and particularly detective stories transfer well to the electronic media.

A landmark interactive game which was published in 1993 is *Myst* (Miller and Miller). It uses computer modeling techniques to create a photographic likeness of an imaginary world—in fact several imaginary worlds, in which a wizard and his sons have disappeared and the user must solve many mechanical puzzles in order to learn more about the story and collect the information necessary to participate in it. Again the organization is spatial and the solution involves mapping parts of the world in order to find hidden clues. The fantasy content is reminiscent of the Brontë's juvenilia, and the plot has the qualities of elaborate childsplay. Yet the game content is hyper-rational and involves understanding mechanical principles and deciphering codes. To play *Myst* is to dwell in the fantasy world of a tinkering child, where mastery over the physical world is practiced over and over again. Obsessively ritualized violent fantasies can be useful in mastering hostile impulses and coping the child's inevitable feelings of powerlessness. The violence of this world (like that of the Brontë's childhood kingdoms of Angria and Gondal, also written by siblings) is of this brooding, formulaic, repetitious kind. Yet in *Myst* the practice of mastery is dissociated from the fantasy content and attached to the gadgets. The gadgets partake in the fantasy world, but most of the interaction is gadget-oriented rather than story-oriented. This is partly the limitations of the technology which only allows a small amount of moving video. Again, books are embedded in the story (as they are in the gameboard games which this derives from, and as stories are embedded in *Tristram Shandy* and *Dictionary of the Khasars*). But the books slow down the game considerably. In fact even if they were made into movies they would still be too passive to enjoy. Interestingly enough the "winning" ending of the story is much less dramatically satisfying than the losing endings. The fictional structure is satisfied when the interactor / player loses is placed in the same predicament as the villains he has foolishly rescued. By contrast, the winning ending, though it has an enchanting visual effect created by embedding video of an actor into the kind of painted photorealistic backgrounds we have otherwise found depopulated, the actor's speech does not bring closure, and we are left at the end wandering around a space whose mysteries we have exhausted. *Myst* is therefore a landmark but only an intermediate step toward a truly satisfying interactive fiction. It does make clear the power of a discovery environment, however, and is very useful in showing students the sense of presence and immediacy that the computer can deliver, especially but not only when sound and photorealistic graphics are added to text.[17]

Because I expect games to play an increasing role in developing the conventions of interactive fiction, I am moving toward including more of them in the course. The important thing here is to emphasize the structural elements that are fiction-making rather than riddle-making.

Student Writing

Before we reach the midpoint of the term, we switch from a reading course to a writing course.[18] Sometimes I introduce the first writing assignment before all the reading has been done. But certainly by the midpoint we are focused on the production rather than the consumption and criticism of nonlinear narrative. There are three major projects due, all computer-based. The first is a small HyperCard stack, up to 15–25 cards, which must show the following properties. The last one is a larger stack (30–50 cards), sometimes an extension of the first project. Students who wish to work in other authoring environments, including their own, are always welcome to depart from HyperCard, but HyperCard is the simplest environment that even those who do not want to do any programming can master.

Here is the kind of assignment offered for the first project:

Write a hypertext story using HyperCard. The story should be at least 15 and no more than 25 card long.

It should be modeled on one of the following forms:

1. A labyrinth with forking paths (or a web with multiple threads)
2. A journey
3. A tour of a simulated place
4. A dictionary or encyclopedia
5. A combination of the above

It must satisfy the following conditions:

1. The writing must be appropriate to the form, pleasurable, and carefully **proofread.**
2. The story or fictional world must be **complete.**
3. There must be at least **3 distinct paths** through the narrative web.
4. It must use **3 or more** of the following devices:
   - progressive digression
   - spatial schema (map, floorplan, labyrinth)
   - single or multiple chronological schema (clock, calendar)
   - multiple points of view on a single event
   - metacomments or deconstruction of the form (like Daffy or Tristram)
   - hot word linking
   - nested stories, interpolated stories
   - interpolated documents

Among the projects that students have created have been:

- a saga of life in a summer colony, accessed through a map of the island, a family tree diagram, and hot word links within each of the interrelated stories ("Reflections on a Lake," Danielle Russell)
- a poem about tossing and turning in bed which reads like a labyrinth, with the syntax allowing movement for a single screen in multiple directions ("Labyrinth," Stephanie Tsai)
- a love story told from the perspective of the lovers and their best friends, with the reader allowed to choose among perspectives ("Getting Together," Richard A. DeCristofaro)
- a love story keyed to the opening measures of each movement of Vivaldi's Four Seasons, with access from keywords in the poem Vivaldi associated with the piece. The audio was included in the stack ("Four Seasons," Jeffrey Morrow)

• a detective story in which you must prevent a murder by investigating a simulated room complete with phone, file drawers, and hidden messages ("Detective," Scott Willcox)

• a cookbook with poison recipes and paperclipped notes which detail a family saga involving many poisonings ("Cookbook," Stephanie Tsai)

• a mock fairy tale in which a young boy takes a journey on a map which the reader chooses from and must find three simpletons, represented by stories at each of the map points ("A Sad Story," Jeffrey Morrow)

• love story which must be read in two synchronized columns, one called "truth" and the other "lies." Only by reading from both does the reader come to understand what happened. ("Lies," Rick Pryll)

• a Pyncheonesque story structured like a trip with multiple detour-digressions, written in Storyspace ("Vacation," Jason Merkoski*)

• An interactive character based on Hal in 2001. (David LeCompte, "Hal")

• A tale of a run-away boy who is circling around through the countryside, returning and running away again, whose story both repeats and changes as we follow in his footsteps ("Circle Creek," Nick Tsai)

• A tour of a nuclear power laboratory which is accessed by map and timeline and in which the interactor plays several roles, in some of which he gets to save the lab from meltdown, with sirens and video of a nuclear explosion included in the stack. ("A Tour of the Microcell Fusion Reactor Research Laboratory and Production Plant ," David Warren)

• A set of stories which all share a subset of dialogue exchanges, bits of conversation which always appear in the same order, but in vastly different contexts. The reader can switch from one story sequence to another. ("Berlin and Barbituates," David Kung)

Some of the projects developed in the first project are expanded for the major project that comes at the end of the term. Students often trade ideas and sometimes a student will develop a piece of code that several students call for, such as the ability to make text slide across the screen.

These stacks get better with successive classes and point to the emergence of certain subgenres which I have now included as the categories in the assignment. Students are always coming up with new forms of organization (such as the labyrinth poem) which I then try to feed back into the class. By having students workshop their ideas and read the work of former class members I am attempting to nurture a tradition of writing. I also encourage students to codify their programming ideas and pass them along in forms that non-programming students can use.

Students are often frustrated by the lack of an authoring environment which would directly reflect the spatial structures they have in mind when they write their narratives. Each year we make progress in thinking about what the right tools would look like. Sometimes students in the course attempt to make the modeling or creation of such authoring tools one of their projects. The goal we take is to make a tool that would facilitate all the kind of stories that fellow students are producing. The difficulty of the task is a measure of the inventiveness of the writers and the fertility of the emerging genre. There is no one structure that would cover all the matrixes, trees, webs, and geographies that writers create when freed from the bindings of the book. There is a pressing need for more flexible tools in order to nurture the growth of this medium that would enable the use of multiple forms of linking and spatialization.

In addition to the HyperCard-based assignments, I ask the students to write an interactive character. First they are given access to a running version of Weizenbaum's *Eliza*, an early experiment in human language processing in the form of an interactive psychologist who reacts to key words such as mother in the user/patient's input and who echoes back the patient's words like a Rogerian shrink ("Why do you say you are feeling sad?"). Weizenbaum's program, though primitive by current computational standards, represents a potential genre of interactive fiction for "flat" characters in E. M. Forster's terms (Weizenbaum).

Despite her irritating difficulties, Eliza succeeds because the predictability and rigidity of her responses echo the predictability and rigidities of certain kinds of therapy. In other words, the limits of the medium serve a literary purpose. Furthermore, the point of Eliza is a procedural one. The lines that she says are funny in themselves but they are twice as funny as responses to the user's input. They are not funny as *statements* but as *behavior*. Eliza is the first literary creation that is about behavior in a dynamic way. As a vehicle for parody the *Eliza* model is particularly extendible. Any comic stereotype—the Jewish mother, the political candidate, the jargon-spouting literary critic—can be made into a parodic conversational interactive character. As a model for successful interaction, *Eliza* is important because her success is based on the match between the medium and the message.

Eliza is interesting in another way: most people immediately know how to interact with her. The psychiatric interview is a familiar pattern that people bring to the interaction. You don't have to give them a list of commands. They know the formula without even thinking about it. When I ask students to play with *Eliza* they spontaneously create imaginary personas to interact with her. In effect they *collaborate* with the program in creating an improvised scene between their character and Eliza. After awhile they anticipate some of the program's responses and get better at supplying straight lines. Here is one example of a student run:

Student: I fantasize that I am a squid.

Eliza: When did you first know that you are a squid?

Student: When mother ran off with an Amway salesman

Eliza: What happened when mother ran off with an Amway salesman?

Student: I was raped by my kitten.

Eliza: Have you been afraid of sex?

Student: Hasn't everyone?

Eliza: Are you sure that you are a piece of beef jerky?

Student: yes! you know it's true.

Eliza: How do you reconcile problems at school?

Student: I write my life decisions on pieces of paper and throw them in the air and scream WHEE! WHEE!

Eliza: I don't understand.

Student: You would say that.[19]

Interestingly enough it's not just thinking up funny things to say to her that makes the scenes work. For contrast I have them feed randomly generated quotations from the newspaper cartoon character Zippy into Eliza (as one can do on MIT's unix system and probably many others) and look for good exchanges. Zippy is always funny but only in a few particularly wild interactions does he feed into Eliza's behavior. Here is an example of one such successful interaction:

Zippy: Look into my eyes and try to forget that you have a Macy's charge card.

Eliza: Does it bother you that I have a Macy's charge card?

But Zippy can almost never have two consecutive meaningful interactions with Eliza.

A human interactor, however, can catch on to the quirks of the program and throw the right pitches. In fact part of the pleasure is in figuring out the program. Interacting is a way of exploring how it works, of gaining mastery over the program while collaborating with it.

After interacting with *Eliza*, students are asked to make their own interactive characters using an authoring system which I created with a former student in the course (Murray and Morrow). This system, *Conversation/ CharacterMaker* allows them to create an interactive character without knowing any programming. It provides a template for making characters who will respond to free input, searching for key words or phrases. The template allows the writer to specify synonyms for the key words, one or more responses, a way of introducing the topic, and things to say if there are no expected key words in the user's input.

Conversation / CharacterMaker is a program in progress. As writers use it, more structure will be added to accommodate ways of building up related topics, and conversational chains. Among the kinds of characters that students suggest for predictability are political candidates, blind dates, and over-persistent ex-lovers. Other students branch out from the stereotypical and attempt to create a self-representation in the computer. The form is also appropriate for detective fiction in which the right questions will lead to a revelation of clues.

Conversational characters are unique in that they are a creative exercise for both the maker and the user. As such they model a potential of interactive fiction which is only beginning to be exploited, the collaboration of author and reader in the shaping of a fictional universe. In order to expose students to the possibilities of creating a character procedurally, I include a survey of artificial intelligence attempts to model human beings, particularly neurotic and paranoid personalities (Boden; Colby 1964, 1975). We talk about recent efforts to create characters as believable agents who interact with one another as well as with the user (Bates, Kelso). We also look briefly at ways in which computer scientists have tried to model storytelling itself as a cognitive activity (Schank and Abelson). Ideally computer-based characters should be teachable by their interlocutors in some way, so that their repertoire grows as a result of their interactions. To play with such ideas, as students do with great facility, brings us to the boundaries of advanced computing environments, which is really outside the realm of the course. I do include the possibility, therefore, of student projects which offer designs for systems too ambitious to build, but which extend in theory the literary potential of the computer.

The Future of an Illusion

The course that I have described here is a composite, and by the time this is published it will probably have significantly changed. For this is an emerging art form and the corpus and the landscape are evolving every day. Within a short time it will not be possible to teach one course covering so broad a field, and I expect to be teaching separate courses: perhaps one on hypertext, one on games and interactive video; one on artificial intelligence and narrative; one on narrative theory and cyberspace. No doubt the narratives we are studying today will seem crude as the medium finds its compelling themes and begins to build more expressive structures.

This is a moment when several disciplines and professions are working in contradictory ways to shape a new artistic form. Although post-structuralist literary critics look at hypertext as a kind of empirical proof of the big bang theory of language, Hollywood looks to interactive movies as merely more of the same, technicolor in three dimensions. Current practitioners range from coterie writers like the Storyspace group to the game-makers and mass marketers of Nintendo. For everyone who looks to the computer to help express the labyrinthine soul, there will be many others who want to exploit its capacity for satisfying voyeurism through exploration of forbidden spaces and simulation of forbidden spectacles. Moreover, the computer itself is now pervasive as an indispensable learning tool, a facilitator of global community, and as the delivery environment for the international war machine. All of this will feed into the process of storytelling, in as yet unknown ways into the process of electronic storytelling.

My hope is that there is a yet to be discovered future between the extremes of coterie theory-mongering and mass shoot-em-ups. Electronic literary forms, like the early novel or cinema, promise to help us fundamentally reshape our understanding of human experience. Here is a concrete medium for modeling infinite desire and finite fate, for experientially expressing the consequences of moral choice or social determinants, for recreating consciousness itself in a way that makes us wonder what makes us different from our toaster ovens, for instantiating multiple points of view and the flow of life, not from beginning to middle to end but around and around in ebbing, flowing, intersecting wavelets.

There is currently no easy way for artists and writers to gain access to the serious power of the computer. Current notions of literary hypertext— writing in screenfuls, linking clumps of text together—represent a relatively trivial use of the machine from an engineer's point of view. But even this first-order use has yet to be served by an authoring system that is easy to use and open to complex structure. Still farther ahead is access by ordinary writers to more powerful functions, such as the building of interactive characters or the manufacturing of generative plot environments. Some would fear the birth of this medium as bringing an end to traditional forms of narrative. But it is really only the addition of another set of tools to serve the core human need to shape life into story. Therefore, while we wait for the machine to be domesticated to serve a wider range of human expression, it is important to encourage young writers to imagine their way to the new beauty and new truths that are waiting to be embodied there.

Bibliography

Bates, Joseph. "Virtual Reality, Art, and Entertainment." *Presence: The Journal of Teleoperators and Virtual Environments 1*, no. 1 (1992): 133–138.

Blank, Marc. *Zork*. Edited by Dave Lebling. 1977.

Blank, Marc. *Deadline*. Infocom, 1984.

Boden, Margaret. *Artificial Intelligence and Natural Man*. New York: Basic Books, 1977.

Bolter, Jay David. *Writing Space: The Computer in the History of Literacy*. Hillsdale, N.J.: Lawrence Erlbaum, 1989.

Colby, K. M. *Artificial Paranoia*. New York: Pergamon, 1975.

Colby, K. M., and J. P. Gilberte. "Programming a Computer Model of Neurosis." *Journal of Mathematical Psychology* (1964): 405–417.

Coover, Robert. "The End of Books." *New York Times Book Review*, June 21, 1992.

Coover, Robert. "Hyperfiction: Novels for the Computer." *New York Times Book Review*, August 29, 1993.

Daley, A. Stuart. "A Chronology of *Wuthering Heights.*" In *Wuthering Heights: A Norton Critical Edition.* Edited by William M. Sale and Richard J. Dunn. New York: W. Norton & Co., 1990.

Friedman, Ted. "Making Sense of Software: Computer Games and Interactive Textuality." In *Community in Cyberspace*, edited by Steve Jones. Sage Publications, 1994.

Joyce, Michael. *Afternoon.* Eastgate Systems, 1987.

Joyce, Michael. "Siren Shapes: Exploratory and Constructive Hypertexts." *Academic Computing*, November 1988: 10–14, 37–42.

Joyce, Michael. *Hypertextual rhythms: (The momentary advantage of our awkwardness*, Part 2). Talk given at the Modern Language Association Convention, New York, December, 1992.

Kelso, Margaret Thomas, Peter Weyhrauch, and Joseph Bates. "Dramatic Presence." *PRESENCE: The Journal of Teleoperators and Virtual Environments* (1993).

Lakoff, George. "Structural Complexity in Fairy Tales." *The Study of Man* 1 (1972): 128–150.

Landow, George. *Hypertext: The Convergence of Contemporary Critical Theory and Technology. Parallax: Re-visions of Culture and Society.* Baltimore and London: The Johns Hopkins University Press, 1992, 242.

Lightman, Alan. *Einstein's Dreams.* New York: Pantheon, 1993.

Miller, Rand and Robyn. *Myst.* Broderbund, 1993.

Moulthrop, Stuart. "Containing Multitudes: The Problem of Closure in Interactive Fiction." *ACH Newsletter* 10 (1988): 1, 7.

Moulthrop, Stuart. "Hypertext and the Hyperreal," In *Hypertext '89*, edited by N. Meyrowitz. New York: Association for Computing Machinery, 1989.

Moulthrop, Stuart. "Hypermedia ● Recursion ● Literature." Ms. 1990.

Moulthrop, Stuart. *Victory Garden.* Eastgate Systems, 1992.

Moulthrop, Stuart. "You Say You Want a Revolution? Hypertext and the Laws of Media." In *Essays in Postmodern Culture*, edited by A. Amiran and J. Unsworth. New York: Oxford University Press, 1993.

Murray, Janet H. *Conversation/CharacterMaker.* Programmer/Codesigner: Jeffrey Morrow. Alpha Version. Macintosh environment. Unpublished, 1994.

Niesz, Anthony J., and Norman Holland. "Interactive Fiction." *Critical Inquiry* 11 (1984): 110–129.

Pinsky, Robert. "A Brief Description of Mindwheel." *New England Review and Bread Loaf Quarterly* 10, no. 1 (1987): 64–67.

Pinsky, Robert, and P. Michael Campbell. "Mindwheel: A Game Sesson." *New England Review and Bread Loaf Quarterly* 10, no. 1 (1987): 70–75.

Rheingold, Howard. *Virtual Community: Homesteading on the Electronic Frontier.* Reading, Mass.: Addison-Wesley, 1993.

Schank, Roger C., and R. P. Abelson. *Scripts, Plans, Goals and Understanding.* Hillsdale, N.J.: Lawrence Erlbaum, 1977.

Turkle, Sherry. *Computers and the Human Spirit.* New York: Simon and Schuster, 1984.

Weizenbaum, Joseph. *Computer Power and Human Reason.* New York: W. H. Freeman, 1976.

Wright, Will. *SimCity.* Maxis, 1987, 1993.

Notes

1. Since I instituted a course on electronic fiction I have received many queries about how it is run, queries that it is impossible to answer merely by providing a syllabus. The following is an overview of the course and its objectives, meant to help those who would like to offer a similar course. The only software requirements are HyperCard (or the IBM equivalent ToolBook for Windows), and (optionally) Storyspace. There are also a handful of existing electronic fictions that can be obtained, most of them from Eastgate Systems *Conversation/CharacterMaker* is available in beta version from me.

2. The text for the course is now the standard for teaching computer science: Harold Abelson and Gerald Jay Sussman, *Structure and Interpretation of Computer Programs,* Cambridge: MIT press, 1985.

3. Among the obvious alternate choices are works by James Joyce, V. Woolf, and Faulkner; Gabriel Garcia Marquez's *Hopscotch,* which comes with an alternate suggested sequencing and selection of chapters; the "choose-your-own-adventure books; the *Back to the Future* film trilogy, and another trilogy, *The Norman Chronicles,* a set of three lays by Alan Ackbourne cover the same period of time in three different areas of the same house, so that exits in one play are entrances in one of the others. One could also choose post-structuralist fiction such as Maurice Blanchot's *Thomas the Obscure,* in order to explore the limits of deconstruction of narrrative. Oral history would also be useful as examples of tightly edited passages that are compact and intersecting. Supplementary readings to this list include Landow, Bolter, Turkle, Moulthrop's essays, Schank, and Bates (see bibliography). In addition, graduate students in the course also usually read some narrative theory, ranging from Aristotle to Todorov to Frye to Barthes, as well as film theory classics like David Bordwell. My feeling is that almost any approach is useful because it is schematization itself that is helpful in building up new structures. Therefore orthodoxies or sophistication of interpretation are largely irrelevant.

4. I use the term "nonlinear" in my course title and in describing these selections with some reservations. Nonlinearity is merely a negative property. In fact there are diverse positive properties that come into focus as linearity is broken down, but we are still groping for ways to characterize them. Nonlinear is therefore a convenient but temporary umbrella term.

5. Of course this is the way the first two books were originally read, since the novel was published in yearly installments. Although the traditionalist in me regrets this abridgment, it works well in the course. Students who love *Tristram* go on to read the whole thing eventually and the ones who find the eighteenth-century diction or the phallocentric mindset unappealing can still enjoy the 170-page selection well enough to stay alert to formalist considerations.

6. I am adopting the term "interactor" from Joseph Bates's "Oz" research group at Carnegie Mellon.

7. "Some of our ideas have a natural correspondence and connection with one another; it is the office and excellency of our reason to trace these, and hold them together in that union and correspondence which is founded in their peculiar beings. Besides this, there is another connection of ideas wholly owing to chance or custom; ideas that in themselves are not at all of kin, come to be so united in some men's minds that it is very hard to separate them, they always keep in company, and the one no sooner at any time comes into the understanding but its associate appears with it; and if they are more than two which are thus united, the whole gang, always inseparable, show themselves together. John Locke, *An Essay Concerning Human Understanding* 2.33.5 (1690).

8. The new potential of the novel for capturing everyday life and personal stories of ordinary people is well stated in Ian Watt's classic study, *The Rise of the Novel* (1957).

9. For the postmodernist theorist/practitioners of hyperfiction, Moulthrop and Joyce, the labyrinth is a controlling image of indeterminacy. Moulthrop in particular is drawn to the Borges as the originator of the labyrinth. See Moulthrop.

10. Although the Oz research group at Carnegie Mellon was disappointed with the results of an attempt to use Propp as the basis for a story-making system because his system does not yield "bushy" enough alternates, unlike, say a chess game for which there are millions of alternative plays (Kelso, Weyhrauch and Bates). A more promising schema is Lakoff's extension of Propp to a story grammar rather than a morphology (Lakoff).

11. Since I usually have graduate students in interactive cinema taking the course along with the undergraduates I include as another formalism, Schank's system of notation for describing stories as "scripts." Students usually find Schank reductive and offensively technical. This may only be the result of encountering computer-speak in a humanities course where they want a respite from symbolic notation. But since they are very open to Propp I think it may have more to do with Schank's overly ambitious claims to be able to represent all of human experience and knowledge in his system (Schank and Abelson).

12. This story was by Adam Crane.

13. See Bolter; Joyce; Landow; Moulthrop.

14. Roland Barthes, S/Z (Paris: Éditions du Seuil, 1970), 11–12; S/Z, trans. Richard Miller (New York: Hill and Wang, 1974), 5–6; quoted in Landow, 1992, p. 3.

15. I want to thank Stuart Malone, Catherine White, and William Murray for sharing with me their insights and offering guidance into the world of electronic games.

16. *SimCity* as a has been well analyzed as a literary artifact by Ted Friedman (1994). One of the exemplary virtues of *SimCity* is that its aesthetics differ with each player. Two programmer friends of mine, a married couple, play it with equally intense involvement. The husband builds high towers in a compact downtown and thinks he is doing neat engineering stuff. The wife builds sprawling suburbs with lots of parks and imaginary grocery stores for people she sees as acting in a narrative.

17. An example of a text-based moment that has a similar power is the screen in *Victory Garden* in which the plane of the page is shattered in patterns like broken glass, indicating that a missile has landed and killed the protagonist Emily.

18. All through the first section students have been asked to make charts and simple HyperCard stacks representing narrative elements and narrative structure. These are somewhat similar to the problem sets that they do for technical courses. They are also expected to be practicing with HyperCard learning how to make a button, a field, background and foreground objects, a simple stack of cards with links. Some students also learn to program in Hyper Talk and there is often trading of tricks and simple code samples and forth.

19. This inventive run was created by Jason Merkoski.

8

Spaces of Experience on Designing Multimedia Applications

Larry Friedlander

Recently, I watched visitors explore an interactive program in a museum, one that contained a vast amount of material—pictures, film, historical explanations, models, simulations. I was impressed by the range of subject matter and by the ambitiousness and polish of the presentation. At every touch of a screen, users were offered multiple choices that lead to ever-expanding pathways and new bits of knowledge. But to my surprise, as I watched visitors going down one pathway after another, I noticed a certain dispirited glaze spread over their faces. They seemed to lose interest quite quickly and, in fact, soon stopped their explorations.

What was the problem? It seems that after the initial excitement and novelty of an interactive system had faded, visitors were simply overwhelmed by the sheer mass of information and were reluctant to continue accumulating facts without a guiding purpose, without some sense of how or why they could use all this material. The technology that delivers immense bundles of data does not simultaneously deliver a reason for accumulating so much information, nor a way for the user to order and make sense of it. That is the designer's task. The pressing challenge of multimedia design is to transform information into usable and useful knowledge.

Computers and Stages

Let us begin with an analogy from theater.[1] In the theater, the audience is confronted with multiple kinds of experience—words, designs, lights, costumes, movements, psychological and narrative occurrences. Unless great care is taken—given there is so much to see, to understand, to integrate—the spectator may be overwhelmed by this abundance. It is the director who is called upon to control these potentially chaotic materials by artfully shaping and combining them into clear unities on the stage. The director is, first of all, a guide who shows us where to look and who teaches us how to understand what we see. But the director is also a Don Juan, a seducer who entices us to enter into the spectacle by creating events that appeal to our fullest selves, to our minds, bodies, hearts, and sense of beauty.

So too, in multimedia, the designer is a kind of theatrical director who must shape a unified, focused, and meaningful experience, moment by moment, out of the richness and potential of the medium. The designer must develop her or his system with the users foremost in mind, making sure that at every point there is a clear, simple and focused experience that hooks them into the welter of information presented in a multimedia system.

However, there is one fundamental difference between theater and interactive systems: in the latter, the spectator can step out of his or her seat, so to speak, and onto the stage. This possibility to penetrate the acting space offers new dimensions to the nature of the experience. What kinds of new spaces are created when the audience undertakes to act? Let me suggest three: space of work, space of penetration, and space of community.

A Space for Work

1. Interactive technology permits users to learn in many different ways, through seeing, hearing, reading, doing, and simulating. The medium itself is capable of engaging us not only intellectually, but aesthetically, dramatically, and sensuously. Too often, however, multimedia programs restrict the learning environment unnecessarily, neglecting the wide variety of ways we actually work with and acquire information.

For example, in the *Shakespeare Project* I designed in the mid-eighties, the focus was on teaching students the processes of theater and how they influenced the interpretation and reception of plays. At the core of the program was a set of comparisons between different versions of the same plays. Students were able to watch a scene and, at any point, move to the same moment in another version. As students noticed the profound differences between different versions of the same script, their attention was drawn to the process of interpretation and enactment that produced such difference, and began them on an exploration of theater from many points of view: the actors', the director's, the critic's, and the reader's.

To extend and complement the range of questions raised in these explorations, the students were asked to engage themselves in a wide spectrum of activities. After all, we can read a play, hear it, see it, criticize it, and participate in it. All these activities are really different forms of learning about the same event. So students were similarly challenged to absorb the dramatic experience by watching, studying, organizing, writing, browsing, imitating, and creating. For example, after they had seen several versions of a scene, and watched the way actors had developed their readings and their sense of character, they were asked to stage the scene on a simulation program I devised called the *TheaterGame*, which permitted them to "block" figures on a stage and make a little movie. Then they could extract clippings from the scene and from their stagings and write multimedia essays on the play. (See Peter Donaldson's discussion in this volume of the latest version of the Shakespeare Project.)

By encountering the same material in a variety of modalities, students grasp the richness and depth of the material. They also extend and refine their own capabilities, becoming better viewers, creators, and critics.

2. Give the user the power to intervene, improve, alter the experience. We can allow users not only to produce something, but to add to or alter the initial program. To leave your mark on a computer is a wondrous thing! The more power the users have to make the information their own, the more powerfully they will be drawn into the interaction. In a program I designed on the history of French theater, called *Paris / Theater*, the user not only explores the relationship between theater and other social and political institutions, but can add and rearrange information. Their research becomes part of the program for other people to use.

The system is organized about a series of maps of Paris from the 12th century to the present. Users can go to any date and specify the kind of building (church, palace, school etc.) and the kind of activity (theater, administration, education etc.) that interests them, and icons showing all buildings of that kind that existed at the time, with their activities, will appear on the map. For example, a church may appear, and if it is colored purple, it means that theater (purple) was performed in that church. Now each of these icons is really a bin holding multimedia information—text, video, graphics. Clicking on the church, for example, might give you a list of all the plays done there, images from those works, descriptive texts, and if the building is still in use, interviews with the personnel in charge.

As the system was designed for graduate students doing research in theater, each bin is an open "holding place." Students can investigate a topic, such as the relationship between the church and other cultural institutions in the period, and then place the results of their research in the bin in the form of text, images or even video. The interface has become a place to collect and display communal work!

3. Create a working partnership between the program and the user. In *Paris / Theater*, students can stage scenes from the classics of the French theater. However, the program helps guide and control choices. The object is to teach students about the historical conditions and restraints that shaped productions: in the 17th century, for example, certain costumes could only be used for tragedy, others for comedy or ballet. So when the user goes through the process of producing a scene, by choosing from a large database a theater, a stage and decor, characters and costumes, at each step her or his choice is monitored by the program. If she or he makes an inappropriate choice, choosing let us say a theater that was closed down that year, s / he will be informed that the choice is not valid and will be told why, so that s / he can search for a better solution.

A Space of Penetration

How can we have the user actually enter into the electronic space and fully participate in the making of that world?

1. When designing a program on Shakespearean theater for the Globe museum, I asked myself what would truly excite someone about Shakespearean acting. The answer was: to be able to play with a great actor oneself. How many of us have dreamed of acting Shakespeare with the stars, of striding the boards of the National Theater with Vanessa Redgrave, or perhaps of playing an intimate little scene with Laurence Olivier in *Hamlet?* This program would allow one to do just that.

Here's how it would work. You would be asked, in a computerized exhibit, to choose your favorite actor or a character in a specific Shakespearean scene. Then, a filmed image of the character / or actor you choose would appear on a large wall screen and begin addressing his or her lines directly to you. When your turn to speak comes, all you would then do is to read out the lines scrolling by at the bottom of the screen. As you did your part, your performance would be recorded by a hidden video camera.

Now, for the magic! Once the scene is completed, a computer takes both films—of you and of the actor—and cunningly combines them on one screen. It thus appears that you and Sir Laurence are working together on the same stage. Finally, you can leave the museum with a taped record of your glorious thespian moment safely tucked under your arm (see end of article for an explanation of how it is done).[2]

2. The program can also draw us into its world less directly than in the *Act With Shakespeare*, but perhaps just as effectively. If we think of the program as a building, we need to create an attractive entry hall, one that invites visitors and also informs them of the purpose and nature of the edifice they are about to explore. Let me give an example from some work I did recently on using interactive technology in a museum.

I was asked to design some interactive programs for the upcoming museum that will lie beneath the new Globe theater situated on the south bank of the Thames in London. This theater will be an authentic recreation of Shakespeare's original playhouse, and the museum will be an important part of the forthcoming complex, serving to introduce visitors to the world of 17th century London and of Shakespearean theater. The museum designers faced many problems. One difficulty was that this exhibition space, unlike most museums, cannot offer any original and rare artifacts. The Globe does not own a copy of Shakespeare's will nor a robe belonging to Queen Elizabeth I. What then can the museum offer the public to entice them to visit? Upon consideration, I reflected that the museum does have one great and unusual strength: it occupies the actual site of the Globe theater. Here, four centuries ago, Shakespeare's plays were performed. And the visitor to the museum stands beneath a reconstruction of that same theater. This wonderful junction of time and space, of the old and the new Globe, of 17th century London and the contemporary city looming across the river, could and should resonate for visitors, luring them into the museum experience, endowing them with the curiosity and energy to explore and appreciate the information the museum does offer.

But how to design the space so that it evoked a sense of wonder in the visitors, that it communicated to them that they were standing in the very place, in the very city, where Shakespeare mounted his works? Perhaps, I though, technology could help.

As the museum is underground, the visitors enter a lobby on street-level before descending *via* stairs to the museum level. Why not make this entry way a descent into the past? Let visitors enter a hall with large windows through which they can see the view of contemporary London, the Thames, St. Paul's, the modern skyline, firmly reminding them of the presence of the modern city. As they descend the stairway, the windows turn into window-like film projections, featuring the same view of London from the Globe but now going back in time. For example, at the first turning they view Edwardian London, at the next Victorian London, and so on. When they reach the floor of the museum proper, and the exhibits of 17th century England, the windows show them Renaissance London.

They are still in London, but have moved miraculously backward in time and space.

Now build on this experience with interactive displays that help our visitors to identify with the Elizabethans who, as they are now doing, also made a journey to the Globe. On the wall, our visitors see filmed projections of Londoners traveling to the theater: rich burgers arriving in coaches, apprentices ambling over the London Bridge, nobleman in ferries being rowed over the Thames. Large electronic maps trace the various routes. Visitors can press buttons to choose a type of theatergoer—noble or worker—and watch each route light up on the wall; and perhaps see a short film of the home and the neighborhood from which they journey. Workstations scattered about could supply more detailed information about the sociology of London; its neighborhoods, its class distinctions, its transportation technology.

This melange of real objects, simulations, and workstations seem to me a powerful way to transform the uses of space, to make the experience of space itself functional—establishing a reason to move forward into the experience of the museum.

Technology can also help guide the visitor out of the museum. Moving upwards out of the museum you would also move forward in time, from the Renaissance to the present, through twisting tunnel-like spaces that dramatically present the history of Shakespearean productions through a mix of large-scale film projections, paintings, sculpture, recordings, texts, and real objects such as costumes. As you are about to leave, you find yourself in "Backstage Alley," an area designed to present the working life of the Globe. Here visitors will look through peepholes at actors rehearsing, at props and scenery being built, at performers at work preparing the production they will go to see that afternoon at the theater just above their head.

Space of Community

Recent advances in technology have opened the door to the creation of virtual spaces that many people, widely separated in space and perhaps in time, can inhabit together. The examples already familiar to us are MUDs, the favorite play space of bored college students, which are virtual environments jointly created by the imaginations of its users. People just sign into this world for the pleasure of meeting and *shmoozing* with others, often under a disguised persona.

But such community-based worlds can also be the repository for information and can be replete with learning tools. We can create meeting places that allow long-distance learning, that allow groups of people to collaborate on creating a world together, or a performance, or a multimedia document. If we imagine such a world connected to a network filled with data, we have perhaps a model for the schools of the next century.

Caring about Design

Once you have enticed the user into the program, the world she or he encounters must be clear, simple, and meaningful. A good interface design is priority number one. Designers must learn to put themselves in the users' shoes. When users open the program, do they see a screen that is inviting, simple, reassuring? Can they intuit with ease how to navigate through the system, what buttons and icons mean, how to get help? Does the design tell the user what the program is about? what it is for? and how to proceed?

Some suggestions. Right at the start provide a clear sense of what the program is meant to accomplish, how long it may take to finish a section or complete a goal, and offer initial guidance. Offer comprehensive directories (and ways to navigate through them) and clear spatial maps of the structure of the program.

The temptation is to make the system so free and interactive that users have complete control at every moment. While this is a praiseworthy goal, users can often feel bewildered and overwhelmed by choices and uncertainty. Instead, find a simple "spine," and organize round it. In general, the more material, information, and procedures in the program, the simpler the basic organizational principle. Some schemes that have worked well are: a trip through a museum or library, where information and activities are stored in appropriate rooms or galleries; maps of locales, cities, interesting spaces; using sets of experts, each of whom introduces and guides the user through a sub-set of the information. Striking a balance is a key to effective design.

Most important, work at developing a format appropriate to your subject matter. Every discipline generates its own appropriate forms for learning. Art appreciation, psychology, and biology—all these require us to develop specific standards of judgment, specific criteria for truth. The program should enhance students ability to think in that discipline.

Computer programs in the humanities, and in higher education as a whole, often fail because they try to fit all disciplines into a framework developed for use in mathematics or the experimental sciences. For example, true or false questions are generally inappropriate to the study of a work of art. Skills needed for developing a sense of history are quite different from those needed to solve equations. When I teach theater, I need to encourage the students' willingness to make daring and unusual choices. Students need to learn not to imitate others, but to develop original and independent solutions to problems. My design should incite their daring, and reward their independence. I need to offer firm information while avoiding rigid categories of right or wrong.

To find an appropriate form for a specific application it is urgent to involve the content expert from the very start, and let the design emerge from his or her real insight into the subject matter. Too often, educational programs are initiated by technological experts who say, "Gee, we have these new gadgets, let's put them to use!" What may result is a fancy, over-designed application which no one wants to use. I began in multimedia out of a long time experience as a teacher of Shakespeare and out of my long time frustration with a specific pedagogical problem. I wanted to make students realize that the text of a play they held in front of them in a large lecture room was not the play itself, but merely the beginning point for the intricate process that would finally lead to a stage production. I knew pretty clearly what I wanted the program to do for me. The choices I made in designing the project flowed directly from my knowledge of the subject and my pedagogical experience.

Caring about the User

Your design should not only be simple, informative, and efficient; it should appeal to the whole user, to the user's sense of beauty, curiosity, and fun. Learning is a form of enthusiasm, an excited reaching out toward the new. The more we are excited and stimulated and intrigued, the more energy we have to direct toward what is new and difficult. A good design allows us to relax and focus attentively on a subject.

The program should look appealing. While this may seem obvious, it is in fact often not heeded. Beauty is a form of positive attention; we look with delight and interest at what attracts us. We also like to be surprised, caught off guard, and amused. Humor too can be an important tool to engage and hold the attention, only be careful that it is not cheap and patronizing.

We should also appeal to the user's sense of fun and to her or his underlying fantasies.

Caring about the Site

Instead of a stultifying sameness of format and function, interactive technology can provide visual and emotional variety in the classroom and museum. In an exhibition space, interactive technology can help vary the visitor's experience, creating a balance between seeing and doing, large and small scale presentations, intensive and casual learning, and different styles of presentation.

Here are some generic forms interactive exhibits can assume:

1. *environments:* The museum space itself can be the experience. Through appropriate technology and design, entire areas, or indeed museums, can make a statement and convey information.

2. *workstations:* These can be separated from the main exhibition area, or placed near relevant exhibits, or combined with exhibits.

3. *information kiosks:* Used for information, sales, publicity.

4. *large-scale displays:* Dramatic and eye-catching displays are not as efficient in conveying information but can startle, entertain, and delight.

5. *playful and informal exhibits:* These can alternate with more serious exhibits to give rhythm and variety to the visit.

6. *traditional-looking exhibits:* The transformational magic of technology can be employed to teach and dazzle without violating the feel of a traditional space.

Above all, be sensitive to the context and environment. Programs suitable to the classroom may be totally inappropriate for a public place. And even within a museum, programs should vary according to site and function. In the museum, for example, electronic displays can bring theatrical dazzle to a space, diverting the eye and breaking the monotony of consistently scaled replicas. Smaller-scale exhibits can provide another kind of magic by projecting animated histories of the kings of England onto dinner plates, and by turning cabinets into speaking pictures, everyday objects become mysterious and surprising.

For example, within the Globe museum, different spaces invite different forms of interactivity. The main exhibit space will contain an intricate reproduction of 17th century London through which visitors can stroll. Modern workstations would be completely out of place in such a traditional-feeling space. But we can introduce interactive exhibits in disguise, hidden in cabinets or under furniture; only the guides will know where they are and how to activate them. For example, a display of an Elizabethan dining featuring a table set with food and utensils can become interactive. The guide begins by asking the group whose dinner they would like to see: the king's, the merchant's, the apprentice's, the yeoman's? When they have chosen, she lifts the cover from a plate and, lo and behold, the appropriate food appears. The trick is simple: a projector is hidden directly underneath the plate and connected to a computer. When the guide presses a hidden button, a computer program finds the appropriate visual images on a video disc, and projects them onto the plate from below.

Such exhibits also allow the guides to sensitively respond to the daily visiting conditions. When the museum is full and people need to be moved through as quickly as possible, the guide does not alert the group to the presence of the interactive exhibits.

At the other extreme from such disguised interactions are exhibits whose whole point is their eye-catching and show-stopping visibility. For a section on Renaissance world images, I designed a huge electronic skyscape, stretching over three dimensional rooftops. The sky will be interactive: when the guide turns a Renaissance model of the universe, the stars in the sky are replace by images of the heavens current in the period—Ptolemaic or Copernican, Platonic or Kabbalistic—providing the audience with a graphic display of the variety and imaginative versatility of 17th century cosmology.

Certain areas can be frankly playful. The "Performance Playground" will be a kind of open, carnivalspace, a lively unstructured area with game-like interactive exhibits centering on theatrical performance. After earnestly studying the densely detailed sections featuring London and court life, visitors can here relax and "fool around." For example, visitors choose a costume from large archive and then see themselves dressed in it. They design lighting for a scene on a simulated stage, watch scenes done by different artists, wander through an multimedia gallery of great actors and performances. (The *Act In a Shakespeare Scene* exhibit would be in this section.)

Place Application in Context

Finally, the application does not exist in a vacuum, it is or should be embedded in the ongoing functions of the class or museum. Indeed, well designed applications can help integrate and unify the numerous activities and functions of these spaces.

The museum is, in fact, a complex of interlocking activities, spaces, and functionalities: exhibits, education, research, marketing, outreach. Explore how these elements can be interconnected. Technology, for example, can link the museum to other areas, in and out of the complex. For example, exhibits within the museum could be redesigned as computer programs for the home and school; or visitors could create projects in the museum and research area which could both be taken home and exhibited within the museum.

If students had multimedia programs about Shakespeare and the Globe to study at school before they came to the Globe, their visit would be richer. Then they could discover, collect, and create information during their visit to take away with them and add to the materials at school, embedding their visit in a larger educational framework.

To help visitors assemble and organize their experience, we might have electronic cards which they could insert in exhibits. Once they are through, they put the cards into stations in the information area, which informs them where they can get printed information on the areas of interest.

The museum shop might also have information kiosks, offering latest news about productions, ticket and seating availability, plus glimpses of productions, interviews with the casts and sample reviews.

In short: integrate the museum into the community; connect the museum to other museums, schools, archives, research centers; integrate the various functions *within* the museum.

Programs for use in the schools, as well, can be integrated into the various classroom activities. For example, in the *Shakespeare Project*, students study different playing versions of a scene, then create their own versions on an animation program, and finally work on the scenes in class, producing and directing their own versions. They then show their work to the other students. The program moves from the computer to the classroom to the stage.

Conclusion

Don't use interactive technology to do what can be more gracefully done elsewhere. Only use the elaborate functions of multimedia to do what cannot be done otherwise. Don't, for example, have users read large chunks of material on the computer, when they can digest this material much more efficiently and pleasantly in a book. Try to find the most economical and dramatic way of presenting an idea or fact. Like TV, this is a medium with a short attention span. In general: discover new ways to present knowledge. Mix traditional presentations with the kind of questioning and investigative formats provided by interactivity. This technology invites us to embrace process, to enjoy the journey as much as the goal. Because it asks its users to intervene with their own choices and opinions, it can challenge authority and help deconstruct received, standard forms of knowledge. So, play with new formats and unusual combinations of elements. The more daring your imagination, the more exciting and stimulating the experience for the user.

Notes

1. The analogy is a natural one for me as I began my career as an actor and director. While initially this may seem strange preparation for designing interactive multimedia applications, the more I work in this field, the more I feel how useful my theatrical background is to the demands of interactive design.

2. How *Act In Shakespeare* works. We film the actor doing the scene both from the front, in a full-face view, and from the side. We leave space on the image for the character to whom he talks. When the visitor plays the scene, he faces the image of the actor shot from the front. Then the visitor is filmed from the side in Chroma-Key. In this video technique a figure is filmed against a well-lit colored background, usually blue. When this image is combined with an image from another source, the blue background disappears and is replaced by the video from the second source. In other words, a foreground object can be opaquely placed in front of a separate background, merging into that background. Thus, the side shot of the visitor is placed on the film that shows the side view of the actor, giving us one image with both the visitor and the actor facing each other. The two images merge seamlessly, giving the convincing impression that the visitor is actually standing on the set and playing a scene with the famous actor.

9

Issues in Accessing and Constructing Multimedia Documents

Geri Gay

Introduction

The promise of the Internet is the potential to allow anyone access to information. Users can now access multiple databases consisting of elements of text, graphics, motion images, and sound. Sophisticated tools are being developed that allow users to capture, represent, integrate, manage information as well as to communicate ideas. Constructing and accessing multimedia documents as well as personal communication using the network raise many complex issues of knowledge construction, interpretation, and communication.

Computing and Social Constructivism

Networked multimedia systems can provide tools for the social construction of meaning and communication: the collection, storage, and classification of multimedia texts, the review and manipulation of these multimedia documents, the exchange and distribution of texts and annotated documents among peers, and the ability of teleconferencing tools to provide conversation. These computing systems provide the opportunity for users to test, reflect and construct meaning from these programs. Participants, even if they hold different views, can feel that some advance has been made in their own understanding or perspectives on reality.

The design and use of the Internet and associated systems are based on principles of constructivism. Constructivism or constructivist principles propose that humans make sense and learn best as a result of doing, creating, building, or reflecting (Dewey, 1938; Papert, 1987). Lave and Wenger (1991) and Brown, Collins, and Duguid (1989) argue that learning involves making sense of some experience, thought, or phenomenon. Another principle associated with constructivism is that our representation or understanding of any concept is not abstract and self-sufficient, but rather is constructed from those situations, social and physical, in which the concept is found and used (Collins, Brown and Newman, 1988; Mahoney, 1988; Simon, 1980).

Emerging Themes from Research and Design Studies

For the past several years, the Interactive Multimedia Group (IMG) at Cornell has been designing and testing interactive systems to begin to support an adequate understanding of what computer devices do in the context of human practice. The results from studies on the ways in which people have used completed programs as well as the ways the computer is used in the context of communication (Norman, 1987; Winograd and Flores, 1986) have enabled us to identify some key issues surrounding human-computer interactions.

The interactive multimedia applications described below include a hypermedia program designed to test tools for accessing a visual database; an interactive multimedia fiction program designed to test individuals' use and interpretation of multimedia story elements and the use of navigation and composition tools; and a networked collaborative design environment devised to test multimedia tools and resources for communication and problem-solving. Each program was designed to meet a different goal, so research data were gathered and enlarged in ways that corresponded to the research questions appropriate for the program as follows:

Navigation and access issues in large multimedia databases
Issues of interpretation and use of multimedia events and objects
Issues of online collaboration and communication
Issues of using online tools and resources to solve problems

Case 1: Issues of Navigation and Access in a Large Multimedia Database
A Field Guide to Insects and Culture, known by its developers more familiarly as the *Bughouse,* is an application that offers users three main navigational and guidance tools to help them to gain access to information. *Bughouse*

presents information about cultural entomology, an area of study that integrates the disciplines of anthropology, art, history, and entomology. The program contains information in a variety of formats and media: text, video, commercial movie clips, segments with actors, photographs, animation, segments of old television commercials, and music. Combined, these media and formats form 160 segments, objects, or "Events."

The content of *Bughouse* is accessible to users in three modes—Index, Browse, and Guide. Traditionally, information in databases is organized and accessible through alphabetical ordering or thematic cross-referencing—the indexing and cross-indexing familiar to most book and library users—and *Bughouse* contains an online Index that users can employ in this standard manner. The Index enables the user to search through a textual description of the topics included in program Events.

Browse mode enables the user to move at will through the program's content by using screen commands to travel, metaphorically, throughout a Victorian country house and its grounds—the movements are analogous to walking from one room to another. Also, the Browse mode provides an online command to bring up maps of the house and surroundings. Students can use the maps to orient themselves, or they can navigate by them, "jumping" to a new location and skipping any intervening rooms or space (figure 9.1).

The third tool to assist in navigation, the Guide, provides the student with an online advisor. The program has a tracking system that records the path of the user, the Events visited. The Guide feature categorizes these events to trace a user's progress and suggests to him/her, if queried, other related Events that are in the category in which the user showed the most interest (figure 9.2).

Research focus: Which search modes do users choose and what effects do the search modes have on how they recalled and organized the information they found?

Method

The first use of the *Bughouse* was introductory. Participants received a general orientation to the interactive multimedia hardware and a brief explanation of the research interests. The students were then free to explore the system as they chose. During both the first and the second sessions,

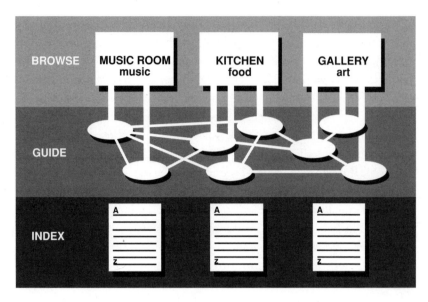

Figure 9.1
Guide, Index, and Browse search mode tools.

students worked through the interactive multimedia program at individual workstations. They were instructed to work at their own pace and to explore the material very much as though they were visiting a museum. The purpose of the first use of the *Bughouse* was to decrease the novelty effect and reduce possible student anxiety concerning use of the system. On the first use, students worked an average of 42 minutes.

At the end of the first session each student was given a questionnaire asking about their overall reactions to the program, any difficulties they were experiencing, perceptions of program organization, and their interest in topics to explore further. Student tracking records were obtained after each student use of the *Bughouse*.

During the second session, each student was given one of three focus questions and asked to explore the information in the program that related to their assigned focus question. The focus questions were designed to require students not only to find relevant information, but to interpret the information found. For example, students could relate information on locust plagues to the development of images of evil or to illustrate the harm done

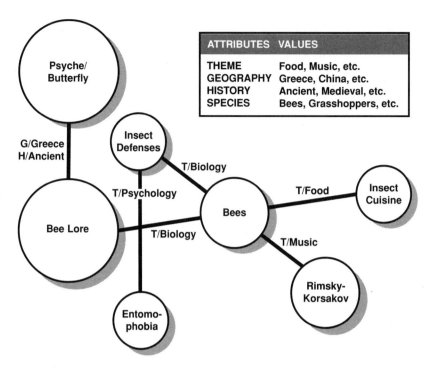

Figure 9.2
Online Guide and tracking system based on attributes of Geography, History, Species and Theme.

by insects. The topics in which students had expressed interest after the first session were referred to when assigning a focus question to each student for the second and purposive use of the *Bughouse* so that, whenever possible, students would be looking for information about a theme of interest to them.

Findings

The analysis of computer tracking data in this study revealed that the Browse mode was more effective at finding information in this visual database than was the traditional Index mode; and the Guide mode, although it was effective too, was not used by as many students. The Guide and Index were text-based systems and, therefore, were not so visually appealing as the navigational features of the Browse mode.

The groups were labeled (based on percentage of time in each mode) as Browsers, Guiders, Indexers, and Mixers. Analysis of the data (Trumbull, Gay and Mazur, 1992; Gay, Trumbull, and Mazur, 1991) pointed out some characteristics and patterns of the users in their search strategies. Indexers, for example, were most confident they had found all the information they needed; but, in fact, of all three groups, they had found the least.

These preliminary findings illustrate ways that designers of hypermedia systems can use tracking data to explore the needs of the user and provide online guidance. The *Bughouse* example highlights the discrepancies that can arise between users' perceptions and their actual use and how tracking data can resolve those discrepancies.

Case 2: Issues of Interpretation and Use of Multimedia Events and Objects in Interactive Fiction

The design of *El Avión Hispano* provides intermediate students of Spanish with a motivating, intriguing context to practice writing by constructing stories. As a pretext for student interaction, the program uses the spatial and thematic metaphor of an airplane flight. The underlying premise of this storyspace is that most people have traveled by plane or train and have imagined stories about other passengers (Gay, 1991). Students are exposed to interactions, characters, and scenarios in the program in much the same way any air traveler experiences them: randomly, as the video proceeds forward inviting the user to stop and select various options; or selectively, as eavesdropping or action attracts interest.

After watching the introductory scene, viewers either proceed through a series of five scenes set on the plane; or they click on objects or people in these main scenes to bring up other video segments which are set in another time and place. The design of the information obtained in these additional program segments is intentionally ambiguous, as are the other video vignettes. The scenes are crafted as *video rorschachs* (Mazur and Gay, 1990) to promote greater possibility of multiple interpretation. Some scenes are nonverbal.

To help students accomplish their creative task, *El Avión Hispano* offers various optional program tools. These include full motion video with controls, a composing space for writing individually or collaboratively with others on the network, a fortune-teller who delivers intriguing details about passengers, an in-flight magazine, and a thesaurus with 7,000 entries.

Students were required to select, combine, and recombine elements from the hypermedia presentation to write a story. Just as no two people in real life can be said to have exactly the same interactions, no two users interact with the program's material in exactly the same sequence.

Research focus: *How do users interpret and use multimedia elements in an interactive fiction program?*

Method
Students from a third semester Spanish class were asked to observe the characters on the fictional airplane and write a story about them. Students' use of text, graphics, and online database resources was documented by MediaTrax. This particular tracking tool records the computer screen and notes any changes in the users stories. These records can be played back and analyzed in real time.

Results
The analysis of the records revealed qualitative differences in the way students explored the program's content. Some students seemed to move from one segment to another in one direction only. Employing a weaving metaphor, Mazur (1993) called this group Spinners, because although they were constructing meaning, the result was but a literal interpretation or description of events in the order in which they were viewed. Others' use was characterized by a back and forth movement among scenes accomplished by use of the video controllers and the program's navigation features. This group was labeled the Weavers.

The "weaving" style of use also correlated to the kind of final stories the students wrote. The students who moved through the program in a linear way wrote stories primarily conveying actions, while students who displayed the non-linear weaving pattern of program use wrote final stories which focused on the motivations or psychology of the characters. The Weavers' stories were more inventive, embellishing content by drawing connections between visual content viewed in particular scenes (figure 9.3).

In addition to revealing styles of use, the log also shows a connection between the cinematic technique and interpretation. Once again we saw that different styles of use related to different ways of making sense of the

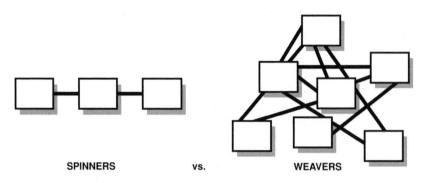

Figure 9.3
Linear (spinners) vs. nonlinear (weavers) use of program options.

program. Some users developed a much richer interpretation and interpreted more complexity. For all students in this particular group, each instance of a close-up shot produced a denotation. Using the pause or resize feature (expanding the video to a full screen picture) on a close-up shot aided the Weaver's linking of visual information. For the Weavers, a move to search for a previously viewed scene (or item in a scene) was preceded by a close-up pause or re-size 43 percent of the time (Mazur, 1993). This finding suggests that designers need to be attentive to incorporating cinematic techniques to support rich visual linkages in hypermedia content to engage and direct viewers' attention.

Case 3: Issues of Collaboration, Access, and Communication in Distributed Hypermedia Environments
Currently under development at the IMG is a networked collaborative design environment to support the activities of students engaged in engineering design tasks. The research purpose that underscores this project will ultimately test the use of networked resources and hypermedia databases to inform engineering design, as well as produce computer tools for augmenting communication that will help coordinate activities and support joint problem-solving. A point highly relevant to this project is that computer-supported cooperative work systems (Bodker, Knudsen, Kyng, Ehn and Madsen, 1988; Ehn, 1988; Greif, 1988; Grudin, 1988) reflect a change from an emphasis on using computers to solve problems to an emphasis on

using computers to facilitate human interaction and communication. The goal of these systems is to assist groups in communicating, collaborating, and coordinating their activities. Specifically, these computer-based systems support groups of people engaged in a common task or goal and provide them with an interface to a shared environment (Ellis, Gibbs and Rein, 1991). Networked systems can now support simultaneous activity and run applications shared by participants. Some desktop conferencing systems support multiple video windows per workstation. This allows display of dynamic views of information, plus dynamic images of participants (Watabe, Sakata, Maeno, Fukuoka and Ohmori, 1990).

Research focus: Are there multimedia and collaboration tools that might optimize collaboration among individuals and groups who are performing design tasks across networks?

Program tools and the online hypermedia databases are undergoing iterative design and testing. Groups of engineering students used the system to complete design tasks in a networked environment. The set-up of the collaborative design environment is shown in figure 9.4. Each station has audio-video links to the other two design stations, a shared computer screen workspace with draw tools, chatbox, and a text editor, and access to an online multimedia database which includes simulations and other resources relating to the design task, and access to Internet resources.

Early phases of the iterative design of this program focused on how students used different communication media at their disposal in order to solve a design problem. A transcription of videotape data collected during this exercise was also used to explore discourse patterns and students' interactions in this complex collaborative environment for use in design and to suggest further areas for research.

Results

In order to closely examine the discourse patterns, the videotapes of interactions during the exercise were transcribed and placed in an Excel 4.0 spreadsheet. This spreadsheet version accommodates multiple data formats and allows for cross-referencing of text and digitized video data. As the multimedia system is used, people interact with the data, leaving their ideas printed in the documents with annotations and footnotes (Geertz, 1973;

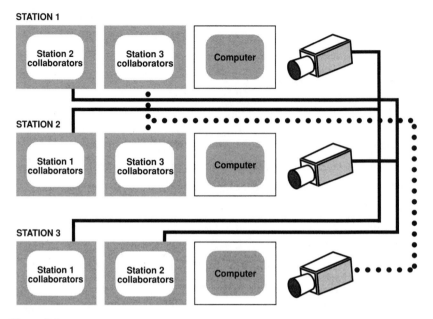

Figure 9.4
Collaborative design environment where students have access to resources including
Internet teleconferencing, texts, simulations, real-time chart and draw tools and
database materials.

Gay, Mazur and Lentini, in press). Moreover, the researchers or viewers can
attach their comments to documents, transcripts, and Quicktime movies for
themselves and others to view. Researchers communicate with the original
material, comments or annotations of others. Gradually, new meanings and
interpretations or themes emerge.

The purpose of the preliminary analysis was to examine what communication channels students used and how they used the channels and resources
during design exercises. Preliminary analysis of students' interaction on the
videotape identified several specific communication activities as students in
the three groups collaborated using the networked systems. Identified activities included orientation, directives, clarifications, social exchanges, ac-
knowledgments, and requests for information. These activities were linked
to use of specific online resources and design activities. The video link was
used most often for requesting information, for clarification by watching the

work of others, and, not surprisingly, for showing structures or objects to direct collaborative work (Greenbaum and Kyng, 1991; Gay and Grosz-Ngate, 1992). It was also discovered that traditional issues of power and control did not seem to disappear in these collaborative design settings.

Distinctions of human coordination can be abstracted from examination of conversation (Suchman, 1987). By examining closely what people are doing when they coordinate their activities, one can observe how students use language to make and break commitments, how students learn new possibilities and interpretations, how students identify what to do, and their interpretation and use of visual images and audio.

Conclusion

Our work has focused on issues of human-computer interface design, the potential of communication media for collaborative work, the ways in which users can make effective use of information in multimedia data bases, the limits and potential of tools for accessing information, and the use and interpretation of representations of content in different media formats. While multimedia can provide for increased experience with concepts, it is not a panacea. Several important conclusions can be made from the research we have completed.

Databases and Internet resources are including more multimedia components. Visual interfaces and navigational tools that allow quick browsing of information layout and database components are more effective at locating information (multimedia) than traditional index or text-based search tools. However, it should be noted that users are less secure in their findings. Users feel that they have not conducted complete searches when they use visual tools and interfaces.

Tracking users' strategies for searching information databases can provide researchers ways of exploring the needs of users by identifying discrepancies between users' perceptions and their actual use of information. Different styles of accessing hypermedia databases are shown to relate to different ways of interpreting and making sense of the information found in the hypermedia environments. These differences need to be taken into account when designing system tools for communicating and learning.

Additionally, certain cinematic techniques used within hypermedia environments seem to be connected with particular interpretations of content organization and visual representations. More research is needed to investigate the use of cinematic conventions, or languages, and the way users interpret events and images in a hypermedia context.

Finally, as users become increasingly acclimated to networked environments, their use of specific online resource and communication tools can be linked to specific communication activities. Identifying these activities will allow researchers to create hypermedia tools that will facilitate human interaction and problem-solving.

Interactive computing systems may provide increased access to information, but these technologies are not the ultimate answer to human communication and understanding. Individuals use these systems in a variety of ways—many unexpected. Our own preliminary research shows that the introduction of new technologies in and of itself will not solve communication problems or make issues relating to status and power disappear. As we continue to analyze the social dynamics in the context of networked multimedia environments, we should be able to both make practical recommendations concerning their use and contribute to the development of a new body of theory.

Acknowledgments

Primary development of the interactive multimedia programs described in this paper and the accompanying research was supported by grants from IBM, Apple Computer, the Cornell University President's Fund, and the National Science Foundation (Cooperative Agreement No. EEC-9053807 and Grant No. RED-9253085). The author wishes to thank Joan Mazur, Marc Lentini, Erika Kindlund and Deborah Trumbull for their comments, insights, and contributions to this piece and research mentioned in the chapter.

References

Bodker, S., Knudsen, J. L., Kyng, M., Ehn, P., and Madsen, K. H. (1988). "Computer support for cooperative design." In *Proceedings of the Conference on Computer Supported Cooperative Work (CSCW 88)*. pp. 377–394). Portland, OR: ACM.

Brown, J.S., Collins, A., and Duguid, P. (1989). Situated cognition and the culture of learning. *Educational researcher* 18: 32–42.

Collins, A., Brown, J. S., and Newman, S. E. (1988). Cognitive apprenticeship: Teaching the craft of reading, writing, and mathematics. In *Cognition and instruction: Issues and agendas*, edited by L. B. Resnick. Hillsdale, NJ: Erlbaum.

Dewey, J. (1938). *Experience and Education.* New York: Macmillan.

Ehn, P. (1988). *Work-oriented design of computer artifacts.* Falkoping: Almqvist and Wiksell International.

Ellis, C. A., Gibbs, S. J., and Rein, G. L. (1991). "Groupware: Some Issues and Experiences." *Communications of the ACM* 34, no. 1: 39–58.

Gay, G. (1991). "Structuring Interactive Multimedia Fiction." In *Hypertext and hypermedia handbook*, edited by E. Berk and J. Devlin. New York: McGraw-Hill.

Gay, G., and Grosz-Ngate, M. (1992). "Collaborative Design in a Networked Multimedia Environment: Emerging Communication Patterns." Submitted for publication.

Gay, G., Mazur, J., and Lentini, M. (in press). "The Use of Hypermedia Data to Enhance Design." Special issue of *SIGGRAPH.*

Gay, G., Trumbull, D., and Mazur, J. (1991). "Designing and Testing Navigational Strategies and Guidance Tools for a Hypermedia Program." *Journal of Educational Computing Research* 7, no. 2: 189–202.

Geertz, C. (1973). "Thick Description: Toward an Interpretive Theory of Culture." In *The Interpretation of Cultures.* New York: Basic Books.

Greenbaum, J., and Kyng, M (1991). *Design at Work: Cooperative Design of Computer Systems.* Hillsdale, NJ: Lawrence Erlbaum Associates.

Greif, I., ed. (1988). *Computer-Supported Cooperative Work: A Book of Readings.* San Mateo, CA: Morgan Kaufman.

Grudin, J. (1988). "Groupware and Cooperative Work: Problems and Prospects." In *The Art of Human-Computer Interface Design*, edited by B. Laurel. Reading, MA: Addison-Wesley.

Lave, J., and Wenger, E. (1991). *Situated Learning: Legitimate Peripheral Participation.* Cambridge: Cambridge University Press.

Mazur, J. (1993). "Interpretation and Use of Visuals in an Interactive Multimedia Fiction Program." Unpublished doctoral dissertation. Cornell University, Ithaca, NY.

Mazur, F., and Gay, G. (1990). "Distinct video crafting of multimedia computing programs for inferactive writing." *Journal of Interactive Instruction Development* 2, no. 4: 18–20.

Mahoney, M. (1988). "Constructive Metatheory: Basic Features and Historical Foundations." *International Journal of Personal Construct Psychology* 1, pp.1–35.

Norman, D. (1987). "User Centered Design." In *The psychology of everyday things*, edited by Donald Norman. New York: Basic Books.

Papert, S. (1987). "Computer Criticism vs. Technocentric Thinking." *Educational researcher* 16, no. 1: 22–30.

Simon, H. A. (1980). "Problem Solving and Education." In *Problem solving and education: Issues in teaching and research*, edited by D. T. Tuma and R. Reif. Hillsdale, N.J. Erlbaum.

Suchman, L. (1987). *Plans and Situated Actions*. New York: Cambridge University Press.

Trumbull, D., Gay, G., and Mazur, J. (1992). "Students' Actual and Perceived Use of Navigational and Guidance Tools in a Hypermedia Program." *Journal of Research on Computing in Education* 24: 315–328.

Vygotsky, L. (1962). *Thought and Language*. Cambridge, MA: MIT Press.

Watabe, K., Sakata, S., Maeno, K., Fukuoka, H., and Ohmori T. (1990). "Distributed Multiparty Desktop Conferencing System: Mermaid." In *Proceedings of the Conference on Computer Supported Cooperative Work (CSCW '90)*, pp. 27–38). Los Angeles, California: ACM.

Winograd, T., and Flores, F. (1986). *Understanding Computers and Cognition: A New Foundation for Design*. Reading, MA: Addison-Wesley.

10

End User as Developer: Free-Form Multimedia

Edward Brown and Mark H. Chignell

Introduction

This chapter introduces a new style of application development environment, free-form multimedia. The free-form approach expands the concept of multimedia, but it also permits a new style of end-user development, allowing users to customize applications to suit their own purposes.

Frequently, the constraints of traditional materials and approaches have the salutary effect of providing a familiar milieu within which author and reader can communicate. Similar structures provided by multimedia environments can substitute for years of experience and provide familiar points of reference for interpreting a wide range of information. However, the use of such structures comes at a price. The end user must accept the constraints imposed by the structures which the software developer has designed for the multimedia environment. This has resulted in a great deal of user interface design effort to present these constraints to users in a form that is palatable and easy to assimilate. This effort has generally proceeded on two fronts. First, the constraints have become enshrined in terms of consistent interfaces where the same interface behavior is shared across a range of applications. These shared constraints then have to be learned only once. The second approach to making constraints more palatable is to embed them within a familiar model or metaphor. Thus there has been a great deal of discussion concerning appropriate user interface metaphors (e.g., Carroll, Mack, and Kellogg, 1988; Waterworth and Chignell, 1989).

New technologies extend the range of choices available to authors, giving them more freedom to express their ideas. However, the technological medium an author uses also defines much of the character of the resulting creation or document. Traditional materials provide well-known structures and constraints for the author to work with. Some of these constraints are associated with different media forms, such as the linear nature of text, the layout of a printed page, the static resolution of a picture, or the practical size limitations of a diagram. In addition, the conventions and culture surrounding those objects provide the reader with certain expectations about how to use them. For example, reading this document one will expect the textual exposition to continue at the top of the next page from the bottom of the current one. Another conventional expectation is that a navigation aid in the form of a table of contents is to be found near the beginning of the volume.

When dealing with multimedia and information presentation, software becomes a means of packaging information for the user. That is, the software defines the "conventions and culture" for the information objects, and determines what a user or "reader" can be expected to do with that information package. In this chapter we will focus on applications that have information presentation as one of their main purposes/activities. We will show how free-form multimedia provides additional creative advantages to authors for conveying their messages.

An alternative approach to handling software constraints has received relatively little attention. This approach allows end user customization so that users can decide for themselves how information should be presented in the application. Differing levels of customization may be used, reflecting different points on the continuum between end-user programming and end user customization. With simple customization, the user is able to individualize the interface—to modify the appearance of icons, the order of menu items, or even to create scripts and macros which can be executed. Essentially, the users are then re-configuring the interface to reflect the way they want information to be presented.

In the remainder of this chapter we will explore methods for achieving the effects of end-user programming, through a relatively simple customization style of interaction. The particular focus will be on the relationship between author and reader in multimedia, with our results being interpreted in terms of information presentation in general. Our approach strives to provide more flexibility to users; not only in the kind of information presented to them, but also in how they choose to structure that information and constrain the interpretation of the multimedia document.

Structuring and Customization in Multimedia

A good user interface achieves a match between the designer's intentions and the user's understanding of the task. Many problems stem from incompatible models of the task that are held by designers and users (Norman, 1988). The interplay between a particular user interface, the nature of the work, and how users relate to the user interface can be subtly altered by components of the software and the user interface, in ways that the designer may not be aware of. The term *psychological overdetermination* (Carroll and Campbell, 1989) has been used to describe highly constrained user interface designs that "characteristically embody multiple, distinct psychological claims" where "virtually every aspect of a systems' usability is overdetermined by independent psychological rationales inherent in its design." Carroll proposed a minimalist approach as an antidote to overdetermination. Our approach is one of *under*determination: leave presentation choices to the end user as part of a customizable user interface, which may itself be part of an environment that contains customizable components. This reduces the role of the developer in determining information structure, and increases the corresponding role of the end user.

Consider the structure of hypertext and multimedia documents. Hypertext links provide a means of structuring information. Authoring choices can be enriched by providing different types of links. Many taxonomies of link types have been devised, such as: semantic (Chaffin and Herrmann, 1984); rhetorical (Trigg, 1983); and lexical (Fox, 1980). The type of a link provides the reader with a cue to how it is used. When the types of the links are obvious or familiar, it may be possible to obtain a basic grasp of the structure without extensive training or practice. In contrast, the ability to decode the structural cues hidden in linear text depends on years of schooling and reading practice. In fact, we are so dependent on our reading ability and are so used to information in this compact medium that new structures (such as hypertext link taxonomies) are introduced through this medium—as written textual material. We should not expect too much from readers who are interpreting hypertext structure and link typing, when typically there has been little prior instruction or educational investment in this type of task.

Customization of link types allows authors to define their own types of information structure in a form that is meaningful to them. In contrast, highly-constrained software limits the freedom of authors to organize information to their own liking. Greater author control of information structure should not be interpreted as an invitation to anarchy. But there is a trade-off: the flexibility of free-form structures versus the special capabilities or operators that can be provided for fixed or pre-defined structures. From our perspective, pre-defined structures are not inherently harmful, but the conventional or consistent form they provide for the document may also interfere with effective communication between author and reader. In most applications new and familiar structures should be judiciously intermixed.

In creating the information structures, authors in a free form environment help define the relationship between readers and themselves. They can also define the nature of the channel that will be used to communicate with readers. The capability to structure discourse becomes intertwined with the structuring of information. In applications where there are multiple authors and readers (where the same individual may sometimes function as both author and reader) the end result is a society of text (Barrett, 1989) where there are multiple threads of discourse and information structuring. The forms that different authors create for communication can then develop along with the forms they use for structuring information. Typically, different software applications, such as electronic mail or conferencing systems, are used to differentiate different forms of discourse. In free-form multimedia, users develop the appropriate forms of interaction as they develop forms for the organization of information. Thus a style of free-form multimedia is created that can serve as a platform for integrating diverse applications within a common environment.

Multimedia Document as Application Program

Free-form multimedia may be defined as *a style of multimedia in which information structure (e.g. node and link meanings) can be realized through the shared intentions of authors and readers.* The "behavior" of the multimedia is then determined by the particular meanings or "types" of nodes and links that are instantiated. Developers and authors are then free to find the form of information structure (or lack thereof) that best suits the application (or family of applications) being developed.

We view free-form multimedia as a new paradigm for end-user application development. Under this paradigm, users can exploit interface constructs in a number of different ways. For instance, in terms of link syntax (the free-form multimedia equivalent of data structure), users may determine links to be one-to-one or one-to-many. They may also be one-way, or bi-directional. There are also a number of interaction styles that may be user-defined. One important aspect of interaction style is the behaviour of the system when a link is selected (traversed) and a target node is opened. The target node may replace the current node, or it may be "added to the screen" with the previous node remaining in its position on the screen. The style in which the new node opens may also be varied. Attributes that may be of interest include the size and position of the window representing the new node, and which portion of the node is shown and/or highlighted. For example, a node may be presented as a scrollable field, and highlighting may be used to indicate that the link anchor or endpoint is a specific region of the target node. Such choices are provided as customization features for the end user.

Viewed from the stance of traditional software engineering and application development, the definition of link syntax (i.e., whether links are one way or bi-directional, one-to-one or one-to-many) specifies the *data structure*, while the definition of link types (link semantics) specifies the *data model*. The composition of the nodes specifies the document *content (information)*. Different versions of free-form multimedia can then be defined based on the degree to which the data model, data structure, and interaction style can be modified. However, our use of the terms "data model," and "data structure" here is informal and meant to serve as an analogy rather than a rigorous mapping.

In general, the more control that is provided to end users over linking and interaction style (figure 10.1), the more they assume the role of application developers. It may seem the design space that can be provided for the end users to develop applications must be relatively small, particularly if the design choices are limited to customizable features. In fact, we have discovered that a reasonable number of syntactic choices, used in combination, open a huge range of possible semantic choices; and that users are content to ascribe new and diverse meanings to different combinations of link and node types as they are needed. For example, a user can decide one type of node is

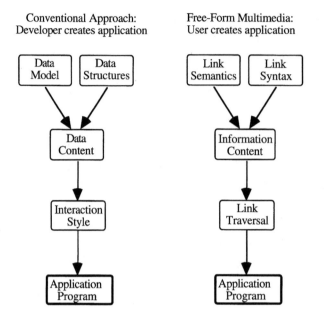

Conventional Approach:
Developer creates application

Free-Form Multimedia:
User creates application

Figure 10.1
The Free-Form Multimedia approach to application development contrasted with the conventional approach.

a topographical map, and link semantics will be zoom in and out of a particular region; and with a subtle change in syntax, a different node type might be ascribed as a footnote, with links as references to the main text. Such ascription of meaning can be seen in the examples shown later in this chapter.

The users of free-form multimedia function as application developers, authors, and readers all at once. Therefore, the structures of discourse and information organization, usually provided by different software applications, are instead created by the users in the course of their work. This provides considerable freedom of expression for users. However, the cost of this freedom is that the user must frequently struggle to find the right form or structure within which to appropriately express the information. Clarke (1990) puts it this way: "Different kinds of relationships—like parts to the whole, cause to effect, or evidence to conclusion—suggest different kinds of graphic organizers. . . . The struggle for form is a struggle for control over an idea" (p. 30).

Free-form multimedia allows different kinds of information to be presented in different ways, using a wide range of possible semantic structures. At the same time, free-form authoring environments need to provide some kind of support for the author's efforts. The question is, what kind of mechanisms will support a large semantic design space without making the author's job too difficult and the struggle for form too elusive?

Free-form multimedia can be achieved without creating new types of operators. Instead, we can generalize the components that are currently used to create document structure. In particular we explore a basic paradigm based solely on the conceptual elements of "nodes" and "links." As our examples will show, carefully designed nodes can "document" or "explain" the meaning and usage of new forms of links created by the author.

One of our guiding assumptions in this work is that development of semantic structures should be part of information organization. Our aim is to provide free-form environments that can blend both activities seamlessly. Thus, the form of information presentation should fall naturally out of the same activity that adds information content.

The Free-Form Environment

The distinction between fixed form and free-form multimedia environments is not just a matter of general linking mechanisms or customizable nodes or anchor points. The HyperCard™ authoring environment, for example, provides a fairly ambiguous type of node and link that is quite malleable in the hands of the author. However, moving much beyond the standard metaphor of an index card (in the case of HyperCard) requires some fairly involved scripting, which takes the author away from the activity of document creation. Thus we do not regard HyperCard and similar authoring/ programming environments as free-form multimedia within the definition proposed here.

Existing hypertext and multimedia systems provide some, but by no means all of the character of free-form multimedia. For instance, Intermedia (Smith, 1988) provides a prodigious number of link types and documents types that made it essentially unrestricted in scope. However, it relies on the classical division of different application software for distinguishing different document types, thereby reinforcing the division between information content and information structure instead of integrating the design of structure with that of content.

Our concept of free-form structure is more akin to the notion of a Box in the BOXER program (diSessa, 1989). The box is a generalized container, that may hold different kinds of entities, from pictures to program script fragments. diSessa uses the word *detuning* to describe a construct that becomes more flexible by dissociating it from a specific semantic context. The resulting functionality may be more diffuse throughout the system, but the expressive power has increased correspondingly.

In a similar way, our concept of a node carries no contextual baggage. While nodes lack special structural facilities, the user is free to use them as individual pieces of text, addenda, or entire documents in their own right. Other than the actual operational characteristics of the node, there is no bias provided in terms of organizational structure. In introducing users to free-form multimedia, we can simply refer to a node as a "place" in the system.

Connections (links) between nodes can be similarly detuned. Since links do not contain content, there are effectively two ways to represent the author's semantics for links. The system could allow the author to change the behaviour of the screen elements, which may then represent different link types. This usually involves some form of programming which is a considerable demand to add to the authoring process, and detracts from our objective of making the creation of form a fluid part of authoring. The alternative is to allow the author to manipulate the *appearance* of link anchors on the screen, thus providing for different semantics to be expressed by different screen objects. Following this latter course, the challenge for the software is to provide link behaviour that is reasonable for many different interpretations of link and node.

In our current research system (called Anchors Aweigh), free-form multimedia provides a reduced syntax, where links are one-to-one and bi-directional. This allows us to examine the semantic power of these syntactic elements in isolation, before new features are introduced. We have experimented with different types of link semantics (e.g., pre-defined link semantics versus user-defined link semantics), and are looking forward to investigating different methods of link traversal (interaction style). We have used a single style of node, which is added to the screen as an extra window. Windows open in a predefined position, but may then be re-positioned by the user. Providing pre-defined nodes (information content) has allowed us to further focus experimental studies on the process by which links are created. However, we also have broader experience using free-form multimedia to develop applications. More syntactic elements would help in creating applications, but the current system is effective for these early explorations.

The free-form nature of our environment depends primarily on three operational characteristics:

1. An unrestricted node model. A node can represent anything—a document, a concept, a physical entity, a diagram, an index, etc.
2. An open-ended linking facility. Links have unrestricted semantics that allow users to develop specific links for different situations, or use them as undistinguished link types.
3. An easy-to-use linking mechanism, without any additional overhead for specifying link semantics.

The user interface in Anchors Aweigh is relatively simple to operate. In particular, the linking mechanism was designed to be obvious and easy to use. To construct a link, the user selects from a palette of anchors (an example of such a palette is shown in figure 10.2) and then clicks the mouse at the two desired locations (start point and end point) for the link anchors. This palette has a handle at the top so that it can be moved by the user around the screen. The link anchor palette allows quick access to alternative anchor icons during link creation. Selecting an anchor symbol from the palette invokes the "stamp tool" and the cursor changes from a hand (signifying browse mode) to a stamp (signifying link authoring mode).

Once the link has been constructed (i.e., the start and end points have been selected) the user returns to browse mode with the cursor changing back from the stamp tool to the hand browser. To browse a link, the user then clicks at an existing anchor and the node of the other associated anchor (i.e., the other end of the link) appears. The basic link operations use only point-and-click mouse operations. No keyboarding or menus are involved. Sound, highlighting, and cursor shape provide feedback regarding what operation the user is performing, and help the user locate anchors and nodes. Our experience indicates that users find this mechanism simple and obvious. At the same time, the palette grouping is designed to adequately convey the

Figure 10.2
Basic link and node editing tools are provided in the form of a palette.

fact that the different symbols do not function differently, but exist so that the user may create their own semantic conventions.

A standard set of drawing and text tools are available for creating the node content. Multiple nodes, appear simultaneously in Anchors Aweigh in overlapping windows, allowing easier navigation and link creation. Anchors appear intermixed with the text and graphics within the nodes. This allows their interpretation and context to be completely flexible.

End User as Developer

Free-form multimedia environments blur distinctions between developers, authors and readers. Participant of end users in the development process is important since end users will typically have the best understanding of their own needs and will best be able to evaluate prototypes during iterative design.

End user development provides a form of participatory design. Through the design of new documents, the semantics the users add effectively create a new application. One of the intriguing aspects of free-form multimedia is that it is simultaneously an application development and a documentation environment. Thus discussions about how to re-define conventions and come up with new applications can take place inside the multimedia system. User/developers can even mail examples of their designs back and forth as part of the discussion, with the mail system (see figures 10.5 and 10.6) itself implemented using specially typed links, as an application of free-form multimedia.

It must be stressed that the activity of the end user in free-form multimedia is very different from other attempts to create end user development; e.g., through visual programming and declarative programming languages. First, the notion of a syntax error is alien to free-form multimedia. Programming occurs implicitly through linking, and each link is valid from the perspective of multimedia as soon as it is created. Thus there is less explicit debugging of errors and more of an evolutionary and exploratory process of modifying links until the right behavior is attained. Second, there is no need for compilation or debugging environments. Each link can be traversed as soon as it is created, and there is no distinction between software programming and software testing. Third, the logic of the application, such as it exists, is driven by the content of nodes and the labels of links, rather than by complex programming logic, conditionals, branches, and loops. Our own observation suggests that application logic based on node content and link labels is much more compatible with human cognition than conventional programming logic.

We are not claiming that every application can or should be built using free-form multimedia, but we can expect end user development in free-form multimedia applications to be useful in some situations. For appropriate applications, the software engineering process should be greatly facilitated as the development of the application becomes self-documenting and cognitively compatible with the mental model of the user/developer (cf. Norman, 1987).

When is free-form multimedia useful? We have suggested that it provides fewer constraints on authors and allows users/readers to customize applications to fit their own needs. These properties should reduce the need for a scripting language in addition to the basic operations of node and link creation. Current scripting languages such as HyperTalk, or programming environments such as Visual Basic are still a long way from the dream of "programming for the rest of us." In fact, scripting languages thus far seem to satisfy neither the novice nor the serious programmer. For the casual user scripting is still a complex procedural programming exercise, and for the serious programmer, there almost always seem to be a need to revert to a more "serious" language once the project goes beyond the stage of developing simple prototypes. Thus free-form multimedia can potentially replace much of the hypertext/scripting effort that characterizes the development of many of today's information presentation applications.

Examples of Free-Form Documents

We have created a number of documents/applications in Anchors Aweigh to explore the properties of free-form multimedia. Figure 10.3 shows a document created in an experimental setting, in which the subjects are given a short amount of time (about 15 to 30 minutes) to generate links among a few, set-content nodes. The documents created in this highly time-pressured type of experiment are probably not representative of hypertext or multimedia authoring activities in general. However, we have been able to show that in generating their own meanings, subjects are encouraged to think about the global themes in the document (Brown, 1993). More generally, we found that subjects using our multimedia system demonstrate more complex cognitive processing under free-format (i.e., user-defined link semantics), than under fixed format conditions (based on verbal protocol analysis).

In other experiments we used Anchors Aweigh to study the mechanisms by which author and reader communicate (Baron, Brown, and Chignell, 1993). We found large individual differences between authors in terms of the types of link that they chose to use during authoring. In particular, when presented with a range of both semantic and rhetorical links, authors tended to emphasize either semantic, or rhetorical links, but not both. That is, some authors tended to have a semantic linking style, while other authors had a rhetorical linking style. We also found that these individual authoring preferences were consistent across two different types of authoring task (authoring for readers with a specific purpose versus authoring a multipurpose document for readers with a range of purposes). We feel these findings, limited as they are, reinforce the notion that hypermedia authors can benefit from control over document structure.

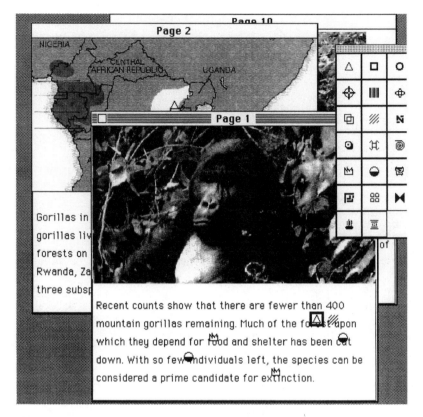

Figure 10.3
Meaningless abstract symbols are used in our research, to understand user's naive use of linking. Such symbols do not bias the subject to any particular meaning, and therefore allow us to investigate what meanings subjects generate spontaneously. The triangle symbol, for example, is reported by this subject to mean "location."

Flexible Hypertext Documents

Providing too much structure to authors may inhibit their own interpretation and understanding of the material. Free-form multimedia environments allow users to generate information structures themselves. An example of how this capability is realized is shown by a node depicted in figure 10.4. The node shown here is part of a concept network in which each node or frame shows one central concept and a number of attached concepts.

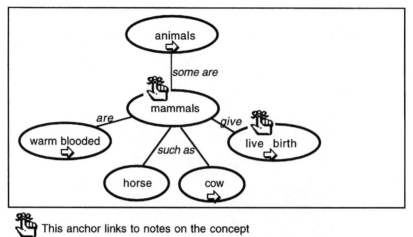

 This anchor links to notes on the concept

⇨ This anchor links to the part of the network centered on that concept

Figure 10.4
Authors create their own semantic structures using simple linking capabilities.

Attached concepts have similar frames which can be accessed by following the appropriate link. For example, in the case of figure 10.4, we can activate a link to bring us to the part of the network centered on the "animals" concept. Thus, the arrow-shape anchor becomes integrated into this specific semantic form, and becomes a navigation tool for traversing the concept-net. Nodes used in this concept-net structure become concept frames. After a little exposure to these conventions, the user stops thinking about the arrow-shape links in general terms and can easily relate to this specific interpretation. Hitting an arrow-shape is no longer perceived as a generic "activate link" action, but has become a "go to this concept" action. The context and appearance of these nodes and links is sufficient to distinguish them from other types of nodes and links.

Our approach to concept-networks was motivated by the SemNet software (Fisher, 1988), which supports a fixed-form environment of this type. It is instructive to compare the more constrained fixed form version against the free form version of the concept-net. The free form has several inherent disadvantages; users must create the lines and ellipses that make up the diagrams, for each frame; mistakes or errors in using the form are not prevented or recognized by the software; redundancies can not be identified, or usage constrained to "sensible" patterns or meanings; and navigation aids or overview screens cannot be automatically generated, they have to be built by a user and connected to the network frame-by-frame.

Many of these disadvantages can be offset with a little judicious design effort. With the ability to copy and edit nodes, as in a word processor or drawing tool, "template" nodes can be created. Consistency is then encouraged by using a standard node template. Continuing with this hypothetical design, a "master menu" of such templates could be created using another node, containing descriptions of each template and links to the templates themselves. The end user or author who wants to create a new node may simply find the correct template from the master menu, follow a link from the menu to the appropriate template, and copy and edit the template, linking the new node to the rest of the multimedia document as desired.

The example of the previous paragraph shows that free-form multimedia can be surprisingly versatile, in spite of relying on relatively few syntactic "customization" constructs. In addition, the inherent advantages of the free-form version are provided with no overhead: authors can extend the system by adding new types of links and nodes, to add commentaries or notations not previously available. This can be done instantly, with no changes to the software environment, as a practical application of end-user development. Similarly, the formalism can be violated in peculiar circumstances, when the situation calls for it. A user can also develop a new kind of navigation tool, rather than being constrained to the particular fixed tools provided by the software.

The free-form version of the network can also be linked and combined with other kinds of structures, such as essays describing the domain, or images showing some aspect of the concepts in the network. A portion of the network might be embedded in another kind of document, or vice-versa. The distinction of free-form multimedia is that these combinations can be created as the new types of document are authored; the new structures are linked-in by the end user, without waiting for a cycle of software development and implementation. They are a natural and integral part of document creation. Thus the transitions between "programming," authoring, and reading have a seamless and transparent feel.

Video Mail

The sense of combining information organization with end-user design is much more apparent in the collaborative uses of the free-form environment. It is in these documents that overt consideration of how information should be organized plays a part in the communication between users. Figure 10.5 represents a simple example of users communicating using the system. This example demonstrates the organizing conventions for an electronic mail system which evolved through consensus under our free-form system. The upper node is a kind of "drop box," which anyone can edit to leave a message for one particular user. Messages can be in any form—text, graphics, or links to other nodes. In this particular case, the user "John" has dropped a link into the mailbox, which connects to a node containing a simple text message.

In this example, conventions have evolved not only around the shape of anchors and what they mean, but also about the usage and meaning of particular nodes. Certain nodes are to be used as mailboxes, and that convention is sufficient to structure the exchange between users. Of course, as with the concept-net example, many convenient features of a mail system are

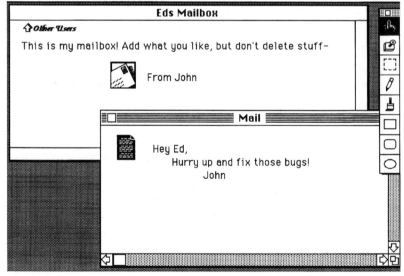

Figure 10.5
A free-form electronic mail system built with generic link and node types.

not or cannot be supported—in particular, it is almost impossible to track discussions—but there is a versatility here that only a free-form environment will provide.

Meaning is not just derived for link icons and nodes types. Users also use the positioning of anchors on the node relative to the node boundaries, text and graphic elements and other link anchors to provide structure. In the mail example, the convention of placing navigation links at the top of the node helps distinguish them from links which comprise the mail messages.

The mail system integrates easily into the other sets of conventions used in other nodes. In figure 10.6, for example, a timeline chart has been "dropped off" by linking it into the mailbox, possibly precipitating a discussion about the structure of the time-line and the milestones contained in it.

There is no confusion regarding which are mail links and which are internal document links, even though the link behaviors are the same:

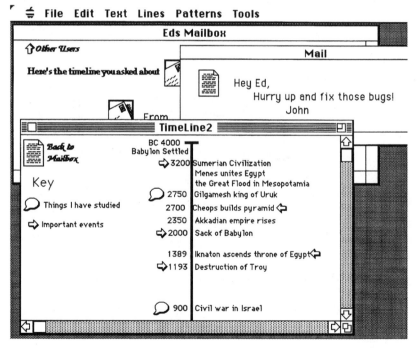

Figure 10.6
A timeline with seven internal links has been dropped (i.e., linked) into my mail.

context, appearance, and most of all the group consensus regarding the semantics of the link anchors all contribute to make the meanings clear. This semantic flexibility may be further facilitated by providing extensive icon libraries, and icon editors (figure 10.7), to permit highly customized representations of different types of link.

In this example, through context and convention, links have become a mail tool. Without changing the behaviour of the link, different mechanisms can be supported and developed by the end-user. Similar conventions can be used to create bulletin board areas, voting mechanisms, document mark-ups, and so on. It is these evolving mechanisms that give the exchange a qualitatively distinct character: the participants control what discussion is about, but at the same time, they also control the way in which discussion is carried out. Thus, in

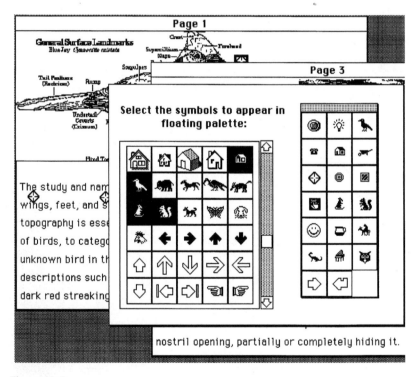

Figure 10.7
With a large icon library and associated icon editors, users have access to a huge range of link anchors for expressing different semantics.

free-form multimedia, semantics evolve through context and convention which supplants the role of data modeling in more conventional software development.

Free-Form Multimedia as Groupware

Free-form multimedia encourages end user development. The end-user is more aware of the needs and characteristics of the task domain as well as the individual characteristics of the target users. The parallel with authorship is obvious; the authors best know the message or series of messages they want to deliver to the audience, thus they are best suited to choosing how that message is delivered.

The assumption behind most software is that the user should be given as much help as possible in structuring the task; thus the goal of user interface design has generally been seen as being synonymous with the goal of making the software easier to use. However, empowerment may be just as important a goal as simplicity for many users. We expect the empowering nature of free-form multimedia to be particularly useful in cooperative and groupware applications. For applications used by individuals (as distinct from groups) the quality of the environment can be measured in terms of how it helps the user's productivity. Elements which might be misunderstood or which distract the user should be redesigned. In such situations understanding may be enhanced by increasing the compatibility of the software interface with the mental models of the users. However, in collaborative applications the software structure and interface should reflect the shared consensus of the group. This is where we expect free-form multimedia to come into its own.

Consider for instance the electronic mail application discussed earlier. If the group wants to emphasize project management information, Gantt charts and project networks can be defined as nodes within the information structure. Nodes within the project network can then be linked to activities and project milestones which in turn can be linked to corresponding budgets, etc. There are a host of details in such an application which are best decided by the group. In such cases an outside developer is unlikely to capture all the nuances of the group and its interests. While it is not as flexible as the free-format multimedia envisioned here, Lotus Notes™ provides an inkling of how flexible information structuring systems can be used quite effectively by groups carrying out heterogeneous sets of tasks.

Free-form multimedia should also prove useful in educational settings, where inquiry may be driven by shared experience of multimedia artifacts. Free-form multimedia allows the collaboration to focus on how information objects should be manipulated. Thought-provoking exchanges occur on how conventions should evolve to delineate different kinds of work, collaboration, communication, and artifacts within a single integrated system. As users create their own protocols for interacting and exchanging ideas, they develop a consensus about which interpretations are agreed upon and which are a matter for debate. We can expect discussions in free-form multimedia to be contentious at times (cf. the phenomenon of flaming in electronic mail), in which cases the information structure can provide a forum for debate, conflict resolution, and decision making.

In contention involving different information structures, and evolving communication forms within the system, users are in effect participating in groupware application development. There is no need to distinguish the development stage from deliverable product, since the development is ongoing and suited to the needs of the immediate discussion. As the users build sets of conventions, they will have a common experience and background to draw on, akin to our experiences in everyday life.

As an analogy, consider an informal discussion that uses a diagram as a focal point. One person might sketch out a graph, and another add various annotations as the interaction continues. They will generally adopt and meld familiar conventions about the meaning of graphs and lines without having to explicitly state them. Furthermore, the tools do not have to constrain them to the particular form—they can shift to another type of presentation if needed.

If the work is not collaborative, but simply the preparation of a document by an individual, then the choices the author makes are not as overtly debated; that is they are not visible as part of the information exchange which appears in the free-form environment as used by a group. The forms do not evolve through a cycle of contention, but are chosen and fixed at a particular time when the author has finished her composition. Furthermore, there is no debate forum or explicit record of decisions as with collaborative use of the system. However, in choosing the forms, the author should undergo some sort of internal process not entirely unlike that of exchange between different individuals; alternatives will be considered and rejected as the author struggles to find an appropriate set of nodes and links for the particular application or information structure being developed.

Summary

In this chapter we introduced the concept of free-form multimedia. We also described the Anchors Aweigh system that we developed to explore the properties of free-form multimedia. It is not our contention that free form document design should replace mainstream applications development. Fixed-form application software can provide powerful operators and context sensitive functionality that the more general model of a free-form system cannot match. However, our experience indicates that authoring with free-form multimedia offers the author much more than simply choosing one form of presentation over another, or the ability to mix media. It allows the author to create new expressive forms to suit each individual document.

Experience with *Anchors Aweigh* leads us to believe that free-form link semantics present no difficulty to authors and users in terms of operating the system. Conversely, use of fixed link types constrains authors and readers. Using a free form system also has the advantage of bringing some of the design decisions normally associated with developing an application under control of the document author. If this approach is valid, as we believe it is, then it foreshadows a radical change in the conception of document creation. Document design becomes environment design.

The natural extension of this view is that fixed-form software constitutes a special case of free-form, which can provide more powerful operators for particular forms that become popular. In general, conventions and careful use of context will provide sufficient structure, making it unnecessary to restrict authors to any particular model of a document or environment.

It is too soon to tell how free-form applications will be used. There is a very real possibility that some free-form applications would eventually become so cluttered with conventions and arbitrary structures that confusion would prevail. However, in favorable situations users will recognize this problem and evolve free-from organizing mechanisms accordingly. Whether such mechanisms evolve naturally, or must be imposed by fiat, has yet to be determined.

Finally, we are convinced that the kind of exchange between users shown here is an important aspect of human communication. The structure of information and the mechanisms by which it is exchanged must be considered in concert with content. This is why we strive in free-form multimedia to make structuring a document as fundamental as is authoring of document content.

Acknowledgments

Portions of this work were completed by the first author while he completed his Ph.D dissertation at the Ontario Institute of Studies in Education. This work was also supported by an operating grant from the National Science and Engineering Research Council of Canada to the second author. Both authors would like to thank Lisa Baron and the HyperGroup at the University of Toronto for their helpful comments and discussion.

Some materials are excerpted from *Mountain Gorilla* by Michael Bright from the project Wildlife series published by Franklin Watts. Copyright © 1989 by Franklin Watts Ltd. Used with permission of Franklin Watts, Inc., New York.

References

Baron, L., Brown, E., and Chignell, M. H. (1993). "Back to Basics: The Role of the Author in Hypertext." Unpublished manuscript. Department of Industrial Engineering, University of Toronto.

Barrett, E. (1989). "Introduction: Thought and Language in a Virtual Environment." In *The Society of Text: Hypertext, Hypermedia, and the Social Construction of Information*, edited by Edward Barrett. Cambridge, Mass.: MIT Press.

Brown, E., and Chignell, M. H. (1993). "Learning by Linking: Pedagogical Environments for Hypermedia Authoring. *Journal of Computing in Higher Education 5*, no. 1: 27–50.

Carroll, J. M., Mack, R. L., and Kellogg, W. A. (1988). "Interface Metaphors and User Interface Design." In *Handbook of Human-Computer Interaction*, edited by M. Helander. Amsterdam: North-Holland.

Carroll, J. M., and Campbell, J. (1989). "Artifacts as Psychological Theories: The Case of Human-Computer Interaction." *Behaviour and Information Technology 8*: 247–256.

Chaffin, R., and Herrmann, D. J. (1984). "The Similarity and Diversity of Semantic Relations." *Memory and Cognition* 12, no. 2: 134–141.

Clarke, J. H. (1990). *Patterns of Thinking; Integrating Learning Skills in Content Thinking.* Boston: Allyn and Bacon.

diSessa, A. (1985). "A Principled Design for an Integrated Computational Environment." *Journal of Human-Computer Interaction* 1, no. 1: 1–47.

Fisher, K. M., Faletti, J., Thornton, R., Patterson, H., Lipson, J., and Spring, C. (1988). "Computer-Based Knowledge Representations as a Tool for Students and Teachers." Annual Meeting of the American Educational Research Association.

Fox, E. A. (1980). "Lexical Relations: Enhancing Effectiveness of IR Systems." *ACM SIGIR Forum* 15, no. 3: 6–36.

Norman, D. A. (1987). "Cognitive Engineering." *In Interfacing Thought*, edited by J. Carroll. Cambridge, Mass.: MIT Press.

Norman, D. A. (1988). *The Psychology of Everyday Things.* New York: Basic Books.

Smith, K. E. (1988). "Hypertext—Linking to the Future." *Online* 12, no. 2: 32–40.

Trigg, R. (1983). "A Network-based Approach to Text Handling for the Online Scientific Community." Ph.D. dissertation. Department of Computer Science, University of Maryland.

Waterworth, J. A., and Chignell, M. H. (1989). "A Manifestor for *Hypermedia* Usability Research." *Hypermedia* 1, no. 3: 205–234.

Waterworth, J. A., and Chignell, M. H. (1991). "A Model of Information Exploration." *Hypermedia* 3, no. 1: 35–58.

11

Salient Video Stills:
Content and Context Preserved

Laura Teodosio and Walter Bender

Digital technology offers the potential to radically transform how media information is received and reused. Once distinct forms of distribution, (i.e., radio, television, print) are now reduced to one common channel—a bitstream. This bitstream representation allows easy searching, parsing, augmentation, compositing, and combining of different forms of media information.

More importantly, beyond new arrangements and combinations of signals, the bitstream representation facilitates signal transformation. Digital data is no longer bound by its original packaging, the audio of a radio broadcast can be transfomed into text; moving images can become information rich stills. These manipulations can be automated and personalized for the human receiver at the point of consumption. The presentation form would change depending on the users particular preferences or what they are doing at any given time, i.e., movies that explain themselves with text, or magazine articles that read themselves on a portable walkman. This type of fluid transformation between presentation modes is called cross-media transcoding.

In order to perform transcoding, a signal must be represented in a way that reveals its content and not just its packaging, to the computer system decoding the information. The signal must have "a sense of itself" [11]—an accessible description that transforms these multitudes of digital bits into a coherent structure. Such signals are not directed at a human recipient, but rather, to a local computational agent acting on the user's behalf. In response to instructions from both the distributor of the signal and the reader, this agent operates upon the signal in manners suggestive of both traditional media and of new forms.

The annotation or content information can be exterior to the signal, in a remote text database, for example, or it can be embedded in the signal, as in the closed captioning of television broadcasts. Network Plus was an early example of the use of closed captioning to aid in decoupling and transcoding a pre-packaged media signal [2]. The system created a personalized augmented summary of the day's news. Although the display environment possessed little video and audio capability, every attempt was made to display features about the data which were considered salient. In an attempt to preserve non-lexical audio cues, the audio track was analyzed for intonation and cadence [10]. This information was used to highlight the words in the transcript that received special acoustic emphasis.

Since there was no detailed log of video information, alternative means were devised to select still images. The results of the audio analysis were used to select images of the newscaster at an emotional moment. Additionally, the video image itself was decoupled from its packaging—the frame. Segments of the image such as the box over a newscaster's shoulder, were extracted from the frame and became images unto themselves. In an attempt to retain contextual coherency and prevent redundancy, the box was only extracted when its contents changed.

These selected images initiated the concept of salient stills. Their creation exemplified the power of a computational agent working on a signal laden with structured content information. This chapter describes in detail some further work on this one type of cross-media transcoding—that of the moving image to still.

The Salient Still

Salient stills do not represent one discrete moment of time, as does a photograph or single video frame. Rather, they reflect the aggregate of the temporal changes that occur in a moving image sequence with the salient features preserved. By the application of an affine transformation and non-linear temporal processing, multiple frames of an image sequence, which may include variations in focal-length or field-of-view, are combined to create a single still image. The still image may have multi-resolution patches, a larger field-of-view, or higher overall resolution than any individual frame in the original image sequence. It may also contain selected salient objects from any one of the sequence of video frames.

Photography is a discrete medium. It suspends the world for one instant, rendering it silently within the two-dimensional boundaries of an image frame. There exists in that photographic representation just one visual point of view and one level of spatial resolution. Video, by contrast, is a temporal medium. The progression of images suggest motion. A sequence of frames may consist of zooms, tilts, pans and other camera movement that over time change the viewer's vantage point, field-of-view and perceived resolution. Changes in the camera settings may cause the viewer's attention to shift from one part of a scene to another. Objects can move in and out of the scene relative to the camera motion.

Any single frame of a continuous sequence of frames accurately portrays only one discrete moment of time, camera focal-length and orientation. While this frame may articulate a moment, it is an incomplete representation of the space/time continuum recorded by the sequence of moving images. The single frame cannot capture the intended expression of the multiple frames.

However, the information in a series of video frames can be culled and transformed into a resulting single still image. The process described below facilitates the creation of a variety of synthetic and composite still images from the multiple discrete frames of a zoom and/or pan sequence. Images are created that are a synthesis of the information extracted from a portion of the entire image sequence. Derived from an intersection of photography and video, the processed images are called salient stills. Salient stills attempt to retain much of the original content (detail) and spatial and temporal extent (context) of the original sequence while condensing data.

One example we will discuss is an image with variable resolution patches. The overall scene is captured at low-resolution. High-resolution patches correspond to areas in the scene where the camera zoomed in. This variation in resolution, rather than being disconcerting, is a narrative tool. Much like the focus-pull of cinema, it draws the user's attention to those salient parts of the scene that commanded the attention of the camera operator or were deemed important by the creator of the salient still. Other examples include images which contain composited objects from the scene, and images with a field-of-view greater than that of any one of the individual video frames— essentially a synthesized panoramic image.

A salient still from zoom is created when multiple frames from a video zoom are combined into a single "multi-resolution" image. A salient still from pan is created when multiple frames from a video pan are combined into a single "panoramic" still image. The methodology does not need to distinguish between the two shot types, so zooms and pans can be intermixed freely in the resulting still image.

Redundancy

Usually when a video camera samples the world in front of it, much of the information captured is repeated in a number of frames. For example, in a sequence in which the camera "zooms in," locations in the physical world are captured many times, but objects central in the scene are imaged with greater resolution in each successive frame. The relative position of the objects in each successive frame may also change; for instance, some objects will be out of the field-of-view and no longer will be imaged. Likewise, since there is usually a great deal of overlap in a pan sequence, the same locations are imaged many times. As in the zoom, the relative position of the objects to the frame changes frame-to-frame; some objects fall out of the field-of-view, while new objects are revealed.

The typical sampling of a scene by a video camera results in a redundant representation, e.g., the same area in the scene may be sampled multiple times, but the redundant samples are not likely to be aligned from frame to frame. The salient still process, which aligns all of the frames in a sequence, is able to exploit this redundancy in four ways: (1) Transient noise can be reduced in the image by examining multiple samples of the same point over time. (2) Additional image resolution can be achieved by combining samples that have been taken at phase shifts that differ either by changes in camera orientation or focal-length. (3) When the camera orientation is changing, an increased field-of-view can be achieved by compositing images that have been correlated by regions of overlap. (4) Transient objects can be located and extracted by comparing the composite image to individual frames.

One result of the salient still process is the extraction of "resolution-out-of-time." In image processing terms, this increased resolution corresponds to a higher bandwidth signal, and, in cognitive terms, it corresponds to an image with more content information than any individual frame in the sequence.

An Example

Four frames from a 12-second zoom sequence of the cellist Yo Yo Ma on stage during a performance at Tanglewood are shown in figure 11.1. Imagine the task at hand is to choose a single image to represent this performance, perhaps to print the image in a newspaper.

One may initially be inclined to chose the close-up frame of Mr. Ma since this is rendered with the most detail per pixel per "area of interest." But this image does not provide the contextual information of the ambiance of Tanglewood, nor does it relay the fact that there is a live audience. In contrast, the far shot retains the ambiance, but it does not provide enough spatial detail of the performer to recognize him as Mr. Ma or to see that he is playing a hypercello. A frame selected from the middle of the zoom contains the musical assistant walking across the stage, detracting from Mr. Ma as the center of focus.

The solution to finding an image with both enhanced visual quality and semantic saliency is not to use any single frame, but to use all of them. The close-up frames render Mr. Ma with the needed detail, the far shot gives context, and middle frames provide enough redundancy in data to assist in the automatic removal of the non-salient musical assistant. Figure 11.2 compares the resolution of the far shot of the sequence with the resolution of the resulting still.

Figure 11.3 shows the resulting image of using data from all the video frames. Notice that the musical assistant is nowhere to be seen. Additionally, the resultant image is much larger than any of the individual frames. The single digitized frames are 640 × 480 pixels, whereas the resulting salient still is 3000 × 1500 pixels. The central portion of the image has the same detail per area of interest as the close-up frames and the resolution decreases towards the edge of the frame.

Figure 11.1
Four frames from a video zoom featuring the cellist Yo Yo Ma.

Figure 11.2
On the left, the "area of interest" extracted from a frame in the original sequence (the right hand image in figure 11.1). On the right, the "area of interest" extracted from the resultant salient still.

Figure 11.3
The salient still.

The resulting picture takes the best features of both an established wide shot and a high detail close-up and merges them into one. Additionally, the high- resolution patch in the center of the image draws the user's attention to the area of interest.

If it is deemed that the musical assistant is a salient feature of the scene, he can be composited into the final still image. Figure 11.4 shows a still of the same sequence where the musical assistant was added back into the image multiple times to show his traversal across the stage. In order to convey the temporal nature of the assistant's actions, the degree of translucency used to render him is a function of time in the scene, i.e., the earlier he appeared in the scene, the more transparent he is in the composite.

Structured Representation

In order to create salient stills we manipulate video in a structured manner moving beyond the frame and into the elements, e.g., foreground and background. Objects and movement get modeled. This decomposition of the signal from its original frame-by-frame packaging allows new degrees of freedom in the compression, manipulation and visualization of this video data. This representation of a visual scene as a series of manipulable objects is the basic model of synthetic images in computer graphics. It has only begun to be explored in the world of "real" images as discussed in [8], [13], [15], [18], [19].

Figure 11.4
Temporal Musical Assistant.

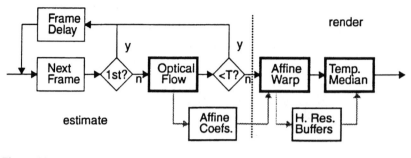

Figure 11.5
System block diagram.

The system for building the still consists of determining global camera motion, building a 3-D space/time representation of the video data, constructing a high-resolution background scene from which other moving objects can be detected, extracting objects, and finally, composing the still. The user is able to assist in the determination of salient features which are to be included in the still.

Methodology

There are three steps to building the high-resolution images: (1) The optical flow between successive frame pairs is calculated. (2) Successive affine transformations, calculated from the flow, are applied. These translate, scale and warp each frame into a single, high-resolution raster. (3) A weighted temporal median filter is applied to the high-resolution image data, resulting in the final image.

Optical Flow
The output of a video camera is a set of discrete samples of a space/time continuum of the world in front of the camera. The creation of a salient still allows the recovery of this continuum. Camera movement between frames is modeled using an optical flow analysis [7], [9], [11], [12]. By characterizing this frame to frame difference as an affine transformation, zooms, as well as translational camera movement, are recovered.

The optical flow can be modeled by a continuous variation of image intensity as a function of position and time:

$$I(x, y, t) = I(x + dx, y + dy, t + dt)$$

Assuming that the motion field is continuous everywhere, the right hand side of the equation can be expanded using a Taylor series, (the higher order terms are ignored):

$$\frac{\partial I}{\partial x}\frac{dx}{dt} + \frac{\partial I}{\partial y}\frac{dy}{dt} = -\frac{\partial I}{\partial t}$$

This equation usually is solved by modeling image motion as translational in the x, horizontal, and y, vertical, directions. This is sufficient to model the pan and tilt of a camera, but it does not model zoom. However, if motion is modeled as an affine transformation, zooms in combination with other camera movement are recovered. The specific algorithm and implementation comes from Bergen et al. [3]. Following their notation, if a pattern is moving with a velocity $p(x,y)$ then modeling only translational changes:

$$p(x, y) = p_x(x, y), p_y(x, y)$$

So, if velocity p is described by six parameters, $a_x, b_x, c_x, a_y, b_y, c_y$, which describe the affine movement, the velocity equations become:

$$p_x(x, y) = a_x + b_x x + c_x y$$
$$p_y(x, y) = a_y + b_y x + c_y y$$

where a_x and a_y are pure translation terms in the x and y directions in units of pixels, b_x is a percentage scaling factor for x in the x direction, c_x is a percentage rotation factor for x in the y direction, b_y is a percentage rotation factor of y in the x direction, and c_y is a scaling factor for y in the y direction. From the above equations, it is observed that a change of focal-length of a camera lens is described by the bx and c_y terms. Pans and tilts are described by the a_x and a_y terms.

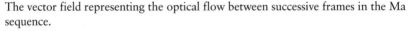

Figure 11.6
The vector field representing the optical flow between successive frames in the Ma sequence.

To determine these affine parameters, first a Gaussian pyramid is constructed for each pair of frames (t and $t + 1$). Computation begins at the lowest level and is refined at each successive level by computing the residual motion.

This method was used principally to detect global camera motion and works well for static scenes where there is only camera motion; unfortunately, the real world of video is not filled with many shots of this type. Therefore a few different methods of reliability were built into the affine estimates, including masking noisy regions, using a priori knowledge of shot type expected to adjust estimates, and smoothing the data by passing a spline through the samples. For a more detailed explanation of these methods see [18]. Figure 11.6 shows a vector field representing the optical flow from successive frames in the Ma sequence.

Warping into Continuous Space/time Raster
A 3-D space/time continuum is built for the video sequence. The result is a video volume where spatial location in the world is on the x and y axes, and

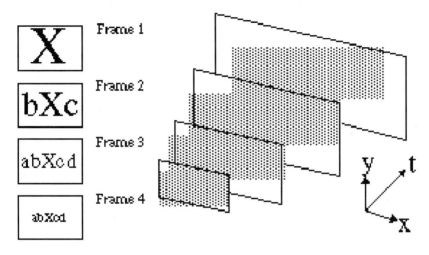

Figure 11.7
The motion between the images is recovered and used to warp all the images into a common raster.

time is on the z axis. A vector passing through the volume perpendicular to the first image plane will pierce the same spatial location in the world of each image. For example, the second image of a pan left sequence is adjusted right so that the two frames line up; the second image of a zoom sequence is scaled so that it appears the two images were captured with the same focal-length lens (see figure 11.7).

The affine transform $(t \rightarrow t+1)$ is used to warp image (t) into the space occupied by image $(t+1)$. Image (t) is further warped into the space occupied by image $(t+2)$ by applying the affine transform $(t+1 \rightarrow t+2)$. The following equations are used to sum the affine parameters:

$$ax_{new} = ax_1 \times bx_2 + ay_1 + ax_2$$
$$ay_{new} = ax_1 \times by_2 + ay_1 \times cy_2 + ay_2$$
$$bx_{new} = bx_1 \times bx_2 + by_1 \times cx_2$$
$$by_{new} = bx_1 \times by_2 + by_1 \times cy_2$$
$$cx_{new} = bx_2 \times cx_1 + cx_2 \times cy_1$$
$$cy_{new} = by_2 \times cx_1 + cy_1 \times cy_2$$

The result of the recursion of this procedure is that all of the frames in the sequence are mapped into a common raster. It is important to note that, following the mapping, the images are no longer at a uniform resolution. Images that were taken with a short focal-length were scaled more than images taken with a long focal-length, thus the former are of lower resolution than the latter. However, there is now a global correspondence between pixel positions and locations in the original scene.

Extraction of High-Resolution or Extended Buffer

From this intermediate space/time volume representation, an extended scene or high-resolution buffer can be created. Various approaches can be taken in the creation of this raster. The still image can be pieced together bit-by-bit using the unaltered pixels as they are rendered in the space/time volume over time. For example, in a pan sequence, the first occurrence of each point in the world is used for the value of the corresponding point in the final altered image. This method works fine for static images, but for scenes containing moving objects or lighting changes the resulting still may be a chaotic rendering of multiply imaged objects. An alternative approach would be to calculate the average value of every sample corresponding to a location in the scene. This method results in "ghosts" while providing no dramatic increase in image resolution. A potential remedy is to apply an operator over a region of pixels as they change over time to determine the corresponding pixel value in the final image. Ideally, this operator will preserve all of the detail found throughout the sequence, while eliminating noise and extraneous motion in front of the camera. We experimented with temporally weighted median operators, and found them effective.

A simple median operation is generally effective at eliminating ghosts [4]. Any transient data, such as a moving object that is stationary for less than half of the frames, are eliminated from the final image. However, a simple median operation is not optimal when zoom sequences are being manipulated, since it gives equal weight to both pixels interpolated between coarse samples (short focal-length) and pixels originating from fine samples (long focal-length). A linear weighting based on the position of each frame in the frame sequence depreciates interpolated pixels. Assuming the zoom is directed outward, the first occurrence of the pixel is weighted more that the last. A refinement, which accounts for variations in the pace and direction of

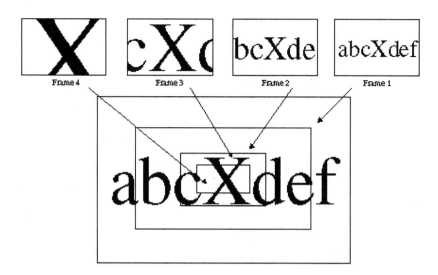

Figure 11.8
Synthetic image created from zoom sequence. The four boxed regions in the composite image are taken from the warped frames shown above. The high-resolution image is created by applying a temporal median over every pixel in the warped frames; i.e., pixels from frames 1 to 4 contribute to the final determination of any pixel in the composite. Since frames 1 through 3 are scaled by interpolation they contribute less to the final image than does frame 4.

the zoom, assigns a weight according to the scale terms, bx and cy, from the affine estimator. Figure 11.8 shows conceptually from where in the image sequence the data in the still image have been derived.

In this resulting image, the center of the salient still is the area of highest resolution. One could imagine, however, a situation where the camera operator zoomed in on an object, zoomed back out, panned to the right, then zoomed back in again. The resulting salient still could have two high-resolution patches.

Enhancements

There have been many enhancements made to the basic salient still process described in section 2, including improvements in the estimation of frame-to-frame correspondence, better image segmentation and compositing, and efficiency considerations.

Auto-Aperture Compensation

Illumination change is one factor in determining the correspondence between frames in an image sequence that is not accounted for by either the optical flow estimation or the affine transformation. By calculating an overall illumination level change between frames, a more accurate estimation of flow is achieved. The normalization of the illumination levels between frames eliminates some discontinuities in the composited still image.

Reduction of Affine Coefficients

Under typical circumstances, the affine shear coefficients, cx and by, are negligible and can be eliminated from the calculations. Also, under typical circumstances, the affine scale coefficients, *bx* and *cy*, should be identical. In practice, the mean of these coefficients is used.

Memory Usage Reduction Due to Inverse Affine

As described in discussion of the methodology, each frame in the image sequence is scaled to a high-resolution buffer from which the salient still is then extracted. Although this works, it is very expensive in terms of image storage; every image in the sequence must be stored at the resolution of the final output image. An alternative is to again inverse the direction of the transformation. After having determined the mapping of each image into the high-resolution space, it is possible to scan this space, and map it back to the appropriate pixels in the original sequence. This method requires the same number of calculations, but only one high-resolution buffer.

$$p'_x(x, y) = \frac{a_y c_x - a_x c_y + c_y x - c_x y}{b_x c_y - b_y c_x}$$

$$p'_y(x, y) = \frac{-(a_y b_x) + a_x b_y - b_y x + b_x y}{b_x c_y - b_y c_x}$$

Chromatic Redundancy

Since the optical flow algorithm is "color blind," all the computations of optical flow, warping and temporal median were done on the Y, or achromatic channel, of a YUV color representation. The same manipulations are then performed on the corresponding pixels in the chromatic channels.

Character Extraction
Since the composite image is a result of a median operator, any object that is stationary relative to the camera motion for more than some duration of time (50% of the frames for a simple median) is incorporated in the composite, whereas objects that are moving relative to the camera "disappear." This somewhat arbitrary selection of foreground objects which are discarded or retained is not always appropriate. Additional contextual cues needed to determine the object's saliency can come from the salient still creator, a log, or description of the video footage.

In the case of the Ma sequence, the character extraction was performed by comparing frames of the sequence with the "actorless" background scene that was extracted from the temporal median process. The regions that differed were considered foreground objects and extracted. There were a few problems with this method, most significant was the temporal variation in the sampled pixels due to the methods of recording, (e.g., aperture change) or changes in the environment such as shadows cast from moving actors. In most cases a noisy segmentation was extracted and then the user was asked to assist in the final segmentation. Other methods of extracting multiple motions can be found in [3] and [6].

Compositing
Once a background scene is extracted, characters or objects considered salient can be composited back into the set. These regions can be composited at higher resolution or with changed color or luminance. In order to ensure a seamless blend of regions as in the Ma temporal composite, a laplacian pyramid blending method is used [1].

Evaluation of Methodology

The results depend upon three factors: the accuracy of the flow vector, the camera attributes and operation, and scene characteristics.

Optical flow incorporates an incomplete model that assumes a world made of a two-dimensional rubber sheet, e.g., all motion is affine (non-perspective) and rigid. While this model is sufficient for many circumstances, it does not work well if there is the possibility of excessive image noise, transient image features, (e.g., actors moving relative to the camera), or changes in perspective between images. Truck and track shots, both of which involve moving the focal plane of the camera relative to the scene, will cause errors due to changes in perspective. The former type of shot will cause the image to bow out from the image plane, whereas the latter will cause objects to unwrap onto the surface of the image plane. In the case of pans and tilts, if the objects in the field-of-view are proximal, there is some perspective distortion. Object occlusion is another source of violation of the optical flow model; whenever the focal-plane of the camera or objects in front of the camera move relative to the scene, occluded or revealed elements distort the estimation of flow.

The theoretical limit of how much resolution can be added to the salient still due to redundant sampling is dependant on both the camera modulation transfer function (MTF) and its operation. While there is no theoretical restriction on using zooms to enhance resolution of points-of-interests, and pans and tilts to cover a wider field-of-view, there is a hard limit on how much additional resolution can be extracted due to tracking the phase shifts between frames. This is discussed in [16].

Discussion of Applications

Salient stills and their methodology are useful in the areas of compression and visualization of temporal video data.

Sometimes it is desirable to have the ability to print a still image from video. But there are inherent problems in this task. First, the spatial resolution of video is below that of a print medium. Additionally, the video image collector is capturing for a temporal medium; following movement often takes precedence over frame composition. As a result, there might not be one frame composed well enough to stand on its own as a still, or perhaps, there is information in the moving image that would be distracting or misleading in a still frame (the multiresolution Yo Yo Ma image is an example of such a still). The salient still process can be used to create still images with increased spatial resolution that are suitable for print publication. The use of variable spatial resolution to indicate regions of interest and temporal transitions is a mechanism whereby the narrative devices of the cinematography can be "transcoded" into those of photography. The patches of high resolution which correspond to the camera's changes in focal length need not be restricted to a single region within the still image, as in the Yo Yo Ma example. If the camera zoomed in on a region and then panned, the result would be a "stripe" of high resolution. If the camera zoomed in and out while panning, the result would be multiple regions of high resolution.

The salient still technology allows for the easy creation of panoramic images without the use of expensive specialized hardware such as a Glubuscope camera. Spaces may be imaged not only 360 degrees out from the focal center of a lens, but also, they may be imaged 360 degrees pointing into a focal center, around a building, for example. The resulting still from this process can also be used as an interface device for the individual frames of video data. This latter process was done in a real-space viewing system of navigable video data of a Russian palace [17].

Salient stills can be used as icons in a digital video database. A video data icon is the synthesis of the salient features of some temporal duration of footage into one image. Saving time, the user of the digital video database would have to glance at only a single salient still rather than view the whole sequence of data. This can be very useful if the database is quite large, for example containing hundreds or thousands of hours of footage. Additionally, the intermediate space/time volume can be used to represent this temporal data as well. The camera motion of the sequence (pans, tilts and zooms) can easily be ascertained from the contours of the space/time volume. An interesting variant on visualizing video databases is described in [5].

The methodology affords new flexibility in the creation of traditional photomontages. From the intermediate space/time volume, the user can traverse the video data and select sections of the volume both in space and time to be used in the synthesis of the final image. Pieces of individual frames can be used for some sections, and temporally processed data can be used in other sections.

This technology can be exploited to create not only single frame representations of moving image data but also more dynamic systems. One could imagine a "video radar," where a camera will continuously film an entire room by panning around 360 degrees [14]. In this scenario, whenever an object is encountered that is not a permanent fixture in the room, the object will be imaged onto the static background image of the space; the system effectively tracks all new activity in the room. The compositing methodology also could be used to highlight characteristics about the activity—the time a person entered the room and the urgency with which she should be noticed.

One by-product of most digital video compression systems is the generation of an inter-frame motion model. Although this model is typically optimized for prediction rather than interpolation, it may be possible to use the model to estimate the inter-frame affine transform required in the salient still process. This would greatly reduce the computational overhead of the process.

Conclusion

We have developed the notion of salient stills as well as methods for constructing them. With the salient still, we are trying to create a high-resolution still image of reproduction quality from video. In this process, we are trying to translate a narrative told in the language of the cinematographer into the language of the photographer. This work is part of a larger body of work in Media Transcoding which is aimed at automatic and fluid conversion of one medium into another. In contrast to McLuhan's maxim, when the message is news or information, the medium is not the message. This ability to adapt media is requisite in a heterogeneous communications environment.

Acknowledgments

This work was sponsored in part by International Business Machines, Inc. The authors would like to thank the Media Laboratory's Entertainment and Information Group, as well as Massimiliano Poletto, Edmond Chalom, John Wang, and Edward Adelson for their assistance.

Notes

1. E. H. Adelson, C. H. Anderson, J. R. Bergen, P. J. Burt, and J. M. Ogden. Pyramid methods in image processing. *RCA Engineer*, Nov/Dec 1984.

2. W. Bender and P. Chesnais. Network Plus. *Proceedings, SPIE Electronic Imaging Devices and Systems Symposium*, Vol. 900, January 1988.

3. J. R. Bergen, P. J. Burt, R. Hingorani, and S. Peleg. Computing Two Motions from Three Frames, David Sarnoff Research.

4. T. Doyle and P. Frencken. Median Filtering of Television Images, Technical Papers Digest, International Conference on Consumer Electronics, June 1986.

5. Edward Elliot. Multiple Views of Digital Video, MIT Media Lab, Interactive Cinema Working Paper, March 1992.

6. Bernd Girod and David Kuo. Direct Estimation of Displacement Histograms. *Optical Society of America Meeting on Understanding and Machine Vision Proceedings*, Cape Cod, MA, June 1989.

7. D. J. Heeger. Optical Flow Using Spatiotemporal Filters, *International Journal of Computer Vision*, 279–302 (1988).

8. Henry Holtzman. Three-Dimensional Representations of Video using Knowledge Based Estimation, Masters Thesis, Massachusetts Institute of Technology, September 1991.

9. B. Horn and B. Schunk. Determining Optical Flow, *Artificial Intelligence*, 17, 1981.

10. Hu, A. Automatic Emphasis Detection in Fluent Speech with Transcription, *Journal of Acoustical Society of America*, Vol 58, No. 4, 1975.

11. J. Jain and A. Jain. Displacement measurement and its application in interframe image coding,. *IEEE Transactions on Communications*, COM-29, 1981.

12. J. Lim and J. Murphy. Estimating the velocity of moving images in television signals, *Computer Graphics and Image Processing*, 4, 1975.

13. Andrew Lippman. Feature Sets for Interactive Images, *Communications of the ACM*, April 1991.

14. Steve Mann. Compositing Multiple Pictures of the Same Scene, *Proceedings IS&T Annual Meeting*, May 1993.

15. Patrick McLean. Structured Video Coding, Masters Thesis, Massachusetts Institute of Technology, June 1991.

16. A. Shepp. Introduction to Images and Imaging, *Image Processes and Materials*, Van Nostrand Reinhold, 1989.

17. Laura Teodosio and Michael Mills. Panoramic Overviews for Navigating Real-World Scenes, *Proceedings ACM Multimedia*, August 1–6 1993.

18. Laura Teodosio. Salient Stills, Master's Thesis, Massachusetts Institute of Technology, September 1992.

19. John Watlington. Synthetic Movies, Master's Thesis, Massachusetts Institute of Technology, September 1989.

12

The Multimedia Prospect:
A Case for Redefinition

Patrick Purcell

Multimedia Contexts

Multimedia as a technology has had an uncertain provenance, veering in reputation between hype and the technical *vade mecum* of the nineties. It has been posited variously as the dynamic growth point of the computer industry market, the ubiquitous interface to telecommunication services, or the new technology for entertainment and education products. It is timely, then, to appraise the current and foreseen climate for multimedia development. The timeliness is further reinforced by the fact that multimedia as a technology has moved in recent years from its hybrid analog/digital origins to being an exclusively digital medium.

The importance of the change to a full digital infrastructure for multimedia is underlined by a recent statement from the European Community, which affirms that "The emergence of digital coding as the common language of communication may fundamentally change our view of the world. The common digital language offers a unique opportunity to leverage converging technologies such as television, computers and telecommunications into global communications. Such an approach would have the potential to offer a vastly augmented range of services to all system users" (RACE, 1993).

To exploit this potential, multimedia techniques will have to absorb new media concepts, such as "dial-up movies," "downloaded TV," "video-on-demand," "broadcatching" rather than broadcasting. Such concepts will demand a radically new approach to the way in which we may conceive, design, and implement future multimedia systems.

It is also timely to appraise some of the currents and trends in other technologies which are beginning to affect the direction, pace and scale of multimedia developments.

These include the best that current technology has to offer, in the form of high band width, enormous computing and signal processing power, intelligent agents, object oriented software, and high fidelity presentation methods. The pace is such that it may be claimed that the most significant advances for multimedia in this decade will be determined by factors previously considered to be quite extraneous to multimedia. Other currents find their output in a variety of industrial and commercial applications. In this chapter, representative exemplars will be presented and compared. The comparison reveals a seemingly dichotomous situation, at once being convergent in shared infrastructure while, at the same time being very divergent in the proliferation of discrete new applications.

A feature of these exemplars, in such diverse fields as television, telecoms, newspapers, movies, museums and art galleries, will be the emergence of the new consortia and industrial partnerships, formed to exploit such new market opportunities.

On another level, this chapter considers the proposition that some of the most interesting developments in the technology in question are not so much "multimedia" as "multimodal," with new modes of interaction and new forms of interface intelligence, to assist the user. Much of this interest has been based on the promise of multimedia to afford access by lay users to many aspects of new information technology and to mediate effectively between these lay users and their increasingly complex information environment.

The following sections are presented to lend evidence to the case for redefining the familiar technology we call "multimedia."

Multimedia Information Systems

"A picture is worth a thousand words," an adage of long standing, is being given a fresh impetus by current developments in imaging technology. During the eighties, visual collections, image libraries and museums embraced optical storage technology to provide better means for accessing the records of very large collections of images (Purcell, 1990). Prototypic projects have been developed, employing mass storage technologies for the display of images in these collections, hitherto housed in slide and photograph cabinets, in large flat files and in museum and gallery storage rooms.

Advances in the technology of digital image collections as a major application area, have a special relevance to ongoing concurrent developments in electronic publishing, in high speed data networks and in advanced telecommunication services (Purcell, 1994).

Today's electronic image libraries, linked to object-oriented databases and accessed by powerful, specially developed search languages, have created a new genre of information technology, namely MMIS (MultiMedia Information Systems). MMIS technology has evolved in those professions, industries and disciplines where the image has a singular significance, for example, in medicine, in advertising, and in the media, in design, in architecture, fine arts, graphic arts, and photography. Art institutions, galleries, museums, and image libraries have provided many of the pioneering applications, in successive generations, through which multimedia information systems have been evolving (Purcell and Smith, 1992).

For some time there has been a real need for support facilities, to help create electronically based image banks based on major cultural resources. In response, a number of platform products have been released, offering digital imaging services and electronic publications to museums, galleries, and the academic community worldwide. Recently, several major initiatives have been launched, such as the Continuum project, created by Microsoft, and the LUNA project by Kodak, the latter having been formed in partnership with the Getty Trust. Both of these services have been launched from a perception of the growing importance of readily accessible imaging technology for scholars and researchers in the visual arts.

Progress in multimedia technology in the world of image libraries and museums is monitored in Europe, by the European Visual Arts Information Network (EVAC, 1992). In the United States the Museum Computer Network represents a major source for reporting progress in this area, nationally and internationally. More recently, the MMCF (Multimedia Communications Forum) has been set in train. One feature of development in this area is the emergence of an EC-funded collaborative research effort that has created consortia of organizations, representing major image holdings, such as the RKD, (the National Dutch image collection in the Hague), in London, the Witt Collection.

Other major museum partnerships have included the Prado Museum in Madrid, the Musee d'Orsay in Paris, and the Ashmolean in Oxford. The membership of the consortia also includes national and multinational telecommunication organizations to support the technical task of linking these organizations into a functioning international art and cultural network.

The substantial amount of current activity being reported highlights the need for the development of standards for formatting and visual indexing, to make for broader and more coherent electronic access to the sources of images possible and to build on the work that has produced existing and emerging standards relevant to electronic imaging, such as MHEG, Hytime and SGML. MIME is a new multimedia standard, which defines a range of media types to support multimedia services across digital telecommunication networks, such as ISDN, (Integrated Services Digital Network)(Adie, 1993).

The most common mode of implementing visual referencing systems has been as a single-site station, with the image collection held on one or more optical storage devices. Institutions such as the Tate Gallery or the National Gallery have pioneered applications in the UK. The Smithsonian, the Metropolitan, and the Getty Trust have pioneered similar systems in the United States.

However, there has recently been an increasing awareness of the potential role of the electronic image library as a multimedia node in a distributed system operating on a broadband data network. A commercial venture with a network of centers in the United States and Europe, the Image Bank, aims to provide the client with read access to high quality image banks. France Telecom's Image Directe project (Fages, 1991) also offers an information retrieval service based on extensive electronic image banks to users.

A new pilot network project in the area of collaborative research across networks, is the TIRONET (Trans Ireland Optical NETwork) project. The TIRONET project is based on an advanced optical fibre network linking Belfast and Dublin and is funded by the EC RACE (R&D in Advanced Communications technologies in Europe) program. The primary goal of this program is to establish the interworking of optical fibre networks between EC member states. The academic partners in TIRONET, apart from University of Ulster are Queens University, Belfast, and University College, Dublin. Several of the applications which form part of the TIRONET project have relevance to the future of educational multimedia on the university campus. They include access to desk videoconferencing facilities and to multimedia educational materials, access to shared library resources, and shared access to supercomputer facilities.

Recently in the UK, plans have gone forward to exploit access to high speed networks such as SuperJANET as a facility for multimedia educational technology. The common digital infrastructure that is shared by value-added services in telecommunications, by online image archives, electronically published journals, and prospectively the new digital broadcasting media, makes for a very promising prospect indeed in terms of future dissemination and publication of image archives. One may anticipate that these innovations will achieve for the world of images and visual information what has already been accomplished by the long established online text databases, for current affairs, business information, and financial services.

The New Television

Compared with, say, automotive design and certain areas of consumer electronics, the television receiver has not been the subject of significant electronic advance. However, the current trends in broadcasting research and development promise to change this situation significantly. The initial proposals for HDTV indicated linear projections of technical advance. Topics included increasing screen resolution and changing the aspect ratio of the screen. A concomitant of these developments (some say politically determined developments), has been the prospect of incompatible TV broadcast standards, technically and geographically isolated, restricting the scale of TV reception and inhibiting international program exchange.

Traditionally, broadcasting has been based on the concept of a single transmitter radiating an identical video signal to a population of passive receivers, adjusted to its frequency. In this single mode of transmission, program origination, transmission, and reception are handled as a tightly coupled triad, all linked in real time operation.

Recently however, other more radical proposals have been entering the arena of future HDTV. They are essentially predicated on the idea that television internationally should take more account of the widespread use of digital techniques that have begun to affect so many applications in the fields of media, communications and information technology. The increasing presence of digital television on the agenda of researchers, engineers, operators, and most significantly on the agenda of the regulators and standard makers, is reflected in the technical literature (IEE, 1992).

In the United States, this alternative view of the future of broadcast television technology was evidenced during the submissions to the FCC, the U.S. government federal communications agency. A proposal by AT&T underlines the union of computers and telecommunications with new broadcasting technology, an approach that informs much current television research and development. This is highlighted in a recent report (Andrews, 1993) that the FCC is to allow the American telephone companies to transmit television programing.

As the technology of television moves away from its analog antecedents towards its digital future, it finds a new alignment with those technologies whose digital infrastructure it shares. Given the view of future TV as an intensive digital processing technology, with much of that processing occurring in the TV receiver, it may be claimed that future television will introduce extensive computing into our homes and daily lives.

Indeed, the modern workstation, with its high-definition graphics processing capability, may be perceived as the TV receiver of the future. Reciprocally, the future television receiver will have much of the functionality of a computer.

This observation is responsible for the paradigm shift that views new television not as a tightly coupled program origination, transmission and reception triad, but as a modular digital system architecture, whose constituent elements have been fully decoupled as an open system, with three discrete functions.

This specification of advanced TV provides it with a basis for convergence with other active research programs such as digital movies and multimedia information systems. Versatility is seen as the cardinal virtue of the open architecture structure. The key features of digital TV and digital video include amenability to data compression, modularity, and scalability, resulting in a television video signal with capacity for variable screen resolutions, frame rates and aspect ratios.

The progressive intersection of the new TV transmission media with other media, including computer and telecommunication networks, is linking television with new forms of electronic publishing, for example, electronic yellow pages, online cartographic information, teleshopping, multimedia information systems and "dial up" movies.

In this development,what we have come to call broadcasting, may in future (with a high degree of user selection) be redefined as "broadcatching." Broadcatching underlines interaction and selection based more on the user's choice and availability than on the broadcasters schedules (Wiseman, 1981). Significant advances in image processing research, have further reinforced the alignment of television delivery with these telecom services, for example in "thin wire TV" on existing phone lines (Snoddy, 1992).

The process of recording on the VCR one's favorite television program for viewing at a more convenient time has become a very familiar process. Digital television will take the proactive viewer into a much enhanced level of choosing, down loading and browsing of favorite programs, such as responding to the command "download for me last night's 'Sixty Minutes!'"

In the same vein, electronic information delivery in the context of future mass media will be highly customized and will be linked with personal computing. Future news systems will not only be personalized, but "updated continuously and provide relevant feedback and have multi-media capabilities" (Bender, 1991). One important role for the computer in this scenario, is to act as a computational intermediary on behalf of the viewer.

Among the technical advantages that we may expect from the new digital television, include more efficient transmission, enhanced audio, ghost-free reception and the incorporation of a variety of multimedia communications interfaces. Apart from the alignment of digital television with other new forms of entertainment and information technologies, we may expect progressive reduction in the need for live broadcast, to the point where newscasts and sportscasts may ultimately become the few regular transmissions tied to the broadcasters program schedule.

In the matter of broadcasting futures, technical and political issues present very different scenarios according to a recent commentary. "To a large degree the research for establishing the technology needed for the near future of broadcast graphics is in good shape. Although there are many hard problems still to be tackled, solutions are not expected to be elusive. The same cannot be said for the political difficulties in establishing worldwide standards while at the same time forging a whole system concept that is going to remain stable for thirty years" (Purcell, 1992b). Cumulatively it seems clear that the new television will play much more extensive and varied roles in the living room of the future, going far beyond entertainment to have a major impact on our work and life styles generally.

Digital Video

In certain respects, the technology of digital HDTV and digital video-on-demand share many corresponding technical features. They include, for example, the techniques of storing, processing, transmitting and reception of digital video.

However, in some cases, applications such as digital television are very different from the technology of digital films and video, as TV requires symmetrical effort in both compression and decoding in situations where the delay between encoding and remote image presentation is minimized for real time transmission.

In the case of "dial up" digital films and video the entire movie sequence may be comprehensively encoded offline and scanned both forward and backward in time, securing optimization of image quality and compression for subsequent transmission and decoding. In the technology of digital movie processing, the issues of image scale, bandwidth, frame rate and screen resolution are all independent variables.

Digital video is not just a versatile medium for the transmission of digital movies. Digital techniques are offering fresh approaches, for example, in shooting films. New techniques include the incorporation of range-sensing cameras into movie making as a feature in the development of 3D movies and the consequent ability to manipulate real world scenes with the freedom usually associated with computer generated 3D models.

In due course, however, the impact of digital techniques will have a profound effect on all aspects of film making, including scripting, shooting, editing, transmission, projection and radically change the way we shall experience digital movies and video both as an entertainment and as an educational medium in the future.

Multimedia and Videoconferencing

Earlier generations of videoconferencing have had a checkered past in terms of success in the market place. With a radically different infrastructure, the new videoconferencing and videotelephony offerings in the market place are having a very different impact. The issues contributing to that impact are several. They include ISDN (Integrated Services Digital Network) and CSCW (Computer Supported Cooperative Working), both of which combine to make this application area a very significant domain for multimedia. New codecs are being developed to service the potential of ISDN based videoconferencing, spanning narrow band and broadband (Purcell, 1993). Advances in CSCW have resulted in bringing together a variety of advanced media to enhance the role that videoconferencing can play in facilitating communication between remotely located members of collaborating groups. Typically, the modalities of interaction include keyboard, voice input, interactive graphics and video.

One of the more significant multimedia developments in recent times has been the development of special codecs to service narrow band ISDN communication in order to facilitate "dial up" videoconferencing in applications as varied as business meetings, distance education and accessing remote conferences and symposia. Distance education is a particularly significant application (Seabrook, 1993).

During 1991, several European telecommunications operators accepted an invitation to participate in a collaborative program on the development of products and services for the videophone market. Six of the telcos, namely British Telecom, Deutsche Bundespost Telekom, France Telecom, Norwegian Telecom, PTT Telecom Netherlands, SIP Italy, took up the invitation, becoming signatories to a five year memorandum of understanding on the European Videotelephone (EV) program.

The main aim of the EV program, is the introduction of a pan-European videotelephone service. Several videophones were designed and interworking tests between them were conducted successfully. One such unit is a compact videoconferencing system, the VC7000 (Seabrook, 1993).

Multimedia and Virtual Presence

The art and technology of visualization has been a long standing prime motivation for research in advanced digital video and autostereo techniques. From its origin in monochromatic vector graphics, the impetus to depict both real and imagined objects and processes has been a major goal. Advances in color, simulation of texture, stereoscopic display, complex digital modeling, specular reflection, simulation of translucency and very high image resolution, has each made its distinct contribution to the realistic depiction of complex objects, scenes and processes. Now computer graphic rendering techniques and computer animation have been conjoined with the physics and chemistry of holography to generate a new range of visually refined and iridescent imagery. The distinctive optical character of these new images reflect both the ultra precise fabrication techniques of holography and the power of modern computer graphic processing engines.

The artifacts, resulting from this conjunction of technologies generally play a role as objects of aesthetic interest in the art gallery or as a powerful medium of visualization in the laboratory. The extension of this composite technology to applications in medicine and in systems for industrial design, architecture and engineering is providing the impetus for further research and development in this interdisciplinary field.

Current research includes full-color three-dimensional portraits, medical visualization of CAT and MRI scans, automotive design and architectural CAD data bases, large scale holograms, wide-angle holography and very recently the first holographic video (St Hilaire, 1991). The ability to generate realistic full color holographic images from CAD/CAM models represents a major advance in design communication, as a form of "design hardcopy." The development of the computer based hologram represents a distinct departure from the "true" hologram, which must be exposed in laser light to an object of nearly the same size as the desired image, size being no constriction for computer modeled objects.

While holographic stereograms have been generated as a series of perspective images and synthesized as a form of "frozen" computer animation, to achieve the "look around" effect, more recent research is directed to combining the role of computer animation with supercomputing to produce moving or animated holographic video in real time. The new resources combine a supercomputer, an acoustic-optical modulator an a custom built rotating display system. It may well be that the impact of current parallel processing techniques will be such as to take holographic imaging further away from its origins, such that computer generated 3D holography-type images will look to classical holography more as an inspiration, than as a source of operating techniques.

Multimedia: The Impending Challenge

The previous sections indicate some of the trends that will affect the course and direction of multimedia in the latter part of the decade. The diverse applications have included multimedia information systems, advanced television, digital cinema, videoconferencing, and visualization technology. While to the casual observer, the operation of a digital movie sequence is superficially similar to an analog sequence, the difference in underlying technology presages a marked difference in terms of future modes of entertainment to be offered, and the provision of electronic information.

Driving the range of such diverse applications are several key developments in such areas of telecoms, computers and electronics, all of which are having an impact on the future of multimedia. Perhaps, the most significant current feature of multimedia communications development is the sheer increase in the scale of operations worldwide. Initiatives such as the Information Highway and AT&T's WorldSource project in the United States and Project Atlantic in Europe serve to indicate the scale of recent global operations.

This burgeoning of the geographic scale of operations is giving rise to a new generation of multimedia value-added services and information systems, with the prospect of global multisite CSCW (Computer Supported Cooperative Working) systems and proposals for full motion video and television on computer networks, such as Internet. As a result, there has been a spate of multinational consortia of broadcasting, communications, computers and media interests to exploit the convergence of the new digital technologies at the global scale. This represents a potent mix of new media technology with media program content. Given the involvement of so many media companies in these international multimedia alliances, it can be validly claimed that the term "media" in "multimedia" refers as much to the media of the "fourth estate" (press, television and radio), as it does to media, defined as the combination of text, audio and video at the user's screen.

The mix of global media technology and program content has obvious positive implications, such as ease of communication at a global scale, the coherence of a single international service, as well as flexibility and versatility in transnational communications. The obverse side of the coin is perhaps less obvious. The perceived threat in Europe of techno-cultural imperialism is one of those issues, where a global Pandora's box of alien cultural offerings is held to overshadow individual national heritages. This threat is felt so strongly in France, for example, that it almost derailed the recent conclusion of the GATT worldwide trade agreement. The "audio/visual sector" crisis, as it was called, has been shelved and still awaits resolution.

The transmission of digital video and TV is often discussed in terms of alternate delivery channels, either via computer networks, terrestrial broadcast, cable, satellite broadcast or telecommunication delivery. In fact, the future availability of digital video should result in a plurality of concurrent options, where the preferred channel for delivery of multimedia information will simply be the location and the convenience of the user, irrespective of whether the user is in the home, classroom or office. An interesting side effect to the plurality of delivery conduits is the "trading places" syndrome, where multimedia data are swapping transmission channels. As more and more television is transmitted in the ground, an increasing proportion of telecom traffic passes through the ether.

In the area of multimedia production, with digital films, video, and television, sharing so much digital infrastructure, a common pool of production techniques is used to create interactive TV, "dial up" movies and video-on-demand. Research in digital movies, for example, is generating potent and distinctive techniques for both scripting and editing digital video (Davenport, 1989) and for shooting three dimensional movies and displaying stereoscopic video. Each of these spectacular technical advances issues a direct challenge to the creative skills of the writers, directors and producers to exploit such innovations. Currently there appears to be little evidence in the world of film and video making that the necessary technical insights exist to any significant degree. This is possibly due to the fact that in this world, digital and analog screens share a superficial resemblance for the casual observer. Consequently a lot of the professional and cultural baggage of video making, is simply being transferred from analog film making to digital film making. To that extent it may be claimed that the world of film and video making is still in a transitional "horseless carriage" period in which familiar techniques, derived from a traditional medium, are simply being pushed into service in the new digital arena.

Multimediation

In the context of the increasing scale and the provision of multiple choice of programs in the new linked environment of "infotainment" (information and entertainment services, sharing the same conduit), the multimedia interface has a new and important role. This new role casts the interface as an agent of mediation, namely, enhancing the user's ability to deal with a veritable "fire hose" of complex and multiple infotainment services. The technology being developed to answer this challenge can be described as "multimodal" rather than multimedia, being multimodal in the sense that the emphasis lies in the multiple modes of interaction between user and computer, which hithero have been based on the conventional keyboard and mouse. The new multimodal interface, in addition to using video, text and audio, also may incorporate speech recognition, gesture modeling, tactile sensation and gesture, to make for greater ease of use between man and machine. Software techniques from artificial intelligence (daemons, autonomous agent and "knowbots"), may also augment the performance of the user at the multimodal computer interface.

The aim of this paper has been to illustrate the current rate of development in communications, in broadcasting, in entertainment and information technologies and the role of multimedia therein. It has served to demonstrate a pattern of change that is simultaneously divergent in terms of the wide range of new applications being created, but equally convergent in terms of the increasing intersection of the channels of information delivery, in which our phone may deliver our television and our television may deliver (and process) our multimedia data. It is an exciting prospect, in which multimedia will play a leading role. The achievement of this prospect will call for considerable agility from the relevant institutions in research and education to respond effectively, to the dynamic of the emerging multimedia scenario. This agility will be expressed in constant revision of the relevant subjects and curricula and in a dynamic and ongoing appraisal of the strategy for research and development in the new multimedia.

References

Adie, C. (1993). "Network Access to Multimedia Information—The RARE Report," Edinburgh Univ Computing Service, Edinburgh, June 1993.

Andrews, E. L. (1993). "FCC Approves TV on Phone Lines," *New York Times,* 17 July 1993.

Bender, W., H. Lie, J. Orwant, L. Teodosio, and N. Abramson (1991). "Newspace: Mass Media and Personal Computing." Proc USENIX '91, Nashville, TN.

Davenport, G., and H. P. Brondmo (1989). "Creating and Viewing the Elastic Charles-Hypermedia Journal." Proc. York Multi Media Conference, York, UK.

EVAC (1992). *ITEM,* no. 3, Publ. European Visual Arts Centre, Ipswich IP4 1LT, UK, 1992

Fages, A. (1991). "Image Directe." *Videotex RNIS Magazine,* no. 49, 1991, Paris.

IEE (1992)."Emerging CCIR Standards for Digital Television Transmission," *Institution of Electrical Engineers* (1990/001) London, UK 1992

Purcell, P. A. (1994). "Media Technology—An Expanding Forum for Advanced Computer Graphics." In *Focus on Graphics,* edited by S. Coquillart. Heidelberg and New York: Springer-Verlag.

Purcell, P. A., and D. I. Applebaum (1990). "Light Table: Interface to Visual Information Systems." In *Electronic Design Studio,* edited by W. McCullogh, P.A. Purcell, et al. Cambridge, MA: MIT Press.

Purcell, P. A., and G. Parr (1993) "Videoconferencing in a Multi-Campus Setting" in *ISDN Applications in Education & Training.* Institution of Electrical Engineers, London

Purcell P. A., and Smith, M. W. (1992). "Developments in Imaging Technology for Arts Information." *Proc. Electronic Imaging for the Visual Arts,* National Gallery, London, UK.

Purcell, P A., and N. Wiseman (1992) "Broadcast Graphics." In *STAR Report, Eurographics '92.* Cambridge University, Cambridge UK.

RACE (1993). "RACE Research Call," CEC Brussels, Belgium, p. 20.

Seabrook, G. (1993). "Towards the implementation of a European videophone service," *BT Journal* 11, no. 1.

Snoddy, R. (1992)."BT assesses TV service using telephone lines" *Financial Times (London), 10 June 1992.*

St Hilaire, P., M. Lucente, S. Benton, et al. (1991) "Electronic Display System for Computational Holography." In *Proc SPIE* 1212 (edited by S. A. Benton), Bellingham, WA.

Wiseman, N. E. (1981). "Improvements to Television," *Information Design Journal* 2, no. 2, pp. 9–11.

13

Wheel of Culture

Ben Davis

Introduction

Dublin, Ireland 1993.

I first came to Ireland in November of 1987 to get far away from my work with multimedia computing technology at MIT. I had been involved with the management of some ten multimedia initiatives and the design and implementation of a radically dynamic prototype for a new multimedia computer language, Athena Muse. At that time, I was intent on roving the countryside outside of Dublin to find standing stones and other ancient and prehistoric monuments of early Ireland. I wanted to feel something powerful from the past, having lived too much in the future.

One object I was keen on seeing was an Ogham stone. The earliest writing in Ireland is said to have begun around 300 A.D. It is inscribed in the alphabet known as Ogham, after Ogmios, the Celtic god of writing. The alphabet is made up of sets of strokes carved on the edge of a vertical standing stone with the edge acting as the central line of the text. The inscription begins at the bottom of the stone and climbs to the top, sometimes continuing down on the opposite sides. These strokes are like digital encoding of the Old Irish language.

The alphabet looks like this:

```
I  II III IIII IIIII I II III IIII IIIII                   /  //  ///   ////  /////
I  II III IIII IIIII                   I II III IIII IIIII /  //  ///   ////  /////
A  O  U  E    I H D T   C  Q  B  L  F  S   N M G  G NG   Z     R
```

(Harbison)

The use of the script continued until the 7th or 8th century. To come upon these stones in a farmer's field in the magic Irish twilight on a cold fall afternoon is a very moving experience. The stones seem like lonely dancers frozen in time with only a secret bar code for identification.

Running your hand over those stones puts human-computer interface theories into perspective. What is an interface but a poetic facade? And how do we think about the thickness of the facade?

> Labour is blossoming or dancing where
> The body is not bruised to pleasure soul,
> Nor beauty born out of its own despair,
> Nor blear-eyed wisdom out of midnight oil.
> O chestnut tree, great rooted blossomer,
> Are you the leaf, the blossom or the bole?
> O body swayed to music, O brightening glance,
> How can we know the dancer from the dance?
>
> —Yeats

But how can we know the stone from the message, the machine from the culture? Or for that matter: How can we know merging skills from oil spills, new communities from new vacuums, the bridging of cultures from high-speed bypassing of the past and present? How has this technology of electronic information become like a Wheel of Culture, turning and turning like a widening gyre? The Wheel of Culture that the new multimedia technology creates is constantly spinning, constantly drawing new information and cultural associations into it because it is a global wheel, dependent on global economy, responsive to market pressures. Knowledge is product, speed is of the essence, and speed kills the competitor.

HyperCulture

Narrative and simulation, "the most effective human communication(s) since the dawn of time" (Whitbey). Is that a Chinese narrative or Chaucerian narrative? Is that simulation a generic communication or does it come with or without museums? The Virtual Curator (Beardon and Worden)? What is this simulation telling us about curators? Virtuality seems pretty well explored in the modern world, often a good deal more than the things it models. The concept of "see what it's like" is the perfect schema for an environmentally troubled world. We can use simulations to predict knowledge and hopefully schedule a technological fix to head off the next disaster.

Inventing the future seems to be about inventing alternative realities, alternative cultures, alternative something new as quickly as possible. The educational possibilities are boundless. I love virtual reality, really I do.

"Building or learning the tools of your trade after you are asked to carry out a task is not business, it is research" (Finney). This quote is in reference to creating soft ware tools after being asked to do a computational task. The old metaphors of tools and work don't actually apply in the post-industrial world. The synthesizer is hardware that allows software tools to be created while the task is at hand. We are most familiar with it as a music generator but what it actually does is create tools (musical structures) while the task is at hand (literally). Synthesizing is building tools in an open-ended task environment. Business is research; research is business in the postindustrial world.

"Instead, users define their own link semantics and icons to be used to anchor the selected links in the multimedia" (Chignell). Hyper-cultural icons for houses, trees, rivers, mountains, tables? How can one person define "link semantics and icons" for someone in a different culture?

"Guided tours can help combat the problem of disorientation" (Dunne and Verbruggen). "Meet the new boss, same as the old boss" (Townsend). "Inferential links allow the navigation on the basis of contextual knowledge. Such inferential links may be defined declaratively, in a rule-based way" (Eliens). Does context have a culture? Just how many rules are needed here? "The ability of the user to interpret information presented to them can be constrained in a variety of different ways, such as cultural background, propensities arising from prior experience, sensory impairment and other factors" (Cameron and Terrins-Rudge).

Please enter: cultural preference, past experience, and how you think you read this.

Multimedia is not a thing, a computer technology. It is the current literacy condition of the environment. Film, video, audio, text, and graphics are ubiquitous; they are being created and distributed twenty four hours a day every day. The air is literally filled with images. These forms are the mechanisms for industrial design, communication, and resource monitoring. The multimedia computer is a way of revealing this environmental condition.

Ogham Type

Digital technologies make information creation and movement into a single substance that is infinitely transformable. Film, vinyl, magnetic tape, paper, photographic paper, ink, graphite, paints—all converted to the digital domain create a new media unlike anything ever invented. This single digital substance can be transformed by the computer (the means of transmission) into any conceivable form. In other words, digital means that anything can be converted into anything else. Sound data can be made into pictures; pictures can be encoded as sound impulses; text can be linked to any form; any still image can be animated; any graphic can be morphed into representational images. All media become data types. We have returned to the Ogham stone, encoding all ideas in binary inscription.

In the information age, multimedia computing is both the means for generating new economies and the means to model those economies. Manufactured objects are no longer "things." They are the embodiments of computed information. A car is no longer a car; it is a Toyota. A television is a Sony. These things are hypermedia computing products. They are researched, designed, modeled, implemented, tested, and marketed with computers. The final product is a manifestation of an information molding process. As this process becomes scaleable, you will see computers running robots that actually make the objects. This is already done at a small scale with plastics and for components of automobiles. Shifts in information technology reinvent products, make new products that are hyper-designed, hyper-managed, hyper-distributed, hyper-consumed, hyper-recycled.

Mechanisms for exploiting multimedia conditions and mechanisms for modeling these exploitations are knowledge-based tools. Knowledge-based tools are cultural artifacts. How then does this process impact the older industrial perception of culture? How does an industrial economy sponsor the emerging information economy, an economy that is based on the free movement of information necessary to create new knowledge when it has always relied on proprietary, secret information for industrial advantage? When does Coca Cola give up its secret formula in order to create new products? And what cultural artifact must be created in order to make this event occur, and occur, and occur? And how do we use the same tool to model possible success?

Current examples of this economic/cultural shift are the sponsoring of multimedia projects by industrial corporations. Public television has been on the leading edge of this for many years: nature programs sponsored by Mobil Oil, controversial drama sponsored by Dow Chemical, arts sponsored by R. J. Reynolds, the list goes on. With the advent of computer-based multimedia technology, we are beginning to see computer manufacturers sponsoring educational experiences, cultural experiences. We are seeing Japanese consumer electronics corporations buying American film companies as software acquisitions for future multimedia entertainment products.

This new global information economy is packaging culture—and the package has an Asian/American/European brand name—and a price.

The MIT Center for Educational Initiatives is a case in point. The current focus of the Center is an internationally sponsored consortium, the Athena-Muse Software Consortium. AthenaMuse is an authoring software for multimedia that is being produced with the influence of Japanese, U.S, and European support. This software is applied to a variety of multimedia experiences.

The design of these materials has been affected by cultural approaches to information structures as diverse as the researchers working with it. These include Japanese, Swiss, Norwegian, Dutch, Colombian, Spanish, Lebanese, and American researchers contributing ideas both to the software and the design of applications. Applications and interface designs are all over the map as well: The Water Resources of Lebanon, Plants and Fruits of Columbia, Media-Literacy in Spain, Tokyo Tanabata Festival.

The design implications are crucial. An effort is being made to "internationalize" software for the production and dissemination of diverse cultural media materials. The intention is to create an open architecture that can be utilized across national boundaries. How does the medium affect the message? How do Eastern concepts of design integrate with Western design considerations?

Multimedia is currently thought of as a process of packaging information. But this process is global and shifts with economic trends and demands. This creates some thing very much like the American television quiz program "Wheel of Fortune," where contestants spin a roulette wheel that allows them to buy letters and solve hidden messages seen only in parts. Depending on their cultural association and education, they can win or lose, but they must choose characters that form fragments of messages quickly and string them together to get at the phrase that wins the prize. Multimedia production is currently in this fragmented guessing game stage of its development where bits and pieces of the technology seem to form a viable product for an emerging global market. Then struggles begin for the best video standard—Japanese, U.S., European? The "wheel" of multimedia takes a cultural turn.

One striking aspect of this turning wheel is that there appears to be an integration of form and content including the form of production. In other words, the style of an information product is closely linked to the character of the content as well as the means to produce the product. For instance, if a multimedia package created to teach Irish does not reflect the way in which Irish is learned locally, does not have a visual design that is easily understood as Celtic in origin, and has not been produced by a team of people intimate with living in Ireland, then the product may teach "about the Irish language" but will probably not "teach Irish."

To achieve the goal of teaching Irish, there must be a close relationship between the form of the product (its metaphors, interactive functions, visual design, intuitive navigation, etc.), its content (Irish language with all the implications of cultural nuance), and the form of production (a team that shares common understandings of things Irish). In short, folk wisdom must prevail in order to have a culturally distinctive product. One must know the dancer from the dance even when they are inextricably mixed.

Because of the global communication technologies that will distribute multimedia products, cultural representation becomes cultural manufacturing. The best analogy is the motion picture business. When a film like *In the Name of the Father* is produced as an Irish product and distributed around the world, then the representation of a culture is actually a thing, a movie. Ironically, the film star is British, Daniel Day Lewis, who is supposedly more marketable than an Irish film star. From this condition the juxtaposition of cultures, the segmentation of cultures, and the integration of cultures all go on simultaneously, making the product as lucrative as possible. The irony here is that the seemingly desirable creation of a relativistic viewpoint, a balanced view, that no one culture is more important than another has been created by dominant cultures that control and maintain the networks, the means of distribution. So making an Irish movie with a British star about life in Ireland all makes sense in terms of marketing a movie. But does the movie really represent the culture? The wheel spins on.

Museums without Cultures

At a recent museum conference on digital imagery, a member of the audience complained that companies like Continuum, a media distribution company partially owned by Microsoft and Bill Gates, was committing cultural crimes by trying to buy and distribute digital museum collections. This was seen as cultural exploitation. The moderator of the panel pointed out to the audience member that the terms "culture" and "museum" were not synonymous, that there were many cultures that had no museums. The point being that the creation of digital cultural programming by large centrally organized institutions represents no culture in particular, rather they represent culture in the abstract. They are "about culture" rather than "being culture." The digital museum as a new kind of institution that preserves and promotes cultural literacy has some very ambiguous aspects. In some respects, it is like the culture that has no museum, no institutionalized repository, because it does not physically exist. It is digital memory that can be accessed and manipulated. The content of the memory, however, is drawn from materials that do physically exist (currently digitizing existing museum collections as distinct from collecting digital imagery created only on the computer).

This condition is further complicated by the fact that digital media types can be equated. Text, graphics, moving and still imagery, and sound are equal data types in this new medium. Being literate no longer means understanding text. Older definitions of literacy return, most notably the language of memory:

Only literates, who could interpret the "shapes indicating voices" (in John of Salisbury's definition of letters), were going to be convinced that writing was superior to the symbolic object. Such objects, the records of the non-literate were therefore preserved along with documents. Another example is the knife by which Thomas of Moulton gave the church of Weston in Lincolnshire to Spalding priory, which was deposited in its archives (in secretario) according to the charter confirming the gift. This latter knife is no longer preserved. To later archivists, knives and other archaic relics meant nothing unless they had inscriptions connected with them; such things were thrown away as medieval rubbish, because the language of memory which they expressed had no significance to literates. (Clanchy)

Cultural material that is digitized can be representations of older physical materials and once in the digital form can be transformed into new combinations and permutations, distributed outside the walls of traditional museums over global networks, and remade into multimedia products that are then redistributed over the same networks. What kind of cultural structure can accommodate these possibilities?

Language of Memory

If, indeed, we are approaching a "Wheel of Culture" condition driven by information technology, then it is important to look at existing language structures that allow for multilevel understanding. This new computer enhanced "language of memory" seems to rely on a strange new principal of overlapping metaphorical structures.

Metaphorical structures in multimedia are cultural indexes. Critical skills are required to understand metaphorical packaging. Never mind for the moment that different cultures have different metaphorical structures. We use the term "foreign" to describe other languages while building a global interactive multimedia networked marketplace that must communicate across borders.

A multimedia product can be for education, entertainment, decision making, reference, skill training, and/or communication. Can we think of an automobile as a communication device that lets information—me or you—get from point A to point B? It may help to think of the automobile with a mobile phone in it. Maybe license plates should be phone numbers. If these metaphors are mixed, what is the resulting "thing?" Is it for getting an education in entertainment or for getting an entertaining education? Is driving a car that is computer enhanced really driving a computer with wheels? Is the car really a kind of architecture?

Multimedia products are built out of familiar structural metaphors. The metaphor that is used for structure is what we usually encounter as the presentation materials. These materials can be represented as a book, a movie, an architecture (a library, museum, theater, maze, vehicle), or an environment (specific geography, worlds). When a new multimedia "object" is made that combines two or more of these metaphors, something else is created. Is it a "hyperthing?"

Interactive metaphors are for knowledge creation and acquisition. You can be given notebooks, calculators, timelines, maps, image albums, steering wheels, etc., so that you can do simulated research, go on a quest, solve a mystery, compete in a game, do an experiment, make juxtapositions, decide on storyline. If you have to do something to get the information, it might be helpful to have a clue how to start which is why the interactive metaphors used are familiar tools that exist outside the computer.

How are the metaphors mixed? You could be taking notes on a mystery novel, a quest in an environment, a game in a maze, a movie of a story, a library of juxtapositions, a world of experiments—some of the above, all of the above.

The interface must make the mix of metaphors understandable, challenging, and exciting. Does the design move from the familiar to the exotic in an intuitive way? Does the design itself teach you how to navigate?

Add to this list the questions:

How are the media integrated? Is an appropriate video/film style used? Is the mix of text, graphics, and sound effective? Is the color good? Finally we must also ask: What culture is this multimedia product coming from? Is it produced primarily by people from that culture? Are the materials and design from that culture? Is it used in that culture? How does it travel?

The language of memory represented by multimedia is a complex interplay of reference, metaphorical structures both for presentation and interaction, and a sensory recollection that relies on form, access, content, and emotion. As different cultures discover this medium it will be obvious that the use of the adjective "foreign" should be removed from language learning. There are no foreign languages, there are only different languages of memory.

Conclusion

I raised these issues of culture and information technology for many reasons. Some of them are the same reasons I went to Ireland to look at those Ogham stones. There is a sense of unease about living and working in the future. The production of these media types and the resultant economies are not trivial, marginal events. They are central to the way, given that electricity doesn't seem to be going out of style, that we will be communicating and generating a living.

Up until very recently, the technologies for editing and combining media were very distinct, analog systems that were distinguishable. A great deal of cultural information is preserved in analog systems. When these systems are converted to digital systems, cultural forms are endangered because they can be converted into any other culture very easily. Things may "look" like they are from another culture, but they may not actually "be" from that culture.

As someone involved in the production and distribution of these kinds of conditions, I have begun to wonder what we are gaining and what we are giving up. I have also realized that the theories and visions of those who do not build these things are very much like the architects who don't know that a two-by-four-inch piece of wood (the standard 2 × 4) is now 1 by 3 inches in reality. There is a great deal of very intricate and difficult work involved in making multimedia because of the high number of variables involved in digital information. What seems like a simple binary, on and off, technology is in reality in the realm of infinite permutations and combinations.

Making an interactive CD ROM, for instance, is a very complicated technical composition problem because of the variety of image resolutions, motion image frame rates, color depth variations, number of aspect ratios, file transfer rates, file compression options, navigation software, etc.—not to mention the design of interfaces.

What the technology is doing that is very positive is making us ask all these questions—some would say too many questions to process in any useful way. But the questions persist. Digital technology allows us to have a very explicit look at the analog world we actually live in and have only recently begun to see as a finite resource. The digital technology is creating both a dialog and a mechanism for discussing itself.

If we are creating a hyperculture that utilizes Ogham type to structure a language of memory, perhaps the condition is more analogous to the Catherine wheel. Originally the wheel of torture for Catherine of Aragon, the term is now associated with a fireworks display that whirls and spins, throwing out dancing lights—the kind of strange multicolored light that defies naming.

References

Beardon, Colin, and Suzette Worden (1993). *Multimedia Technologies and Their Role in Museums,* Abstract: Culture, Technology, Interpretation: The Challenge of Multimedia, Conference, Dublin.

Cameron, Eric, and Deirdre Terrins-Rudge (1993). *An Epistemological Approach to the Interpretation and Representation of Objects in a Distributed Multimedia Environment.* Abstract: Culture, Technology, Interpretation: The Challenge of Multimedia, Conference, Dublin.

Chignell, Mark (1993). *Free-Form Multimedia for Learning and Design.* Abstract: Culture, Technology, Interpretation: The Challenge of Multimedia, Conference, Dublin.

Clanchy, M. T. (1979). *From Memory to Written Record England, 1066–1077,* p. 207, Cambridge, MA: Harvard University Press.

Dunne, Chris, and Renaat Verbruggen (1993). *Intelligent Navigation in Hypermedia Documents Using Dynamically Generated Guided Tours.* Abstract: Culture, Technology, Interpretation: The Challenge of Multimedia, Conference, Dublin.

Eliens, Anton (1993). *Deja-Vu: A Distributed Hypermedia Application FrameWork.* Abstract: Culture, Technology, Interpretation: The Challenge of Multimedia, Conference, Dublin.

Finney, Andy (1993). *Give Me the Job and I'll Do the Tools (or is it the other way around?).* Abstract: Culture, Technology, Interpretation: The Challenge of Multimedia, Conference, Dublin.

Harbison, Peter (1970). *Guide to the National Monuments of Ireland,* p. 11, Dublin: Gill and McMillan.

Lennon, John (1989). The John Lennon Collection, *Imagine,* New York: Capital Records.

Townsend, Peter. (1971). Who's Next?, *Won't Get Fooled Again,* New York: MCN Records.

Whitby, Max (1993). *Return of the Narrative: Storytelling in an Interactive Age.* Abstract: Culture, Technology, Interpretation: The Challenge of Multimedia, Conference, Dublin.

Yeats, William Butler (1983). *The Poems of W. B. Yeats.* Edited by Richard J. Finneran. Among School Children, p. 217, New York: Macmillan.

Index of Key Terms

Contributors

Edward Barrett
Senior Lecturer
Program in Writing and Humanistic Studies
MIT

Colin Beardon
Rediffusion Simulation Research Centre
Faculty of Art, Design & Humanities
University of Brighton
U.K.

Walter Bender
MIT Media Laboratory

Edward Brown
Department of Computer Science
Memorial University of Newfoundland

Mark H. Chignell
Department of Industrial Engineering
University of Toronto

Glorianna Davenport
Associate Professor of Media
Technology
MIT

Ben Davis
Research Associate
MIT Center for Educational Computing
Initiatives

Peter S. Donaldson
Ann Fetter Friedlander Professor of
Humanities
MIT

Larry Friedlander
Professor of English
Stanford University

Geri Gay
Associate Professor, Communication
Director, Interactive Multimedia Group
Cornell University

Ricki Goldman-Segall
Director, MERLIN
Department of Curriculum Studies
Faculty of Education
University of British Columbia

Janet H. Murray
Director, Laboratory for Advanced
Technology in the Humanities
MIT

Patrick Purcell
University of Ulster
Northern Ireland
U.K.

Marie Redmond
Director, Multimedia Centre
Trinity College, Dublin

Michael Roy
Harvard University

Niall Sweeney
Trinity College, Dublin

Laura Teodosio
BAM! Software, Inc.
New York, N.Y.

Suzette Worden
Rediffusion Simulation Research Centre
Faculty of Art, Design & Humanities
University of Brighton
U.K.